财政部规划教材
全国高等院校财经类教材

VALUATION PRINCIPLES

(Bilingual)

资产评估原理

(双语)

陈 蕾 / 编著

中国财经出版传媒集团
中国财政经济出版社
北京

图书在版编目（CIP）数据

资产评估原理 =VALUATION PRINCIPLES (Bilingual)：汉、英 / 陈蕾编著. -- 北京：中国财政经济出版社，2023.9

财政部规划教材　全国高等院校财经类教材

ISBN 978-7-5223-2473-9

Ⅰ.①资… Ⅱ.①陈… Ⅲ.①资产评估—高等学校—教材—汉、英 Ⅳ.① F20

中国国家版本馆 CIP 数据核字（2023）第 163840 号

责任编辑：樊　闽	责任印制：张　健
封面设计：卜建辰	责任校对：胡永立

资产评估原理
ZICHAN PINGGU YUANLI

中国财政经济出版社 出版

URL：http://www.cfeph.cn
E-mail：cfeph@cfeph.cn

（版权所有　翻印必究）

社址：北京市海淀区阜成路甲 28 号　邮政编码：100142
营销中心电话：010-88191522
天猫网店：中国财政经济出版社旗舰店
网址：https://zgczjjcbs.tmall.com
北京富生印刷厂印刷　各地新华书店经销
成品尺寸：185mm×260mm　16 开　24.5 印张　612 000 字
2023 年 9 月第 1 版　2023 年 9 月北京第 1 次印刷
定价：71.00 元
ISBN 978-7-5223-2473-9
（图书出现印装问题，本社负责调换，电话：010-88190548）
本社图书质量投诉电话：010-88190744
打击盗版举报热线：010-88191661　QQ：2242791300

前　言

当今世界的经济全球化与一体化趋势日益加强。随着国家与地区之间经济合作的相互依赖和相互渗透，对外投资、境外并购等国际化业务蓬勃发展，资产评估机构参与国际竞争与合作的需要也空前加强，资产评估行业正进入一个新的发展时期。面对日趋激烈的行业竞争和宝贵的发展契机，扎实的专业技能、较高的综合素养以及卓越的外语水平已经成为资产评估高级专门人才的必备素质。与此同时，根据《国家中长期教育改革和发展规划纲要》，"适应国家经济社会对外开放的要求，培养大批具有国际视野、通晓国际规则、能够参与国际事务和国际竞争的国际化人才"是国家教育体制改革的重要目标之一，这对资产评估专门人才的培养也有了更新、更高的要求。为适应这一趋势，部分开设资产评估专业本科生或研究生教育的高等院校，已尝试设置与此相关的全英文、双语或专业英语课程，立足于培养能够在合资或外资的资产评估机构、会计师事务所等中介机构以及在政府资产管理部门、企事业单位、金融证券投资公司中从事资产评估及相关工作的应用型、复合型、国际型高素质人才。

作为一名资产评估专业教师，为了使学生"零距离"地接触到国际一流的学术成果，自2011年以来，编者一直选取国外原版教材或评估准则的相关内容从事资产评估专业的全英文或双语教学，包括"资产评估""评估学原理""资产评估专业英语""国际评估准则"等课程。然而，资产评估对象的多样化使得资产评估知识范围极其广泛，现有英文原版教材或聚焦于企业价值评估，或立足于无形资产评估，或关注于不动产评估、以财务报告为目的的评估等其他类型资产评估，其专业性较强但基础性和全面性稍显不足，给部分课程的教材选用带来一定难度。所以，对于大多数初学者或需要提高专业英语水平的专业人士而言，迫切需要一本基础性的资产评估原理的双语教材，能够在内容框架方面与现行《资产评估基础》《资产评估原理》等入门级中文教材内容相匹配，以帮助读者更快、更好地消化和吸收其精髓知识，并作为从专业基础理论逐渐向资产评估高级专业化应用过渡之不可或缺的一环。

本书名为《资产评估原理（双语）》，从资产评估专业培养目标出发，力求成为一本实用的资产评估专业双语教材，并采用有助于提高学生专业知识和启发学生思考运用的编写形式，以期能使学生成为满足国际交流需求的资产评估高素质人才，对于资产评估专业课程体系的完善、资产评估国际化人才的培养等具有积极意义。

本书按资产评估专业基础主干课程的构架设置11个专题，分别是"资产评估概述""资产评估方法""机器设备评估""不动产权益评估""无形资产评估""企业价值评估""以财务报告为目的的评估""税基评估""其他资产评估""资产评估报告""资产评估准则"；以及2个附录，"术语表""资产评估行业组织及实用网站"。每一专题均先以"名人名言"开始，以培养学生的主动学习兴趣与开阔视野意识；随后介绍"基本知识"，重点体现资产评估专业的基本理念与核心内容；接下来是"知识扩展"，多是围绕所在专题而精选的阅读素材，以进一步丰富教学内容；最后是"思政微课堂"，通过对课程思政元素的融入，帮助学生了解资产评估行业相关的国家战略、法律法规及政策规范，引导学生关注现实问题、深入评估实践，培育学生经世济民、诚信执业、德法兼修、勤勉尽责的综合素养，提升与之相关的家国情怀、法治意识、专业使命感和社会责任感。其中，"基本知识"和"知识扩展"均设有中文摘要作为导读内容，同时设有"核心术语"和"问题与讨论"专栏，强化学习效果。本书最后的附录设置有助于学生对教学内容的举一反三与思考探索。

本书既可满足高等院校资产评估专业本科生或研究生"资产评估""评估学原理""资产评估理论与方法""资产评估专业英语"等相关课程的全英文或双语教学需要，也可作为从事资产评估的实际工作者提升专业英语水平的工具用书，还可为从事资产评估相关研究人员提供案头参考。

本书从构思酝酿到编撰成书，从课堂试用到修改完善，从2017年《评估学原理（英文）》到2023年《资产评估原理（双语）》，实现了章节扩充、内容更新和资源升级。陈蕾负责内容框架的设计和全书的总纂。钟笑雪、李和荟协助进行了部分资料整理工作；席乐、孙凯萌、王叶参与了少量资料搜集工作。

本书获首都经济贸易大学及财政税务学院教材建设项目资助，在此郑重致谢。同时，中国财政经济出版社编辑樊闽女士为本书的出版付出了辛勤的劳动，在此一并感谢。

受编者学识和经验所限，书中难免存在疏漏之处。在本书即将付梓出版之际，诚挚希望各位读者对本书中的错误及不当之处提出批评和建议，编者将在今后再版时更正。

编　者
2023年9月

CONTENTS

Chapter 1　Introduction to Valuation
资产评估概述

Wisdom 名人名言 _1

Rudimentary Knowledge 基本知识 _2

  Abstract 中文摘要 _2

  Text 正文 _3

  Core Words and Expressions 核心术语 _15

  Questions and Discussion 问题与讨论 _17

More Knowledge 知识扩展 _17

Topic: Valuation under Uncertainty 评估的不确定性 _17

  Abstract 中文摘要 _17

  Text 正文 _18

  Core Words and Expressions 核心术语 _28

  Questions and Discussion 问题与讨论 _29

Information Extension 思政微课堂 _30

Chapter 2   Valuation Approaches
资产评估方法

Wisdom 名人名言 _31

Rudimentary Knowledge 基本知识 _32

Topic 1: The Market Approach 市场法 _32
    Abstract 中文摘要 _32
    Text 正文 _33
    Core Words and Expressions 核心术语 _41
    Questions and Discussion 问题与讨论 _43

Topic 2: The Cost Approach 成本法 _43
    Abstract 中文摘要 _43
    Text 正文 _45
    Core Words and Expressions 核心术语 _57
    Questions and Discussion 问题与讨论 _59

Topic 3: The Income Approach 收益法 _60
    Abstract 中文摘要 _60
    Text 正文 _61
    Core Words and Expressions 核心术语 _71
    Questions and Discussion 问题与讨论 _72

Topic 4: The Choice of Valuation Approaches/Methods
    资产评估方法的选择 _73
    Abstract 中文摘要 _73
    Text 正文 _74
    Core Words and Expressions 核心术语 _76
    Questions and Discussion 问题与讨论 _76

More Knowledge 知识扩展 _77

Topic: Methods Application in Business Valuation
　　资产评估方法在企业价值评估中的应用 _77
　　　　Abstract 中文摘要 _77
　　　　Text 正文 _78
　　　　Core Words and Expressions 核心术语 _81
　　　　Questions and Discussion 问题与讨论 _83

Information Extension 思政微课堂 _83

Chapter 3　Plant and Equipment Valuation
机器设备评估

Wisdom 名人名言 _85

Rudimentary Knowledge 基本知识 _86
　　　　Abstract 中文摘要 _86
　　　　Text 正文 _87
　　　　Core Words and Expressions 核心术语 _90
　　　　Questions and Discussion 问题与讨论 _91

More Knowledge 知识扩展 _91

Topic: Fair Value Measures of Plant and Equipment
　　机器设备的公允价值计量 _91
　　　　Abstract 中文摘要 _91
　　　　Text 正文 _92
　　　　Core Words and Expressions 核心术语 _95
　　　　Questions and Discussion 问题与讨论 _96

Information Extension 思政微课堂 _96

Chapter 4　Real Property Interests Valuation
不动产权益评估

Wisdom 名人名言 _97

Rudimentary Knowledge 基本知识 _98

  Abstract 中文摘要 _98

  Text 正文 _99

  Core Words and Expressions 核心术语 _107

  Questions and Discussion 问题与讨论 _108

More Knowledge 知识扩展 _109

Topic: The Diversity of Real Estate Valuation
  不动产评估的多样性 _109

  Abstract 中文摘要 _109

  Text 正文 _109

  Core Words and Expressions 核心术语 _113

  Questions and Discussion 问题与讨论 _114

Information Extension 思政微课堂 _114

Chapter 5　Intangible Assets Valuation
无形资产评估

Wisdom 名人名言 _116

Rudimentary Knowledge 基本知识 _117

  Abstract 中文摘要 _117

  Text 正文 _118

  Core Words and Expressions 核心术语 _127

  Questions and Discussion 问题与讨论 _129

More Knowledge 知识扩展 _130

Topic 1: Intellectual Property Valuation 知识产权评估 _130
  Abstract 中文摘要 _130
  Text 正文 _130
  Core Words and Expressions 核心术语 _135
  Questions and Discussion 问题与讨论 _135

Topic 2: Intangible Assets Valuation Process
  无形资产评估程序 _136
  Abstract 中文摘要 _136
  Text 正文 _137
  Core Words and Expressions 核心术语 _145
  Questions and Discussion 问题与讨论 _146

Topic 3: Amortization and Impairment of Intangible Assets
  无形资产的摊销和减值 _146
  Abstract 中文摘要 _146
  Text 正文 _147
  Core Words and Expressions 核心术语 _153
  Questions and Discussion 问题与讨论 _154

Information Extension 思政微课堂 _154

Chapter 6　Business Valuation
企业价值评估

Wisdom 名人名言 _156

Rudimentary Knowledge 基本知识 _157
  Abstract 中文摘要 _157
  Text 正文 _158

Core Words and Expressions 核心术语 _174

Questions and Discussion 问题与讨论 _177

More Knowledge 知识扩展 _178

Topic1: Business Information Collection and Analysis 企业信息收集与分析 _178

Abstract 中文摘要 _178

Text 正文 _179

Core Words and Expressions 核心术语 _185

Questions and Discussion 问题与讨论 _186

Topic2: M&A Valuation Process 企业并购估值流程 _186

Abstract 中文摘要 _186

Text 正文 _187

Core Words and Expressions 核心术语 _193

Questions and Discussion 问题与讨论 _193

Information Extension 思政微课堂 _193

Chapter 7　Valuations for Financial Reporting 以财务报告为目的的评估

Wisdom 名人名言 _196

Rudimentary Knowledge 基本知识 _197

Abstract 中文摘要 _197

Text 正文 _197

Core Words and Expressions 核心术语 _207

Questions and Discussion 问题与讨论 _208

More Knowledge 知识扩展 _208

Topic 1: Fair Value and Financial Reporting
公允价值与财务报告 _208
 Abstract 中文摘要 _208
 Text 正文 _209
 Core Words and Expressions 核心术语 _213
 Questions and Discussion 问题与讨论 _214

Topic 2: Goodwill and Impairment 商誉和减值 _214
 Abstract 中文摘要 _214
 Text 正文 _215
 Core Words and Expressions 核心术语 _221
 Questions and Discussion 问题与讨论 _221

Information Extension 思政微课堂 _221

Chapter 8 Tax Base Assessment
税基评估

Wisdom 名人名言 _223

Rudimentary Knowledge 基本知识 _224
 Abstract 中文摘要 _224
 Text 正文 _224
 Core Words and Expressions 核心术语 _230
 Questions and Discussion 问题与讨论 _231

More Knowledge 知识扩展 _231

Topic 1: Mass Appraisal of Real Property 房地产批量评估 _231
 Abstract 中文摘要 _231
 Text 正文 _232

Core Words and Expressions 核心术语 _237

Questions and Discussion 问题与讨论 _238

Topic 2: Automated Valuation Models (AVMs) 自动评估模型 _238

Abstract 中文摘要 _238

Text 正文 _239

Core Words and Expressions 核心术语 _241

Questions and Discussion 问题与讨论 _242

Information Extension 思政微课堂 _242

Chapter 9　Other Assets Valuation
其他资产评估

Wisdom 名人名言 _244

Part Ⅰ: Financial Instruments Valuation 金融工具评估 _245

Abstract 中文摘要 _245

Text 正文 _245

Core Words and Expressions 核心术语 _254

Questions and Discussion 问题与讨论 _255

Part Ⅱ: Non-Cash Flow Producing Assets Valuation 无法产生现金流量的资产的评估 _245

Abstract 中文摘要 _255

Text 正文 _256

Core Words and Expressions 核心术语 _258

Questions and Discussion 问题与讨论 _258

Part Ⅲ: Mineral Rights Valuation 矿业权评估 _259

Abstract 中文摘要 _259

Text 正文 _259

Core Words and Expressions 核心术语 _263

Questions and Discussion 问题与讨论 _264

Information Extension 思政微课堂 _264

Chapter 10　Valuation Reporting
资产评估报告

Wisdom 名人名言 _266

Rudimentary Knowledge 基本知识 _267

Abstract 中文摘要 _267

Text 正文 _268

Core Words and Expressions 核心术语 _273

Questions and Discussion 问题与讨论 _273

More Knowledge 知识扩展 _274

Topic: Reporting under Valuation Standards_274

Abstract 中文摘要 _274

Text 正文 _274

Core Words and Expressions 核心术语 _279

Questions and Discussion 问题与讨论 _280

Information Extension 思政微课堂 _281

Chapter 11　Valuation Standards
资产评估准则

Wisdom 名人名言 _283

Rudimentary Knowledge 基本知识 _284

Abstract 中文摘要 _284

Text 正文 _285

Core Words and Expressions 核心术语 _287

Questions and Discussion 问题与讨论 _288

More Knowledge 知识扩展 _288

Topic 1: Chinese Valuation Standards (CVS) 中国评估准则 _288

Abstract 中文摘要 _288

Text 正文 _291

Core Words and Expressions 核心术语 _295

Questions and Discussion 问题与讨论 _296

Topic 2: International Valuation Standards (IVS) 国际评估准则 _296

Abstract 中文摘要 _296

Text 正文 _298

Core Words and Expressions 核心术语 _301

Questions and Discussion 问题与讨论 _302

Topic 3: European Valuation Standard (EVS) 欧洲评估准则 _302

Abstract 中文摘要 _302

Text 正文 _304

Core Words and Expressions 核心术语 _311

Questions and Discussion 问题与讨论 _312

Topic 4: Uniform Standards of Professional Appraisal Practice (USPAP) 美国评估准则 _313

Abstract 中文摘要 _313

Text 正文 _315

Core Words and Expressions 核心术语 _319

Questions and Discussion 问题与讨论 _320

Topic 5: RICS Red Book 英国评估准则 _320

Abstract 中文摘要 _320

Text 正文 _322
Core Words and Expressions 核心术语 _329
Questions and Discussion 问题与讨论 _330

Information Extension 思政微课堂 _330

Appendix I   Glossary 术语表 _333

Appendix II   Appraisal Industry Associations and Useful Websites (selected) 资产评估行业组织及实用网站 _365

References 参考文献 _370

Chapter 1
Introduction to Valuation
资产评估概述

Wisdom
名人名言

善治财者，养其所自来，而收其所有余，故用之不竭，而上下交足也。

——司马光

天下不患无财，患无人以分之。

——管仲

Price is what you pay. Value is what you get.

Warren Buffett

A cynic is a man who knows the price of everything and the value of nothing.

—Oscar Wilde

Nobody can go back and start a new beginning, but anyone can start today and make a new ending.

—Maria Robinson

Rudimentary Knowledge
基本知识

Abstract 中文摘要

资产评估是指由资产评估机构及其资产评估专业人员依据一定的执业标准对资产的价值进行评定估算的专业化活动。《中华人民共和国资产评估法》定义的资产评估是"评估机构及其评估专业人员根据委托对不动产、动产、无形资产、企业价值、资产损失或者其他经济权益进行评定、估算,并出具评估报告的专业服务行为"。

关于资产评估的英语用法,一般而言,"appraisal, appraise, appraiser"在早期属于美式英语用法,主要在美国及受美国影响较大的国家使用;而"valuation, value, valuer"在早期属于英式英语用法,主要在英国以及一些英联邦国家使用。因此,在阅读早期的评估报告、专业书籍或者文章时,我们可以根据专业词汇的选择使用情况对其历史渊源进行辨别,但随着时间的推移和国际化进程的推进,二者混用的情况日益普遍。中国即属于上述用法混用的情况,这也充分体现了我国资产评估行业发展的综合性特征。此外,还有一些用以表示资产评估的其他常用词汇,如"survey、assessment、rate、evaluation"等,但其在不动产、税收、金融等不同专业领域的适用性方面存在差异。此外,资产评估专业人员还应正确把握资产的价格、成本和价值之间的关系。

资产评估的基本要素通常包括评估主体、评估客体、评估依据、评估目的、评估原则、价值类型、评估假设、评估程序、评估方法、评估基准日等构成要素。其中,价值类型是指资产评估结果的价值属性及其表现形式。不同的价值类型从不同的角度反映资产评估价值的属性和特征;不同属性的价值类型所代表的资产评估价值不仅在性质上不同,而且在数量上往往也存在较大差异。资产评估价值类型一般包括市场价值和市场价值以外的价值类型。市场价值是指自愿买方和自愿卖方在各自理性行事且未受任何强迫的情况下,评估对象在评估基准日进行正常公平交易的价值估计数额;市场价值以外的价值类型又称非市场价值,是一系列价值类型集合的概括性称呼,通常包括投资价值、在用价值、清算价值、残余价值、公平价值、特殊价值、协同价值、保险价值、课税价值、市场租金、抵押贷款价值等。作为资产评估的基本要素之一，评估假设的合理选择和设定也是十分必要和重要的。评估假设是依据现有知识和有限事实，通过逻辑推理，对资产评估所依托的事实或前提条件作出的合乎情理的推断或假定。评估假设也是资产评估结论成立的前提条件。评估假设一般包括假设和特殊假设，不同的资产评估准则对评估假设的划分方法可能略有差异。常见的评估假设有交易假设、公开市场假设、持续经营假设、清算假设等。

资产评估准则是规范和指导资产评估专业人员执业的技术规范和职业道德规范的总称，是保证其执业质量的行业公认标准。根据发布主体及应用范围，资产评估准则可分为国际组织评估准则、区域组织评估准则、中国评估准则和外国评估准则。例如，国际评估准则（IVS）作为目前最具国际影响力的国际组织评估准则，主要用于规范资产评估执业行为，保证执业质量，明确执业责任，维护社会公共利益和资产评估各方当事人合法权益，以满足财务报告、国际资本市场和国际经济领域的需要。而中国资产评估准则体系是由财政部制定的资产评估基本准则和中国资产评估协会根据资产评估基本准则制定的资产评估执业准则和资产评估职业道德准则构成。中国资产评估准则体系的制定和发布，对于推动我国资产评估行业健康发展、使其更好服务于改革与发展大局具有重要意义。

Text* 正文

1. Valuation Concept

1.1 Value and Valuation

Webster's Third International Dictionary defines "value" in part as follows: "a fair return on equivalents in goods, services or money for something exchanged; the monetary worth of something; marketable price; relative worth, utility, or importance; something intrinsically valuable or desirable."

Any discussion of value must begin with the realization that there are many

---

* *Partly from:* The International Valuation Standards Council (IVSC), *International Valuation Standards*, 2007 Edition, 2007; The International Valuation Standards Council (IVSC), *International Valuation Standards*, 2011 Edition, 2011; The International Valuation Standards Council (IVSC), *International Valuation Standards*, 2022 Edition, 2021; The European Group of Valuers' Associations (TEGOVA), *European Valuation Standards*, 8th Edition, 2016.

different types, including:

(a) social value;

(b) ethical value;

(c) moral value;

(d) sentimental value;

(e) economic value;

(f) commercial value.

In the *International Glossary of Business Valuation Terms*, the term "valuation" is defined as "the act or process of determining the value of a business, business ownership interest, security, or intangible asset." Valuation focuses on two of the types of value listed above: economic and commercial value. Economic value is the value of an asset derived from its ability to generate income. It is the financial return that can be generated through ownership. Commercial value is defined as "pertaining to business; done with a profit motive". Therefore, commercial value relates to business profits. Combining the definitions above, valuation is the process used to determine the economic or commercial value or range of values for subject assets.

In International Valuation Standards (IVS), valuation is defined as "the process of estimating value". The word "valuation" refers to the estimated value (the valuation conclusion) or the preparation of the estimated value (the act of valuing).

1.2 Appraisal and Valuation

Appraisal and valuation are the most common words in this field. There is no huge difference between them. Webster's International Dictionary defines appraisal as "the act of estimating the value of an asset or assets, goods, etc.; an estimate of value, as for sale, assessment, or taxation". In Uniform Standards of Professional Appraisal Practice (USPAP), appraisal is defined as "the act or process of developing an opinion of value; an opinion of value".

In general, appraisal is similar to valuation in professional language. American English prefers the derivatives from Appraise, while British English prefers the ones from Value. Generally, the words used in reports only suggest the writer's origin.

Therefore, appraisal, <u>appraise</u> and <u>appraiser</u> are mainly used in American English-speaking areas, the US and other countries affected by America; while valuation, value and <u>valuer</u> are largely used in British English-speaking areas, the UK and the commonwealth countries. Basically, through the words we can find out the country from which the reports or other materials come.

In China, Assets Valuation has been influenced by both British and the United States. <u>China Appraisal Society (CAS)</u> is the authoritative valuation association in China and <u>Public Valuer (PV)</u> stands for the professionals. In this aspect, we could find the comprehensive feature of China's assets valuation industry.

1.3 Survey, Assessment, Rate and Evaluation

Survey aims at measurement; and survey also has the meaning of valuation in early England and some commonwealth countries. In certain cases, surveyors are also called valuers. Assessment and rate are mostly used for tax purposes and evaluation is for financial purposes.

1.4 Price, Cost and Value

Price is the monetary amount asked, offered, or paid for an asset. The price may differ from the value of an asset because of complications such as financial capabilities, motivations or the special interests of a given buyer or seller.

Cost is the monetary amount required to acquire or create an asset. The cost appears when an asset has been acquired or created. The price paid for an asset is the cost to the buyer.

Value is not a fact but a perception of the most probable price to be paid for an asset in an exchange, or the economic benefits of owning an asset.

A value in exchange is a hypothetical price, and the <u>hypothesis</u> on which the value is estimated is determined by the purpose of the valuation. A value to the owner is an estimate of the benefits that would accrue to a particular party from ownership.

2. Basis of Value

A <u>basis of value</u> is a statement of the fundamental measurement assumptions of a valuation. It describes the fundamental assumptions on which the reported value will be based, e.g., the nature of the hypothetical transaction, the relationship and motivation of the parties and the extent to which the asset is exposed to the market. The appropriate basis will vary depending on the purpose of the valuation.

A basis of valuation can fall into one of three principal categories:

The first is to indicate the most likely price that would be achieved in a free and open market. Market value falls into this category.

The second is to indicate the benefits that a person or an entity enjoys from ownership of an asset. The value is specific to that person or entity, and may have no relevance to market participants in general. Investment value and special value fall into this category.

The third is to indicate the price that would be reasonably agreed between two specific parties for the exchange of an asset. The asset is not necessarily exposed in the market and the price agreed by both parties may be the figure that reflects the specific advantages or disadvantages of the ownership to the parties involved rather than to the market at large, although both parties may be unconnected and negotiating at arm's length. Equitable value falls into this category.

Besides, valuations may require the use of different bases of value that are subjected to criteria such as regulation, private contract, or other documents. Although such bases may appear similar to the bases of value defined in some valuation standards, their application may require a different approach from that described in them. Such bases have to be interpreted and applied in accordance with the provisions of the source document.

2.1 Market Value

Market value is the estimated amount for which an asset should exchange on the valuation date between a willing buyer and a willing seller in an arm's length transaction, after proper marketing. Meanwhile, the parties should participate knowledgeably, prudently and voluntarily. The definition of market value shall be applied in accordance with the following conceptual framework:

Chapter 1 Introduction to Valuation 资产评估概述

(a) "The estimated amount" refers to the estimated value for an asset rather than a predetermined amount or actual sale price. Market value is the most probable price reasonably obtainable in the market on the valuation date in keeping with the market value definition. It is the best price reasonably obtainable by the seller and the most advantageous price reasonably obtainable by the buyer. This estimate excludes an estimated price subject to special terms or circumstances, such as atypical financing, sale and leaseback arrangements, special considerations or concessions granted by anyone associated with the sale, or any element of special value.

(b) "An asset should exchange" refers to the asset being exchanged between buyers and sellers in market transaction. The value of an asset is the price in a transaction that meets all the elements of the market value definition at the valuation date.

(c) "On the valuation date" requires that the value is time-specific to a given date. Because markets and market conditions may change, the estimated value may vary with time. The valuation amount should reflect the actual market state and circumstances as of the effective valuation date, not as of either a past or future date.

(d) "Between a willing buyer" refers to voluntary buyers. This buyer is neither overestimated nor determined to buy at any price. This buyer is also one who purchases in accordance with the realities of the current market and with reasonable market expectations, rather than in relation to an imaginary or hypothetical market that cannot be demonstrated or anticipated to exist. The assumed buyer would not pay a higher price than one that the market requires. The present owner is included among those who constitute "the market".

(e) "A willing seller" is neither an overestimated nor a forced seller prepared to sell at any price, nor one intended to hold out for an unreasonable price in the current market. The willing seller is motivated to sell the asset at market terms for the best price attainable in the open market after proper marketing, whatever price may be. The factual circumstances of the actual owner are not a part of this consideration because the willing seller is a hypothetical owner.

(f) "In an arm's length transaction" exists between parties who lack a special relationship, e.g., parent and subsidiary companies or landlord and tenant, that may make the price level uncharacteristic of the market or inflated because of an element of special value. The market value transaction is presumed to be between independent parties.

(g) "After proper marketing" means that the asset would be exposed to the market in the most appropriate manner to effect its disposal at the best price reasonably obtainable in accordance with the market value definition. The method of sale is deemed to be that most appropriate to obtain the best price in the market to which the seller has access. The length of exposure time may vary according to the type of asset and market conditions. The only criteria is that there must be sufficient time for the asset to attract an adequate number of market participants. The exposure period occurs prior to the valuation date.

(h) "Where the parties had each acted knowledgeably, prudently" presumes that both the willing buyer and the willing seller are reasonably informed about the nature and characteristics of the asset, the actual and potential uses of it, and the state of the market as of the valuation date. Each is further presumed to use that knowledge prudently to seek the price that is most favourable for their respective positions in the transaction. Prudence is assessed by referring to the state of the market at the valuation date, not with benefit of hindsight at some later date. For example, it is not necessarily imprudent for a seller to sell assets in a market with falling prices at a price that is lower than previous market levels. In such cases, as are true for other exchanges in markets with changing prices, the prudent buyer or seller will act in accordance with the best market information available at the time.

(i) "And without compulsion" establishes that each party is motivated to undertake the transaction, and neither is forced nor unduly coerced to complete the transaction.

The concept of market value presumes a price negotiated in an open and competitive market where the participants are acting freely. The market value of an asset will reflect its highest and best use. The highest and best use is the use of an asset that maximizes its productivity that is technically possible, legally permissible and financially feasible. The highest and best use may be for the continuation of the asset's existing use or for some alternative use. This is determined by the use that a market participant would have in mind for the asset when formulating the price that he/she would be willing to bid.

2.2 Investment Value

Investment value is the value of an asset to the owner or a prospective owner for individual investment or operational objectives. This subjective concept relates specific property to a specific investor, group of investors, or entity with identifiable investment objectives and/or criteria. Although the value of an asset to the owner may be the same as the amount that could be realized from its sale to another party, this basis of value reflects the benefits received by an entity from holding the asset and, therefore, does not necessarily involve a hypothetical exchange. Investment value reflects the circumstances and financial objectives of the entity for which the valuation is being produced. The valuation is often used for measuring investment performance. The investment value of an asset may be higher or lower than the market value of the asset. The difference between the investment value of an asset and its market value motivates buyers or sellers to enter the market place.

2.3 Equitable Value

Equitable value is the estimated price, for the transfer of an asset or liability between identified knowledgeable and willing parties, that reflects the respective interests of those parties. Equitable value can be distinguished from market value. Equitable value requires the assessment of the price that is fair between two identified parties, considering the respective advantages or disadvantages that will be gained from the transaction. It is commonly applied in judicial contexts. In contrast, market value that requires any advantages unavailable to market participants generally will be disregarded.

Equitable value is a concept broader than market value. Although in many cases the fair price may equate to the price obtainable in the market, the assessment of equitable is likely to consider matters that have to be disregarded in the assessment of market value, such as any element of special value arising because of the combination of the interests.

Examples of the use of equitable include: determination of a price that is fair for a shareholding in a non-quoted business, where the holdings of two specific parties may mean that the price that is fair between them is different from the price that might be obtainable in the market; determination of a price that would be fair between a leaser and a lessee for either the permanent transfer of the leased asset or the cancellation of the lease liability.

2.4 Special Value

Special value is the amount that reflects particular attributes of an asset that are only of value to a special purchaser. A special purchaser is a particular buyer for whom a particular asset has special value because of advantages arising from its ownership that would not be available to other buyers in the market.

Special value can arise if an asset has attributes that make it more attractive to a particular buyer than to any other buyers in a market. These attributes can include the physical, geographic, economic or legal characteristics of an asset. Market value requires the disregard of any special value because at any given date it is only assumed that there is a willing buyer, rather than a particular willing buyer. When special value is identified, it should be reported and clearly distinguished from market value.

2.5 Synergistic Value

Synergistic value is the additional element of value created by the combination of two or more assets or interests and the combined value is more than the sum of the separate values. If the synergy is only available to one specific buyer, then it is an example of special value.

2.6 Value in Use

Value in use is the value that a specific property has for a specific use to a specific user and therefore non-market related. This value type focuses on the value that specific property contributes to the entity of which it is a part, regardless of the property's highest and best use or the monetary amount that might be realized upon its sale. The accounting definition of value in use is the present value of estimated future cash flows expected to arise from the continuing use of an asset and from its disposal at the end of its useful life.

2.7 Liquidation or Forced Sale Value

Liquidation or forced sale value is the amount that may reasonably be received from the sale of a property within a time frame too short to meet the marketing time frame required by the market value definition. In some states, forced sale value in particular may also involve an unwilling seller and a buyer or buyers who buy with knowledge of the disadvantage of the seller.

2.8 Salvage Value

Salvage value is the value of a property, excluding land, as if disposed of for the materials it contains, rather than for continued use without special repairs or adaptation. It may be given as gross or net of disposal costs and, in the latter case, may equate to net realizable value. In any event, components included or excluded should be identified.

2.9 Market Rent

Market rent is the estimated amount for which an interest in real property should be leased on the valuation date between a willing lessor and a willing lessee on appropriate lease terms in an arm's length transaction, after proper marketing and where the parties had each acted knowledgeably, prudently and without compulsion.

Market rent may be used as a basis of value when valuing a lease or an interest created by a lease. In such cases, it is necessary to consider the contract rent and, where it is different, the market rent.

2.10 Insurable Value

Insurable value is the value of property provided by definitions contained in an insurance contract or policy.

2.11 Assessed, Rateable, or Taxable Value

Assessed, rateable, or taxable value is the value that contains applicable laws relating to the assessment, rating, and/or taxation of property. Although some jurisdictions may cite market value as the assessment basis, methods used to estimate the value may produce results that differ from market value. Therefore, assessed, rateable, or taxable value cannot be considered to comply with market value unless explicitly indicated to the contrary.

2.12 Mortgage Lending Value

Mortgage lending value is the value of a property as determined by professionals assessing the future marketability of the property by taking into account long-term sustainable aspects of the property, the normal and local market conditions, and the current use and alternative appropriate uses of the property. Speculative elements may be excluded in the assessment of mortgage lending value. The mortgage lending value shall be documented in a transparent and clear manner. Mortgage lending value is one of a number of risk analysis techniques, which may be used to calculate the risk weighting that may be attached to mortgaged security held by a bank. This is a long-term risk assessment technique, which is not a suitable basis for establishing value at a given point in time. In this way, the mortgage lending value differs fundamentally from other bases of value.

2.13 Fair Value or Fair Market Value

International Financial Reporting Standards (IFRS) defines fair value as the price that would be received to sell an asset or paid to transfer a liability in an orderly transaction between market participants at the measurement date. For financial reporting purposes, over 130 countries require or permit the use of International Accounting Standards (IAS) published by the International Accounting Standards Board (IASB).

The Organisation for Economic Co-operation and Development (OECD) defines fair market value as the price a willing buyer would pay a willing seller in a transaction on the open market. OECD guidance is used in many engagements for international tax purposes.

Many national, state and local agencies use fair value as a basis of value in a legal context. The definitions can vary significantly and may be the result of legislative action or those established by courts in prior cases.

3. Valuation Assumptions

In addition to stating the basis of value, it is often necessary to make an

<u>assumption</u> or multiple assumptions to clarify either the state of the asset in the hypothetical exchange or the circumstances under which the asset is assumed to be exchanged. Such assumptions can have a significant impact on value. Besides, the valuer may have to make special assumptions in order to complete the valuation effectively, often in the absence of particular information. In either case those assumptions should be clearly stated.

3.1 Assumptions

The valuer makes an assumption that something on a matter of fact which he/she does not or cannot know or reasonably ascertain.

The valuer must undertake inspections and investigations to the extent necessary to produce a professional valuation for the purpose instructed. The valuer may need to make assumptions to enable an opinion of value to be reported in the absence of full data or knowledge. Assumptions may relate to facts, conditions or situations affecting the valuation. In the absence of full information, valuation under assumptions is considered to be most likely correct. For matters that may be beyond the valuer's ability to check independently, the assumption may be accompanied by a recommendation that the client has the facts established by those with the appropriate specialist skills. When assumptions made are subsequently found to be incorrect, the valuer may need to review and amend the figures reported and refer to that possibility in the report.

The following is an indicative, but not exhaustive, list of matters that may be reported as matters where assumptions have been made in arriving at an opinion of the value of property:

(a) A detailed report on title that sets out any encumbrances, restrictions or liabilities that may affect the value of the property may not be available. In such a case, the valuer would have to assume a position considered most likely happened, also state that he is not responsible for the true interpretation of the legal title;

(b) The extent of the inspection should be clearly set out in the report, consistent with the nature of the instruction and the type of property. It may be necessary to make the assumption that, while any obvious defects have been noted, other defects may exist, therefore a more detailed survey or the appointment of specific experts are required. Moreover, it is necessary to follow a comment that the opinion of value stated is based on the condition as reported and therefore any additional defects that exist may require the figures to be amended;

(c) Assumptions may be needed with regard to the necessary statutory consents for the current buildings and use together with reference to any policies or proposals by statutory bodies that could impact positively or adversely on the value;

(d) The competence of the valuer to report on any potential risk of contamination or the presence of hazardous substances needs to be considered. It may be necessary to make assumptions in providing an opinion of value that either no such risks exist or that the valuer rely on information prepared by specialist consultants;

(e) The valuer may, on occasion, need to assume that all main services provided are operational and sufficient for the intended use;

(f) It may be necessary to make an assumption as to whether the property has not, or will not be expected to flood or whether other environmental matters may bear on the opinion of value;

(g) Wherever the property is let and to be valued as such, it may be necessary to assume that detailed enquiries about the financial status of tenants would not reveal matters that might affect the valuation;

(h) The valuer may need to assume that there are no planning or highway proposals that might involve the use of any statutory powers or otherwise directly affect the property;

(i) The valuer may assume that items of plant and equipment normally considered being part of the service installations to a building would pass with the property.

3.2 Special Assumptions

Assumption differs from facts existing at the date of valuation becomes a <u>special assumption</u>. Special assumptions are often used to illustrate the effect of possible changes on the value of an asset. They are designated as "special" so as to highlight to a valuation user that the valuation conclusion is contingent upon a change in the current circumstances or that it reflects a view that would not be taken by market participants generally on the valuation date.

This may often be to inform the client about the effect of changed circumstances on the valuation. Examples include the valuer being instructed to make special assumptions as to the value of the property:

(a) were it vacant when in fact the property is let;

(b) were planning permission to be obtained for a particular use.

Assumptions and special assumptions must be reasonable and relevant with regard to the purpose for which the valuation is required. Assumptions should be recorded in the terms of engagement and in the valuation report.

Core Words and Expressions 核心术语

value	价值，评估
economic value	经济价值
commercial value	商业价值
valuation	评估，估值
International Valuation Standards (IVS)	国际评估准则
appraisal	评估的
Uniform Standards of Professional Appraisal Practice (USPAP)	专业评估执业统一准则
appraise	评估
appraiser	评估专业人员，评估师
valuer	评估专业人员，评估师
China Appraisal Society (CAS)	中国资产评估协会
Public Valuer (PV)	资产评估师
hypothesis	假说，假设，前提
basis of value	价值类型

market value	市场价值
market participants	市场参与者
investment value	投资价值
special value	特殊价值
equitable value	公平价值
valuation date	评估基准日
a willing buyer	自愿买方
a willing seller	自愿卖方
an arm's length transaction	公平交易
equitable value	公平价值
shareholding in a non-quoted business	非上市公司股权
synergistic value	协同价值
value in use	在用价值
liquidation or forced sale value	清算价值，强迫出售价值
salvage value	残余价值
market rent	市场租金
insurable value	保险价值，可保价值
assessed, rateable, or taxable value	课税价值
mortgage lending value	抵押贷款价值
International Financial Reporting Standards (IFRS)	国际财务报告准则
fair value	公允价值
International Accounting Standards (IAS)	国际会计准则
International Accounting Standards Board (IASB)	国际会计准则理事会

Chapter 1 Introduction to Valuation 资产评估概述

Organisation for Economic Co-operation and Development (OECD)	经济合作与发展组织
fair market value	公允市场价值
assumption	假设
special assumption	特殊假设

Questions and Discussion 问题与讨论

1. What is your understanding of value?

2. As for understanding market value, what do we need to focus on?

3. How can we know that an asset is being highest and best used?

4. Please list the common bases of value.

5. What is the function of valuation assumptions?

6. What is the difference between assumptions and special assumptions in the context of valuation?

More Knowledge
知识扩展

Topic: Valuation under Uncertainty 评估的不确定性

Abstract 中文摘要

资产评估属于价值判断范畴。无论是金融资产、不动产还是其他类型的资产，任何资产都有其价值。为了更好地投资和管理资产，资产评估是必不可少的关键步骤。不同类型的资产适用不同的评估方法，但其基本原则却是相似的。在对一项资产进行评估时，不能仅仅依赖于主观认识，而是要注重联系实际，通过收集不同的信息并对其进行分析和计算来确定资产的价值。

资产评估专业人员在评估过程中也不可避免地会遇到不确定性问题，因而应当尽可能将不确定性因素纳入评估模型中。但与其他分析性学科一样，资产评估领域也存在着一些有待检验的看法，甚至是理解误区。例如：

（1）因为评估模型是量化的，所以评估价值一定是客观的；

（2）经过系统分析，运用正确的评估方法所得到的评估结果的正确性，不会随着时间推移而改变；

（3）一次充分、正确的评估一定能给出被评估资产最准确的价值；

（4）评估的模型量化程度越高，评估的质量越高；

（5）为了从评估中获利，必须假设市场是低效率的；

（6）真正重要的是评估的结果而不是过程。

资产评估在诸如证券投资、并购分析、公司财务等许多不同的领域都发挥着重大的作用。在证券投资分析中，不同的投资者对评估往往有着不同的应用程度与应用方式；在并购分析领域，资产评估则一直占有相当重要的地位。随着企业管理的目标逐渐趋向于企业价值最大化，资产评估在公司财务方面也越来越受到相应的重视。

Text* 正文

Every asset, financial as well as real, has a value. The key to successfully investing in and managing these assets lies in understanding not only what the value is but also the sources of the value. Any asset can be valued, but some assets are easier to value than others and the details of valuation may vary from case to case. Thus, the valuation of a share of a real estate property requires different information and follows a format different from the valuation of a publicly traded stock. What is surprising, however, is not the difference in valuation techniques across assets, but the degree of similarity in basic principles. There is undeniably uncertainty associated with valuation. The uncertainty often comes from the asset being valued, though a valuation model

---

* Partly from: Damodaran A. Investment valuation: Tools and Techniques for Determining the Value of Any Asset.3rd Edition, John Wiley & Sons, Inc., 2012: 1-9.

may add to that uncertainty.

This part lays out a philosophical basis for valuation, together with a discussion of how valuation is and can be used in a variety of <u>frameworks</u>, from <u>portfolio management</u> to corporate finance.

1. A Philosophical Basis for Valuation

It was Oscar Wilde who described a cynic as one who "knows the price of everything, but the value of nothing". He could describe some equity research analysts and many investors, a surprising number of people who subscribe to the "bigger fool" theory of investing, which argues that the value of an asset is irrelevant as long as a "bigger fool" is willing to buy the asset from them. While the above-mentioned argument may provide a basis for some profits, it is a dangerous game to play, since there is no guarantee that such an investor will exist at the same time.

A postulate of sound investing is that an investor pays no more for an asset than its worth. This statement may seem logical and obvious, but it is forgotten and rediscovered in every generation and in every market. A disingenuous one could argue that value is in the eyes of the beholder, and that any price can be justified if other investors are willing to pay that price. That is patently absurd. Perceptions may be all that matter when the asset is a painting or a sculpture, but investors do not (and should not) buy most of the assets for aesthetic or emotional reasons. The financial assets are acquired for the <u>cash flows</u> expected on them. Consequently, perceptions of value have to be backed up by reality, which implies that the price paid for any asset should reflect the cash flows that it is expected to generate. The models of valuation usually attempt to relate value to the level and expected growth in these cash flows.

The details of valuation are often debated, including how to estimate true value and how long it will take for prices to adjust to true value. But there is one opinion with consensus. Asset prices cannot be justified by merely using the argument that there will be other investors around willing to pay a higher price in the future.

2. Generalities about Valuation

Similar to all analytical disciplines, valuation has developed its own set of myths over time. This section examines and debunks a selection of these myths.

Myth 1: Since valuation models are quantitative, valuation is objective

Valuation is neither the science that some of its proponents do not make it out to be nor the objective search for the true value that idealists would like it to become. The models that we use in valuation may be quantitative, but the inputs leave plenty of room for subjective judgments. Thus, the final value that we obtain from these models is coloured by the bias that we bring into the process. In fact, in many valuations, the price gets set first and the valuation follows.

The obvious solution is to eliminate all bias before starting on a valuation, but this is easier said than done. Given the exposure we have to external information, analyses and opinions about a firm, it is unlikely that we embark on most of the valuations without bias. There are two ways of reducing the bias in the process. The first is to avoid taking strong public positions on the value of a firm before the valuation is complete. In far too many cases, the decision on whether a firm is under or overvalued precedes the actual valuation, leading to seriously biased analyses. The second is to minimize the stake we have in whether the firm is under or overvalued, prior to the valuation. Institutional concerns also play a role in determining the extent of bias in valuation. For instance, it is an acknowledged fact that equity research analysts are more likely to issue buy rather than sell recommendations, i.e., they are more likely to find firms to be undervalued than overvalued. This can be traced partly to the difficulties they face in obtaining access and collecting information on firms that they have issued sell recommendations and to the pressure that they face from portfolio managers, some with supposable large positions in the stock. In recent years, this trend has been exacerbated by the pressure on equity research analysts to deliver investment banking business.

When using a valuation done by a third party, the biases of the analyst should be considered before decisions are made on its basis. For instance, a self-valuation done by a target firm in a <u>takeover</u> is likely to be positively biased. While this does not make the valuation worthless, it suggests that the analysis should be viewed with scepticism.

Myth 2: A well-researched and well-done valuation is timeless

The value obtained from any valuation model is affected by firm-specific as well as market-wide information. As a consequence, the value might change as new information is revealed. Given the constant flow of information into financial markets, a valuation done on a firm age quickly, and has to be updated to reflect current information. The information may be specific to the firm, affect an entire sector or alter expectations for all firms in the market. The most common example of firm-specific information is the earnings report that contains news not only about a firm's performance in the most recent time period but also about the business model that the firm has adopted. The dramatic drop in value of many new economy stocks from 1999 to 2001 can be traced, at least partially, to the realization that these firms had business models that could deliver customers but not earnings, even in the long term. In some cases, new information can affect the valuations of all firms in a sector. Thus, pharmaceutical companies that were valued highly in early 1992, on the assumption that the high growth from the eighties would continue into the future, were valued much less in early 1993, as the prospects of health reform and price controls dimmed future prospects. With the benefit of hindsight, the valuations of these companies (and the analyst recommendations) made in 1992 can be criticized, but they were reasonable, given the information available at that time. Finally, information about the state of the economy and the level of interest rates affects all valuations in an economy. A weakening of the economy can lead to a reassessment of growth rates across the board, though the effects on earnings are likely to be the largest at cyclical firms. Similarly, an increase in interest rates will affect all investments, though to varying degrees.

When analysts change their valuations, they will undoubtedly be asked to justify them. In some cases, the fact that valuations change over time is viewed as a problem. The best response may be the one that Lord Keynes gave when he was criticized for changing his position on a major economic issue: "When the facts change, I change my mind. And what do you do, sir?"

Myth 3: A good valuation provides a precise estimate of value

Even at the end of the most careful and detailed valuation, there will be uncertainty about the final numbers, coloured as they are by the assumptions that we make about the future of the company and the economy. It is unrealistic to expect or demand absolute certainty in valuation, since cash flows and discount rates are estimated with error. This also means that one should leave a reasonable margin for error in making recommendations on the basis of valuations.

The degree of precision in valuations is likely to vary widely across investments. The valuation of a large and mature company, with a long financial history, will usually be much more precise than the valuation of a young company, in a turmoil sector. If this company happens to operate in an emerging market, with additional disagreement about the future of the market thrown into the mix, the uncertainty is magnified. Besides, the difficulties associated with valuation can be related to where a firm is in the life cycle. Mature firms tend to be easier to value than growth firms, and young start-up companies are more difficult to value than companies with established produces and markets. The problems are not associated with the valuation models we use, though, but with making estimates for the future.

Many investors and analysts use the uncertainty about the future or the absence of information to justify not doing full-fledged valuations. In reality, though, the payoff to valuation is the greatest in these firms.

Myth 4: The more quantitative a model, the better the valuation

It may seem obvious that making a model more complete and complex should yield better valuations, but it is not necessarily to do so. As models become more complex, the number of inputs needed to value a firm increase, bringing potential input errors. These problems are compounded when models become so complex that they become "black boxes" where analysts feed in numbers into one end and valuations emerge from the other. All too often the blame gets attached to the model rather than the analyst when a valuation fails. The refrain becomes "It was not my fault. The model did it."

There are three points we will emphasize on all valuation. The first is the principle of parsimony, which essentially states that you use no more inputs than absolutely need to value an asset. The second is the <u>trade-off</u> between the benefits of building in more detail and the estimation costs (and error) with providing the detail. The third is that the models do not value companies, you do. In a world where the problem that we often face in valuations is not too little information but too much, separating the information that matters from the information that does not is almost as important as the valuation models and techniques that you use to value a firm.

Myth 5: To make money on valuation, you have to assume that markets are inefficient

Often implicit in the act of valuation is the assumption that markets make mistakes and that we can find these mistakes, often using information that other investors can access. Thus, the argument, that those who believe that markets are inefficient should spend their time and resources on valuation whereas those who believe that markets are efficient should take the market price as the best estimate of value, seems to be reasonable.

This statement, though, veils the internal contradictions in both positions. Those who believe that markets are efficient may still feel that valuation has something to contribute, especially when they are called upon to value the effect of a change in the way a firm is run or to understand why market prices change over time.

Furthermore, it is unclear how markets would become efficient in the first place, if investors did not attempt to find under and overvalued stocks and trade on these valuations. In other words, a pre-condition for market efficiency seems to be the existence of millions of investors who believe that markets are not. However, those who believe that markets make mistakes and buy or sell stocks on that basis ultimately must believe that markets will correct these mistakes, i.e., become efficient, because that is how they make their money.

We approach the issue of market efficiency as wary sceptics. On the one hand, we believe that markets make mistakes but, on the other, finding these mistakes requires a combination of skill and luck. This view of markets leads us to the following conclusions. First, if something looks too good to be true – a stock looks obviously undervalued or overvalued – it is probably not true. Second, when the value from an analysis is significantly different from the market price, we start off with the presumption that the market is correct and we have to convince ourselves that this is not the case before we conclude that something is over or under valued. This higher standard may lead us to be more cautious in following through on valuations.

Myth 6: The product of valuation (i.e., the value) is what matters; the process of valuation is not important.

There are risks in focusing exclusively on the valuation outcome, i.e., the value of the company, and whether it is under or overvalued, and missing the valuable insights that can be obtained from the process of the valuation. The process can reveal the determinants of value and answer some fundamental questions: What is the appropriate price to pay for high growth? What is a brand name worth? How important is it to improve returns on projects? What is the effect of profit margins on value? Since the process is so informative, even those who believe that markets are efficient (and that the market price is therefore the best estimate of value) should be able to find some use for valuation models.

3. The Role of Valuation

Valuation is useful in a wide range of tasks. The role it plays, however, is different in different areas. The following section lays out the relevance of valuation in portfolio management, acquisition analysis and corporate finance.

3.1 Valuation and Portfolio Management

The role that valuation plays in portfolio management is determined mostly by the investment philosophy of the investor. Valuation plays the minimal role in portfolio management for a passive investor, and a larger role for an active investor. Even among active investors, the nature and the role of valuation differ for various types of active investment. Market timers use valuation much less than investors who pick stocks do, and the focus is on market valuation rather than on firm-specific valuation. Among security selectors, valuation plays a central role in portfolio management for fundamental analysts and a peripheral role for technical analysts.

The following sub-section describes, in broad terms, different investment philosophies and the role played by valuation in each.

3.1.1 Fundamental Analysts

The underlying theme in fundamental analysis is that the true value of the firm can be related to its financial characteristics: its growth prospects, risk profile and cash flows. Any deviation from this true value is a sign that a stock is under- or overvalued. It is a long-term investment strategy, and the underlying assumptions are:

The relationship between value and the underlying financial factors can be measured.

The relationship is stable over time.

Deviations from the relationship are corrected in a reasonable time period.

Valuation is the central focus in fundamental analysis. Some analysts use discounted cash flow models to value firms, while others use multiples such as the price-earnings and price-book value ratios. Since investors using this approach hold a large number of "undervalued" stocks in their portfolios, they hope that, on average, these portfolios will do better than the market.

3.1.2 Franchise Buyer

The philosophy of a franchise buyer is best expressed by a successful investor. Franchise buyers concentrate on a few businesses they understand well, and attempt to acquire undervalued firms. Often, franchise buyers wield influence on the management of these firms and can change financial and investment policy. As a long-term strategy, the underlying assumptions are:

(a) Investors who understand a business well are in a better position to value assets correctly.

(b) These undervalued businesses can be acquired without driving the price above the true value.

Valuation plays a key role in this philosophy, since franchise buyers are attracted to a particular business because they believe it is undervalued. They are also interested in how much additional value they can create by restructuring the business and running it right.

3.1.3 Chartists

Chartists believe that prices are driven by investor psychology as much as by any underlying financial variables. The information available from trading, like price movements, trading volume, short sales, etc., gives an indication of investor psychology and future price movements. The assumptions here are that prices move in predictable patterns, that there are not enough marginal investors taking advantage of these patterns to eliminate them, and that the average investor in the market is driven more by emotion rather than by rational analysis.

While valuation plays little role in charting, there are ways whereby an enterprising chartist can incorporate valuation into analysis. For instance, valuation can be used to determine support and resistance lines on price charts.

3.1.4 Information Traders

Prices move on information about the firm. Information traders attempt to trade in advance of new information or shortly after it is revealed to financial markets; buy on good news and sell on bad. The underlying assumption is that these traders can anticipate information announcements and gauge the market reaction to them better than the average investor in the market.

For an information trader, the focus is on the relationship between information and changes in value, rather than on value, per se. Thus, an information trader may buy an overvalued firm if he/she believes that the next information announcement is going to cause the price to go up, because it contains better-than-expected news. If there is a relationship between how undervalued or overvalued a company is and how its stock price reacts to new information, then valuation could play a role in investing for an information trader.

3.1.5 Market Timers

Market timers note, with some legitimacy, that the payoff to calling turns in markets is much greater than the returns from stock picking. They argue that it is easier to predict market movements than to select stocks and that these predictions can be based on observable factors.

While valuation of individual stocks may be useless to a market timer, market timing strategies can use valuation in at least two ways:

(a) The overall market itself can be valued and compared to the current level.

(b) A valuation model can be used to value all stocks, and the results from the cross-section can be used to determine whether the market is over or under valued. For example, as the number of stocks that are overvalued, using the dividend discount model increases relative to the number that are undervalued, therefore there may be reasons to believe that the market is overvalued.

3.1.6 Efficient Marketers

Efficient marketers believe that the market price at any point in time represents the best estimate of the true value of the firm, and that any attempt to exploit perceived market efficiencies will cost more than it will make in excess profits. Efficient marketers assume that markets aggregate information quickly and accurately, that marginal investors promptly exploit any inefficiencies and that any inefficiencies in the market are caused by friction, such as transaction costs, and cannot be arbitraged away.

For efficient marketers, valuation is a useful exercise to determine why a stock sells for the price that it asks. Since the underlying assumption is that the market price is the best estimate of the true value of the company, the objective is to determine what assumptions about growth and risk are implied in this market price, rather than on finding under or overvalued firms.

3.2 Valuation in Acquisition Analysis

Valuation should play a central part of acquisition analysis. The bidding firm or individual has to decide a fair value for the target firm before making a bid, and the target firm has to determine a reasonable value for itself before deciding to accept or reject the offer.

There are also special factors to consider in takeover valuation. First, the effects of synergy on the combined value of two firms (target plus bidding firm) have to be considered before a decision is made on the bid. Valuers who suggest that synergy is impossible to value and should not be considered in quantitative terms are wrong. Second, the effects on value, of changing management and restructuring the target firm, should be taken into account in deciding a fair price, which is of particular concern in hostile takeovers.

Finally, there is a significant problem with bias in takeover valuations. Target firms, especially facing hostile takeover, may be over-optimistic in estimating value, and they try to convince their stockholders that the offer price is too low. Similarly, if the bidding firm has decided, for strategic reasons, to do an acquisition, analysts bear strong pressure to come up with an estimate of value that backs up the acquisition.

3.3 Valuation in Corporate Finance

If the objective in corporate finance is to maximize the firm value, the relationship among financial decisions, corporate strategy and firm value has to be delineated. In recent years, management consulting firms have started offered companies advice on how to increase value. Their suggestions have often provided the basis for the restructuring of these firms.

The value of a firm can be directly related to the corporate decisions on which projects are taken, on how projects are financed, and on the dividend policy. Understanding this relationship is the key to making value-increasing decisions and to sensible financial restructuring.

4. Conclusion

Valuation plays a key role in many areas of finance, such as corporate finance, mergers and acquisitions and portfolio management. Valuation is not an objective exercise, and any preconceptions and biases that an analyst brings to the process will find its way into the value.

Core Words and Expressions 核心术语

framework	框架，结构
portfolio management	投资组合管理
cash flow	现金流
takeover	收购
business model	企业模型
trade-off	权衡

market timer	择时交易者
fundamental analyst	基本面分析者
price-earnings ratio	市盈率
price-book value ratio	市净率
franchise buyer	特许买家
chartist	图表分析专家
trading volume	交易量
short sale	卖空
support line	支撑线
resistance line	压力线
market timing	选时交易
cross-section	横截面
dividend discount model	股利折现模型
transaction cost	交易成本
arbitrage	套利
bid	出价
effect of synergy	协同效应
restructuring	重组
hostile takeover	恶意收购

Questions and Discussion 问题与讨论

1. What is the value of an investment?

2. How do you understand valuation?

3. People claim that value is only based upon investor perception, while cash flows and earnings do not matter. Do you agree with it or not? Why?

Information Extension
思政微课堂

中国资产评估行业诞生于 20 世纪 80 年代末，见证了我国国企改革推进和资本市场发展的步伐。1988 年 3 月，大连会计事务所对大连炼铁厂与香港企荣贸易有限公司合资过程中投资的建筑和机电设备出具了评估报告，这是我国首例资产评估业务。1991 年 11 月，以国务院第 91 号令发布的《国有资产评估管理办法》是我国第一部规范国有资产评估和资产评估行业管理的行政法规，标志着我国资产评估行业走上法制化的道路。2004 年 2 月，财政部发布《资产评估准则——基本准则》《资产评估职业道德准则——基本准则》（财企〔2004〕20 号），成为推动我国建立资产评估准则体系的重要标志。

2016 年 7 月 2 日，十二届全国人大常委会第二十一次会议审议通过《中华人民共和国资产评估法》，自 2016 年 12 月 1 日起施行。该法律对资产评估一系列重大问题作出了明确规定，全面确立了资产评估行业的法律地位，标志着我国资产评估行业进入了法制化发展的新阶段。随后，财政部于 2017 年 4 月 21 日出台《资产评估行业财政监督管理办法》（财政部令第 86 号），并于 2017 年 8 月 23 日发布《资产评估基本准则》（财资〔2017〕43 号），推进资产评估行业财政监督管理和资产评估准则体系建设的与时俱进。

多年来，我国资产评估行业走出了一条适合中国特色社会主义市场经济的专业化道路，其服务领域遍及市场经济各行各业、涉及各种所有制和资产形态，为维护国有资本权益、规范资本市场运作、防范金融系统风险、保障社会公共利益和国家经济安全作出了重要贡献。

Chapter 2
Valuation Approaches
资产评估方法

Wisdom
名人名言

万物得其本者生,百事得其道者成。

——刘向

纸上得来终觉浅,绝知此事要躬行。

——陆游

The problem in valuation is not that there are not enough models to value an asset. It is that there are too many models. Choosing the right model to use in valuation is as critical to arriving at a reasonable value as understanding how to use the model.

—Aswath Damodaran

At twenty years of age, the will reigns; at thirty, the wit; and at forty, the judgment.

—Benjamin Franklin

Rudimentary Knowledge
基本知识

Topic 1: The Market Approach 市场法

Abstract 中文摘要

市场法也称为市场比较法、销售比较法等，指以市场近期售出的相同或类似资产的交易价格为基础，通过比较被评估资产与最近售出的相同或类似资产的异同，将类似资产的市场价格进行调整，从而确定被评估资产价值的一种资产评估思路。市场法的基本原则包括供求原则、替代原则、平衡原则、外部性原则等。

市场法有两个重要的适用前提：一是评估对象的可比参照物具有公开的市场，市场上有足够多的自愿买者和卖者，并存在活跃的交易行为；二是可比参照物的交易信息可以获得，市场成交价格基本上可以反映市场行情，由此估测得到的评估结果则会更贴近市场，也更容易被资产交易各方所接受。

市场法的基本应用步骤如下：（1）明确评估对象并选择可比参照物：选取在功能、市场条件以及交易时间与评估对象可比的参照物，参照物的数量越多，越能够充分和全面反映资产的市场价值；（2）在评估对象与参照物之间选择比较因素：影响资产价值的基本因素理论上大致相同，所以运用市场法时，应根据不同种类资产的价值形成特点和影响价值的主要因素，形成综合反映参照物与评估对象之间的比较参数体系和对比指标；（3）指标对比和量化差异：根据上述选定的对比指标，资产评估专业人员在评估对象和参照物之间进行指标的比较，并将其差异量化或者货币化；（4）分析确定已经量化的对比指标之间的差异：资产评估专业人员通过对比指标之间的差异，形成对评估对象价值的调查结果，并得到初步评估结果；（5）综合分析确定评估结果：若有多个参照物，则需对多个初步评估结果进行综合分析，可以采用算数平均法或者加权平均法形成最终的评估结果。

市场法的具体方法包括直接比较法、类比调整法、价值比率法等。按照所调整因素差异的不同，市场法可以进一步表现为用于调整时间因素差异的价格指数法、用于调整区域因素差异的打分法（或间接比较法）、用于调整功能因素差异的功能价值法、用于调整交易条件差异的价格折扣法、用于调整实体新旧程度差异的成新率法等；按照所选价值指标的不同，市场法可以进一步表现为市盈率法、市净率法、市销率法等。

市场法能够客观地反映资产目前的市场情况，其使用的参数和指标都是直接从市场获得，体现了市场性和公正性，也是最易于被各方当事人接受和理解的方法，因此具有较强的适用性，应用范围较广。但是，市场法的应用需要具备公开活跃的市场和足够多的相同或相似交易案例，这也可能因缺少可比数据而导致方法的适用性受限。

Text* 正文

1. Introduction

The market approach is a comparative approach that considers the sales of similar or substitute properties and related market data and establishes a value estimate by processes involving comparison. The market approach is also called comparable sales method, market comparison approach, sales comparison approach or direct market comparison method.

Under this approach, appraisers produce a value indication by comparing the subject property with similar properties, which is called comparable sales. A major premise of the market approach is that the value of a property is related to the prices of comparable properties. The sales prices of the properties that are judged to be most comparable tend to indicate a range in which the value indication for the subject property may fall.

The comparative techniques of analysis applied in the market approach are fundamental to the valuation process. The appraiser estimates the degree of similarity or difference between the subject property and the comparable sales by considering various elements of comparison, including but not limited to variations in the following: property right appraised, the motivations of buyers and sellers, financing

---

* Partly from: The Appraisal Foundation (TAF), 2010-2011 Uniform Standards of Professional Appraisal Practice, 2009; Wang Chengjun, Professional English, Appraisal Journal of China, 2007.

terms, market condition at the time of sale, size, location, physical characteristics, and economic characteristics. Elements of comparison are tested against market evidence to estimate which elements are sensitive to change and how they affect value. The market approach often uses market multiples derived from a set of comparable sales, each with different multiples. The selection of the appropriate multiple within the range requires judgement, considering qualitative and quantitative factors.

It is necessary to adjust the price information from other transactions to reflect any differences in terms of the actual transaction and the basis of value and any assumptions to be adopted in the valuation being undertaken. The amount or percentage of adjustments is then applied to the known sale price of each comparable property to derive an indicated value for the subject property. Through this comparative procedure, the appraiser renders an opinion of the value that was defined in the problem identification as of a specific date.

2. Basic Premises and Procedures

2.1 Basic premises

The market approach provides an indication of value by comparing the asset with identical or comparable (that is similar) assets for which price information is available. There are two basic premises to be met before the application of the market approach:

(a) The market approach is based on the open market hypothesis. There should be an active, free and open market, from which appraisers can collect the information of related reference assets.

(b) There should be enough comparable sales and properties in the open market, so that requirements of valuation can be fully met. To apply the market approach effectively, at least three comparable sales highly similar to the estimated property should be selected.

The open market refers to a fully competitive market, in which there are numerous willing buyers and sellers. Under the premise of full exchanged or disclosure trading information, there is relatively sufficient time for the buyers and sellers to trade equally. Excluding the chance of individual transactions, the market transaction price can basically reflect the market situation. The more active the transaction is in the open market, the easier it is to obtain the comparable sales. The market approach is efficient when a number of similar properties have recently been sold or are currently for sale in the subject property's market.

2.2 Procedures

The Procedures of the market approach are followed:

(a) Identify the subject property and select comparable sales. The first step is to consider the prices for transactions of identical or similar assets that have appeared recently in the market. If few recent transactions occur, it may also be appropriate to consider the prices of identical or similar assets that are listed or offered for sale provided the relevant information is clearly established and critically analysed;

(b) Select appropriate elements of comparison between the subject property and the comparable sales. Elements for comparison including but not limited to variations in the following: function, market condition, physical characteristics, trading time and location;

(c) Estimate the difference of the elements between the comparable sales and the subject property. The valuer should perform a comparative analysis of the similarities and differences between the comparable assets and subject asset, from both qualitative and quantitative aspects;

(d) Adjust the price information from comparable sales to reflect any differences in the elements of comparison. It will often be necessary to make adjustments based on the comparative analysis. Those adjustments must be reasonable and valuers should document the reasons for the adjustments and how they were quantified;

(e) Weigh and reconcile the alternative value indications into final value estimate by means of arithmetic average and weighted average, etc.

3. Appraisal Principles

Principle of Substitution: The principle of substitution holds that the value of a property tends to be set by the price that would be paid to acquire a substitute property within a reasonable amount of time. This Principle implies that the reliability of the market approach is diminished if substitute properties are not available in the market.

Principle of Supply and Demand: Property price results from negotiations between buyers and sellers. Buyers constitute market demand, and the properties offered for sale make up the supply. This assumes a market with many buyers and sellers acting in their own interests. To estimate demand, appraisers consider the number of potential users of a particular type of property, their purchasing power, and their tastes and preference. To analyse supply, appraisers focus on existing unsold properties as well as properties that are being constructed, or planned.

Principle of Balance: The supply and demand moves toward market equilibrium, but absolute equilibrium is almost never attained. Due to shifts in population, purchasing power, consumer tastes and preferences, and demand may vary greatly over time. The construction of new buildings and the demolition of old buildings cause supply to vary as well.

Principle of Externalities: Positive and negative external forces affect all types of property. Periods of economic development and economic depression influence property value. An appraiser analyses the market area of the subject property to identify all significant external influences. The adjustments made for location reflect these external forces to a great extent. Two competitive properties with identical physical characteristics may have quite different market values if one of the properties has less attractive surrounding.

4. Applicable Scope

Since the parameters and indicators used in this approach are obtained directly from the market, the market approach tend to objectively reflect the current market situation of assets. Thus, it can relatively reflect the marketability and fairness and be easily accepted and understood by all parties and has strong applicability.

However, the application of the market approach requires an active market and sufficient transaction cases which are identical or similar with the asset, so the lack of comparable data may also limit the applicability of this methodology.

5. Concrete Methods

In this section three concrete methods of market approach will be introduced: direct comparison method, analogical adjustment method and value ratio method.

5.1 Direct comparison method

Direct comparison method is based on the market transaction price of the comparable property, comparing the differences between the main characteristics of the comparable property with the subject property so that the value of the subject property can be estimated.

$$\text{Value of the subject property} = \frac{\text{Main characteristic of the subject property}}{\text{Main characteristic of the comparable property}} \times \text{Price of the comparable property}$$

The direct comparison method is intuitive, simple and easy to operate, but it usually requires higher comparability between the subject property and the comparable property. The difference between them should be mainly reflected in some obvious factors, such as the trading time, trading location, function, trading (market) conditions, newness rate, etc. According to the different factors, the specific methods of direct comparison method are also different.

Formulas of common adjustment coefficients are stated as follow:

(a) Adjustment coefficient of trading time (e.g., Price Index Method)

$$\text{Adjustment coefficient of trading time} = \frac{\text{Price index on the valuation date of subject property}}{\text{Price index on the trading date of comparable property}}$$

Note: The application of this formula assumes that the relationship between the price index and the asset value is linear.

(b) Adjustment coefficient of trading location (e.g., Scoring Method/Indirect Comparison Method)

$$\text{Adjustment coefficient of trading location} = \frac{\text{Centesimal score of the trading location of subject property}}{\text{Centesimal score of the trading location of comparable property}}$$

Note: The application of this formula assumes that the relationship between the trading location score and the asset value is linear.

(c) Adjustment coefficient of function (e.g., <u>Function-Value Method</u>)

$$Adjustment\ coefficient\ of\ function = \frac{Production\ capacity\ of\ subject\ property}{Production\ capacity\ of\ comparable\ property}$$

Note: The application of this formula assumes that the relationship between the production capacity and the asset value is linear.

(d) Adjustment coefficient of market conditions (e.g., <u>Price Discount Method</u>)

$$Adjustment\ coefficient\ of\ market\ conditions = 1 - Price\ discount\ rate\ (\%)$$

Note: The price discount is usually determined by the valuer through statistical analysis or empirical judgment.

(e) Adjustment coefficient of physical characteristics (e.g., <u>Newness Rate Method</u>)

$$Adjustment\ coefficient\ of\ physical\ characteristics = \frac{Newness\ rate\ of\ subject\ property}{Newness\ rate\ of\ comparable\ property}$$

Note: The application of this formula assumes that the relationship between the newness rate and the asset value is linear.

Example 1-1

Consider the following property: The annual production capacity of the subject property is 30 tons, while the annual production capacity of the comparable property is 40 tons. The market price of the comparable property on the valuation date is 100,000 yuan. Assume all other factors that might affect the value of the property are same, try to estimate the value of the subject property.

The value of the subject property=100,000× 30/40=75,000(Yuan)

Example 1-2

Consider the following property: The newness rate of the subject production line is 50%, while the newness rate of the comparable production line is 80%. The price for transaction of the comparable production line is 26,000 yuan. Assume all other factors that might affect the value of the property are same, try to estimate the value of the subject production line.

The value of the subject production line $=26{,}000\times 50\%/80\%=16{,}250(Yuan)$

5.2 Analogical adjustment method

Analogical adjustment method is the most widely used method in the application of the market approach. This method is to compare and analyse differences between the subject property and the comparable property, calculating the value of the subject property by multiplying adjustment coefficients of comparable elements by the price of it.

$$\begin{aligned}
\text{Value of the subject property} &= \text{Price of the comparable property} \\
&\quad \times \text{adjustment coefficients of comparable elements} \\
&= \text{Price of the comparable property} \\
&\quad \times (1 \pm \text{adjustment rates of comparable elements})
\end{aligned}$$

$$\begin{aligned}
\text{Value of the subject property} &= \text{Price of the comparable property} \\
&\quad \times \text{Adjustment coefficient of trading time} \\
&\quad \times \text{Adjustment coefficient of trading location} \\
&\quad \times \text{Adjustment coefficient of function} \\
&\quad \times \text{Adjustment coefficient of market condition} \\
&\quad \times \text{Adjustment coefficient of physical characteristics}
\end{aligned}$$

The adjustment coefficients can be selected and set differently according to the different subject properties. The specific methods and formulas depend on the selection of adjustment coefficient.

Example 1-3

An excavator was purchased on June 1, 2019. The information for valuation is as follows:

Adjustment coefficient	The comparable excavator	The subject excavator
Price	600,000 yuan	-
Market conditions	Open market	Open market
Trading time	June 1, 2016	June 1, 2022
Production capacity	50,000 tons per year	60,000 tons per year
Newness rate	80%	60%

The survey found that the price index of similar equipment increased by 1% every year, try to estimate the value of the subject excavator on June 1, 2022.

Adjustment coefficient of trading time=106%/100%=1.06

Adjustment coefficient of production capacity =60,000/50,000=1.2

Adjustment coefficient of newness rate =60%/80%=0.75

The value of the subject excavator=600,000×1.06×1.2×0.75=572,400(Yuan)

5.3 Value ratio method

The value ratio method refers to valuate the subject assets by comparing the differences of economic parameters or economic index between the subject assets and the reference assets. The value ratio method is widely used in business valuation. In order to enhance comparability, comparable "value connection" need to be used to link the value of the subject enterprise and the comparable enterprise, since the scale, profitability and other aspects of enterprises may be different. This connection can be reflected by economic parameters or economic index, which can get the value ratio of subject business after adjustment.

There are many kinds of alternative value ratios:

(a) the value ratio of profit indicators, such as earnings before interest and tax (EBIT), cash flow after tax, and earnings per share (P/E ratio);

(b) value ratio of income indicators, such as sales revenue (P/S ratio);

(c) the value ratio of asset indicators, such as net assets (P/B ratio), total assets;

(d) the value ratio of other indicators, such as the cost to market ratio, the mineable reserves, etc.

Take P/E ratio for example. P/E ratio is the ratio of market price per share to earnings per share, which indicates the profitability of enterprises. The application of P/E ratio in the value ratio method is followed:

Value of the subject property = Income of the subject property
$$\times \frac{P}{E} \text{ ratio of the comparable property}$$

The following conditions should be applied and afforded significant weight in the value ratio method:

(a) sources and reliability of the data related with the comparable businesses;

(b) determination of the comparable standard and comparable businesses;

(c) the number of the comparable businesses;

(d) the selection of the value ratio.

Example 1-4

Consider the following property: The annual net profit of a subject business is 10 million yuan. The average price earnings ratio of similar businesses in the capital market is 17 times. Try to value the value of the subject business.

The value of the subject business=10×17=170 million yuan

Core Words and Expressions 核心术语

market approach	市场途径
similar or substitute properties	相似或可替代资产
related market data	相关市场数据
value estimate	价值估计
comparable sales method	可比交易法
market comparison approach	市场比较途径
sales comparison approach	销售比较途径
direct market comparison method	直接市场比较法
value indication	价值结论
comparable sales	可比交易（案例）
major premise	重要前提
indicate a range	形成区间

valuation process	评估程序
elements of comparison	比较因素
variation	变量
property right	资产权益
financing terms	融资条件，金融条款
market evidence	市场证据
open market hypothesis	公开市场假设
disclosure/disclose	披露
principle of substitution	替代原则
principle of supply and demand	供求原则
potential users	潜在使用者
purchasing power	购买力
existing unsold properties	现存未出售的资产
principle of balance	平衡原则
equilibrium	均衡
principle of externalities	外部性原则
periods of economic development and economic depression	经济发展和经济衰退的周期
direct comparison method	直接比较法
analogical adjustment method	类比调整法
value ratio method	价值比率法
price index method	价格指数法
scoring method	打分法
indirect comparison method	间接比较法

function-value method	功能价值法
price discount method	价格折扣法
newness rate method	成新率法
earnings before interest and tax (EBIT)	息税前利润
P/E ratio	市盈率
P/S ratio	市销率
P/B ratio	市净率
mineable reserves	矿山可开采储量

Questions and Discussion 问题与讨论

1. What are the procedures of the market approach?

2. Please conclude the appraisal principles of the market approach.

3. Do you think the market approach is suitable for a special equipment? Why?

4. Please list the concrete methods in the application of the market approach.

Topic 2: The Cost Approach 成本法

Abstract 中文摘要

成本法是指首先估测评估对象的重置成本，然后估测评估对象业已存在的各种贬损因素及贬值额，再将其从重置成本中予以扣除而得到评估对象价值的评估方法。其中，重置成本包括复原重置成本和更新重置成本两种形式；贬值可以划分为实体性贬值、功能性贬值和经济性贬值。

成本法有三个重要的适用前提：一是评估对象处于持续使用状态或假定处于持续使用状态；二是评估对象能够通过重置途径获得，用以测算其重置成本的历史信息和相关数据也可以获得；三是评估对象所发生的价值贬损能够被合理地估算。

成本法的基本应用步骤如下：（1）明确评估对象；（2）收集评估对象的相关历史资料，并分析其成本结构；（3）测算评估对象的重置成本；（4）测算评估对象所发生的各项贬值；（5）综合分析，并从重置成本中扣减各项贬值以确定评估结果。

成本法的应用重点涉及四种基本要素，即资产的重置成本、资产的实体性贬值、资产的功能性贬值和资产的经济性贬值。其中，复原重置成本是指采用与评估对象相同的材料、建筑或制造标准、设计、规格及技术等，以现时价格水平重新购建与评估对象相同的全新资产所发生的费用；更新重置成本是指采用与评估对象并不完全相同的材料、建筑或制造标准、设计、规格和技术等，以现时价格水平购建与评估对象具有同等功能的全新资产所需的费用；实体性贬值，也称有形损耗，是指资产由于使用和自然力的作用导致资产的物理性能损耗或下降引起的资产价值损失；功能性贬值是指由于技术进步引起的资产功能相对落后而造成的资产价值损失；经济性贬值是指由于外部条件的变化引起资产收益、资产利用率发生持续减少，下降或者闲置等而造成的资产价值损失。

成本法的具体方法体系实际就是在成本法总的评估思路的基础上，围绕四种基本要素所采用的具体测算方法构成。例如，资产重置成本的测算可以采用重置核算法、价格指数法、功能价值法、规模经济效益指数法、统计分析法等具体方法；实体性贬值的测算可以采用观察法、使用年限法等具体方法；功能性贬值的测算具体针对超额投资成本和超额运营成本两种类型分别展开；经济性贬值的测算可以具体通过测算经济性贬值率或经济性贬值额得到。

基于市场参与者对价值与成本的关系认识，成本法被视为是资产评估中最基本且应用较广泛的方法之一。根据成本法的应用思路，资产的价值大小与资产的成本高低紧密相关；而资产在被具体使用的过程中，其价值又会受到各种因素的影响而出现贬值。因此，资产的价值不会超过在现有条件下重置该项资产的费用支出。成本法尤其适用于交易不活跃市场和新品市场中的资产评估。但是，成本法的应用也存在一定的局限性，特别是实体性贬值的估算对资产评估专业人员的主观估测依赖性较大，测算经济性贬值的技术难度也较大，这都对资产评估工作的详尽程度和人力及时间消耗提出了很高要求。

Text* 正文

1. Introduction

The <u>cost approach</u>, one of the most generally recognized valuation approaches, is based on the value theory of classical economic school. The classical economic school formulates a value theory that attributes value to the cost of production. In *The Wealth of Nations* (1776), Adam Smith considered value as an objective phenomenon. The nature price of an object reflected how much the item cost to produce. In <u>contemporary appraisal practice</u>, the classical theory of value has influenced the cost approach. The cost approach is based on the understanding that market participants relate value to cost.

In the cost approach, the value of a property is derived by estimating the <u>replacement cost</u> or <u>reproduction cost</u> of property and then abstracting the amount of <u>depreciation</u> (e.g., <u>deterioration</u> and <u>obsolescence</u>) in the property from all causes. Replacement cost is the cost of replacing a comparable new item assuming using modern materials, techniques and designs; while reproduction cost is the cost to create a virtual <u>replica</u> of the existing structure, employing the same design and similar materials. Therefore, the replacement cost is generally that of a modern equivalent asset, which is one that provides similar function and equivalent utility to the asset being valued, but with current design and constructed or made using current <u>cost-effective</u> materials and techniques. And the reproduction cost is particularly appropriate in circumstances that the utility offered by the subject asset could only be provided by a replica rather than a modern equivalent.

There are three kinds of depreciation: <u>physical depreciation</u>, <u>functional depreciation</u>, and <u>economic depreciation</u>. Physical depreciation of assets can also be known as tangible loss. It means that the decline or wastage of the physical property, which is caused by using and natural power, reduces the value of assets. Functional depreciation of assets is also called intangible loss or technical obsolescence. It means that the relatively backward functionality, which is caused by the development of

---

* *Partly from: The Appraisal Foundation (TAF), 2010-2011 Uniform Standards of Professional Appraisal Practice, 2009; Wang Chengjun, Professional English, Appraisal Journal of China, 2005.*

technology, reduces the value of assets. Economic depreciation of assets is also called external obsolescence. It means that idle assets and decline of profit caused by the change of external conditions (e.g., society, politics, policy, etc.) leads to the reduction of assets' value.

2. Basic Premises and Procedures

2.1 Basic premises

The following basic premises should be afforded significant weight before the using of cost approach:

(a) The subject asset is in or assumed in <u>sustained use</u>. It has significance to estimate the replacement cost or reproduction cost and all relevant forms of obsolescence only in the case that the asset is in or assumed in sustained use, which indicates that the asset has the value in use. The sustained use of assets is not only a physical concept, but also contains the economic significance of effective use of assets. Only when the assets can sustain to be used and bring economic benefits to potential owners or controllers, will the replacement cost of assets be recognized and accepted by <u>potential investors</u> and the market;

(b) The <u>historical information and data</u> are available. The historical information and data are the basis of the cost approach, which is widely used to analyse the cost structure and calculate relevant data (e.g., replacement or reproduction cost, depreciation) of the subject property. It is tough to apply the cost approach if the historical information and data is unavailable;

(c) The depreciation can be estimated. The cost approach analyses and reflects the value of assets from the perspective of assets' depreciation. This approach is useful only when the depreciation can be estimated and can be abstracted from the replacement cost or reproduction cost of property.

2.2 Procedures

This approach provides an indication of value by calculating the current replacement or reproduction cost of an asset and making deductions for physical deterioration and all other relevant forms of obsolescence. The procedures of the cost approach are:

(a) Identify the subject property;

(b) Collect the historical information and analyse the cost structure of the subject property;

(c) Estimate the replacement/reproduction cost of the subject property. Calculate all of the incurred cost by a typical participant seeking to create or obtain an exact replica or an asset providing equivalent utility;

(d) Determine whether there is any deprecation related to physical, functional and economic obsolescence associated with the subject asset, and then calculate the newness rate of the subject property by estimating the depreciation from all causes;

(e) Deduct total deprecation from the total costs and form the final value estimate for the subject asset.

3. Appraisal Principles

The cost approach provides an indication of value using the economic principle that a buyer will pay no more for an asset than the cost to obtain an asset of equal utility, whether by purchase or by construction. This approach is based on the principle that the price that a buyer in the market would pay for the asset being valued would, unless undue time, inconvenience, risk or other factors are involved, be not more than the cost to purchase or construct an equivalent asset. Generally, the asset being valued is less attractive than the alternative that could be purchased or constructed because of age or obsolescence. Wherever this is the case, adjustments may need to be made to the cost of the alternative asset depending on the required basis of value.

4. Applicable Scope

The cost approach is particularly important when a lack of market activity limits the usefulness of the market approach and when the subject properties are not amenable to be valued by the income approach. For example, when market transactions of comparable property are unavailable, or when transactions are non-existent, the cost approach is the preferred valuation procedure. Therefore, the cost approach is usually used to develop an opinion of market value of proposed construction, special-purpose or specialty properties, and other properties that are not frequently exchanged in the market. If comparable sales are not available, current market indication of depreciated cost or the costs to acquire an existing property are the best reflections of market perception and market value. This means that the cost approach is particularly useful in valuing properties that are not frequently exchanged in the market.

The cost approach is also considered to be more important in estimating the market value of new or relatively new property, because cost and market value are usually more closely related to each other when properties are new. Meanwhile, the cost approach can be applied to older properties given adequate data to measure depreciation. However, an appraiser should be aware that the physical deterioration, functional obsolescence, and economic obsolescence of the property are more difficult to estimate for considerably older properties.

In addition, cost approach techniques can also be employed to derive information needed in the market and income approaches to value, such as the costs to cure items of deferred maintenance.

5. Concept Analysis: Depreciation

The cost approach considers the possibility that one could construct, as a substitute for the purchase of a given property, another property that is either a replica or one that could furnish equal utility. One would not be justified in paying more for a given property than the cost of acquiring equivalent property, unless undue time, inconvenience, and risk are involved. In practice, the approach also involves an estimate of depreciation for older and/or less functional properties if an estimate of cost for new unreasonably exceeds the likely price that would be paid for the appraised property.

The term depreciation is used in different contexts in valuation and in financial reporting. In the context of asset valuation, depreciation refers to the adjustment made to the cost of reproducing or replacing the assets to reflect physical deterioration and functional (technical) and economic (external) obsolescence in order to estimate the value of the asset in a hypothetical exchange in the market when there is no direct sales evidence available.

In the financial reporting, depreciation refers to the charge made against income to reflect the systematic allocation of the depreciable amount of an asset over its useful life. It is specific to the particular entity and its utilization, and is not necessarily affected by the market. To appraisers, accrued depreciation is a function of an accounting convention and do not necessarily reflect the market.

Therefore, in applying the cost approach, an appraiser estimates the market's perception of the differences between the property being appraised and a newly constructed property with optimal utility.

6. Concrete Methods

Broadly, there are four elements need to be estimated in the application of cost approach: replacement/reproduction cost, physical depreciation, functional depreciation, and external depreciation.

6.1 Measurement of replacement/reproduction cost

6.1.1 Replacement Cost Calculation Method

The replacement cost calculation method is used to calculate all of the costs that would be incurred by a typical participant seeking to create or obtain an asset providing equivalent utility. It is a method to calculate the replacement cost according to the cost structure of the subject property with the current market price. Estimating the direct cost and indirect cost of the reconstruction assets using current market price and then sums them up, the replacement cost will be calculated as follow:

Replacement cost = Direct cost + Indirect cost

For constructed property, the direct cost includes material cost, labour cost, manufacturing cost, capital cost, reasonable profit, etc. When the subject property is purchased property, the direct cost includes purchase price, installation and commissioning cost, incidental expenses, labour cost, etc. The indirect cost includes administrative expense, training expense, design expense, etc. Current price for estimated assets is the premise of this method and this method can be used to calculate both replacement cost and reproduction cost.

Example 2-1

Consider the following property: The subject property is a device whose current market price is 50,000 Yuan each. The Transport fees is 1,000 Yuan. The direct installation cost is 800 Yuan including raw materials cost 300 Yuan, labour costs 500 Yuan; Indirect costs of installation cost for each labour cost is 0.8 Yuan. Try to estimate the replacement cost of the equipment.

the replacement cost of the equipment = 50,000+1,000+800+500×0.8 = 52,200(Yuan)

6.1.2 Price Index Method

The price index method is based on the <u>book value</u> of the subject property, which is applied to calculate the reproduction cost by adjusting the historical cost of property with the price index:

Reproduction cost = historical cost × Price index

The widely used indexes are fixed base price index and chain price index. The price index method can be only used to calculate the reproduction cost.

Example 2-2

Consider the following property: The asset is constructed in 2007 and the book value of it is 50,000 Yuan; Price index when constructing the asset is 95%; Price index when valuating the asset is 160%. Please estimate the reproduction cost of the equipment.

The reproduction cost of the equipment=50,000×160%/95%=84,211(Yuan)

Replacement cost calculation method and price index method are commonly used in replacement cost estimation, but there are obvious differences between them:

(a) The cost estimated by price index method only considers the factors of price change, so it can only determine the reproduction cost; while the replacement cost calculation method considers not only the price factor, but also the factors of production technology progress and labour productivity, so it can be used to estimate the replacement cost.

(b) The price index method is based on the price change level of one or all assets in different periods, while the replacement cost calculation method is based on the purchase and construction cost accounting with current price level.

6.1.3 Function-Value Method

The function-value method provides an indication of replacement cost by seeking comparable asset and its function index, and then adjust the replacement cost of comparable asset with the proportion of the function index (e.g., production capacity) of subject asset to the function index of comparable asset. The formula is as follows:

$$Replacement\ cost\ of\ estimated\ asset = Replacement\ cost\ of\ comparable\ asset \times \frac{Production\ capacity\ of\ estimated\ asset}{Production\ capacity\ of\ comparable\ asset}$$

Example 2-3

Consider the following property: comparable asset is a new machine performs the same function as the subject asset, the prevailing market prices of the comparable asset is 50,000 Yuan, the annual output of the comparable asset is 5,000 pieces, the annual output of the subject asset is 4,000 pieces. Try to calculate the replacement cost for the subject asset.

The replacement cost of the subject asset=50,000×4,000/5,000=40,000(Yuan)

6.1.4 Scale Economic Benefit Index Method

When the replacement cost of asset is not linear with its production capacity, the scale economic benefit index method can be applied to calculate the replacement cost of estimated asset. The formula is as follows:

$$\frac{Replacement\ cost\ of\ estimated\ asset}{Replacement\ cost\ of\ reference\ asset} = \left(\frac{Production\ capacity\ of\ estimated\ asset}{Production\ capacity\ of\ reference\ asset}\right)^{x}$$

$$Replacement\ cost\ of\ estimated\ asset = Replacement\ cost\ of\ reference\ asset \times \left(\frac{Production\ capacity\ of\ estimated\ asset}{Production\ capacity\ of\ reference\ asset}\right)^{x}$$

"X" refers to scale economic benefit index, which is an empirical data calculated by mathematical statistics.

Example 2-4

Consider the following property: The replacement cost of the comparable asset is

100,000 Yuan, the annual output of the comparable asset is 300,000 pieces, the annual output of the subject asset is 600,000 pieces, and the scale economic benefit index is 0.7. Try to calculate the replacement cost for the subject asset.

The replacement cost of the subject asset $=100,000 \times (600,000/300,000)^{0.7}=162,450(Yuan)$

6.1.5 Statistical Analysis Method

Statistical analysis method is not an independent calculation method, but a method can simplify valuation and improve efficiency. This method calculates the replacement cost using statistical principles, whose procedure is as follows:

(a) Classify the subject assets according to certain standards;

(b) Make sample inspection on representative asset, and choose appropriate method to calculate its replacement cost;

(c) Compute k as the adjustment coefficient of historical cost;

$$k = \frac{Replacement\ cost\ of\ sample\ assets}{Historical\ cost\ of\ sample\ assets}$$

(d) Calculate the replacement cost of subject assets using k.

$$Replacement\ cost\ of\ subject\ assets = \sum Historical\ cost\ of\ subject\ assets \times k$$

6.2 Measurement of Physical Depreciation

Physical depreciation is the loss of utility due to the physical deterioration of the asset or its components resulting from its age and usage. Physical depreciation can be measured in two different ways:

6.2.1 Observational method

The observation method refers to the on-the-spot investigation of the main parts of the subject asset by the engineering and technical personnel with professional knowledge and rich experience, and the comprehensive analysis of the design, manufacture, use, wear, maintenance, repair, major repair, transformation and physical life of the assets, so that the newness rate of the subject asset and the physical depreciation of the assets can be estimated.

Physical depreciation = Replacement cost × (1 − Newness rate)

" *(1 − Newness rate)* " can be also named "*physical depreciation rate*". Then,

Physical depreciation = Replacement cost × physical depreciation rate

Example 2-5

The subject equipment whose purchase cost was 100,000 Yuan each. The prevailing market prices of the equipment is 150,000 Yuan each. Judged by experts, the physical depreciation rate of the equipment is 20%. Without considering other factors, try to estimate the physical depreciation of the equipment.

the physical depreciation of the equipment=150,000×20%=30,000(Yuan)

6.2.2 Life-based method

The life-based method calculates the physical depreciation by analysing the practical service life of the subject property.

$$Physical\ depreciation\ rate = \frac{Practical\ service\ life}{The\ total\ service\ life} \times 100\%$$

$$Physical\ depreciation = \frac{Practical\ service\ life}{The\ total\ service\ life} \times (Replacement\ cost - Residual\ value)$$

If the residual value can be ignored, then the formula would change to:

$$Physical\ depreciation = \frac{Practical\ service\ life}{The\ total\ service\ life} \times Replacement\ cost$$

The total service life refers to the sum of the practical service life and the remaining service life:

The total serviced life = Practical serviced life + Remaining serviced life

Practical serviced life = Nominal serviced life × Asset utilization

The remaining service life is the expected service life of the asset according to the tangible loss factor. The nominal service life refers to the period from the purchasing time to the valuation time. The nominal service life can be determined through accounting records, asset registers and registration cards. The practical service life is estimated based on the actual loss of assets in use. The difference between the practical service life and the nominal service life can be adjusted by the asset utilization rate.

Asset utilization rate
$$= \frac{\textit{The accumulated actual use of time up to the date of the valuation}}{\textit{The accumulated legal use of time up to the date of the valuation}}$$

When the asset utilization rate is greater than "1", it means that the asset is overloaded, and the practical service life of the asset is longer than the nominal service life; when the asset utilization rate is equal to "1", it means that the asset is fully loaded, and the practical service life of the asset is equal to the nominal service life; when the asset utilization rate is less than "1", it means that the operation is insufficient, and the practical service life of the asset is less than the nominal service life.

Example 2-6

An asset was purchased in February 2011. When it was valued in February 2021, its nominal service life was 10 years. According to the technical standard of the asset, it should work 8 hours per day under normal use, and the asset actually works 7.5 hours per day. Assuming that the whole year is calculated by 360 days, and the subject asset can be used for another 10 years, try to estimate the physical depreciation rate of the asset.

Asset utilization rate= (10×360×7.5)/(10×360×8) ×100%=93.75%

Practical serviced life=10×93.75%=9.375(Years)

Physical depreciation rate=9.375/(9.375+10) ×100% =48.39%

6.3 Measurement of Functional Depreciation

Functional depreciation is the loss of utility resulting from inefficiencies in the subject asset compared to its replacement due to the outdate of its design, specification or technology. There are two forms of functional obsolescence:

6.3.1 Excess investment cost

Excess investment cost can be caused by changes in design, materials of construction, technology or manufacturing techniques, which may result in the availability of modern equivalent assets with lower investment costs than the subject asset.

$$\text{Excess investment cost} = \text{Reproduction cost} - \text{Replacement cost}$$

6.3.2 Excess operating cost

Excess operating cost can be caused by improvements in design or excess capacity, which may result in the availability of modern equivalent assets with lower operating costs than the subject asset. To calculate the excess operating cost, the procedure is as follows:

Firstly, calculate the annual excess operating expense of subject assets;

$$\begin{aligned}\text{Annual excess operating expenses} = &\text{ Annual operating cost of subjet asset} \\ &- \text{Annual operating cost of modern equivalent asset}\end{aligned}$$

Secondly, calculate the annual net excess of operating cost;

$$\begin{aligned}\text{The annual net excess of operating cost} = &\text{ Annual excess operating expenses} \\ &\times (1 - \text{income tax rate})\end{aligned}$$

Then, estimate the remaining service life of subject assets;

Finally, discount the annual net excess of operating cost using appropriate discount rate.

$$\text{Functional depreciation} = \text{The annual net excess of operating cost} \times \left(\frac{P}{A}, r, n\right)$$

Example 2-7

The subject property was a device purchased in 2021. Compared with the new equipment of the same production capacity on the valuation date, the subject property requires more than 4 workers and consumes the power of more than 40,000 kilowatt hours per year. And the annual wages of each operator are 60,000 Yuan, the price of each kilowatt hour is 0.8 Yuan, the equipment can still be used for 5 years, the discount rate is 10%, the corporate income tax rate is 25%. Then please estimate the functional depreciation of the equipment.

Functional depreciation=(4×60,000+40,000×0.8) ×(1-25%)×(P/A,10%,5)=773,323(Yuan)

6.4 Measurement of Economic Depreciation

External or economic depreciation is the loss of utility caused by economic or locational factors external to the asset. This type of depreciation can be temporary or permanent. Economic obsolescence may arise when external factors affect an individual asset or all the assets employed in a business and should be deducted after physical deterioration and functional obsolescence.

Examples of economic depreciation include but not limited to: adverse changes to demand for the products or services produced by the asset, oversupply in the market for the asset, and a disruption or loss of a supply of labour or raw material.

Economic depreciation can be calculated in two ways: <u>economic depreciation rate</u> and <u>economic depreciation amount</u>.

6.4.1 Economic depreciation rate

$$Economic\ depreciation\ rate = \left[1 - \left(\frac{Practical\ production\ capacity}{Design\ product\ capacity}\right)^X\right] \times 100\%$$

If the capacity of subject asset is linear with its value, then the formula changed to:

$$Economic\ depreciation\ rate = \left[1 - \left(\frac{Practical\ production\ capacity}{Design\ product\ capacity}\right)\right] \times 100\%$$

Practical production capacity refers to the production capacity that is expected to be actually utilized considering the insufficient start-up and idling. "X" is known as scale economic benefit index calculated through mathematical statistics, which is usually between 0.6 and 0.7. When the economic depreciation rate is used to calculate the economic depreciation amount, the calculation should be based on the replacement cost of the subject assets or the result of the replacement cost minus the physical depreciation and functional depreciation.

6.4.2 Economic depreciation amount

Economic depreciation amount is the loss in revenue generated during the sustained use of subject asset.

$$Economic\ depreciation\ amount = Annual\ revenue\ loss \times (1 - Income\ tax\ rate) \times \left(\frac{P}{A}, r, n\right)$$

Example 2-8

The designed production capacity of a subject production line is 20,000 sets per year. Due to the change of market demand structure, the annual output is estimated to be reduced by 6,000 sets in the future service life. Assuming that the economic benefit index of scale is 0.6, try to estimate the economic depreciation rate of the production line.

Assuming that the profit of each product is 100 yuan, the production line can be used for another three years. The return on investment of the industry where the enterprise is located is 10% and the income tax rate is 25%. Try to estimate the economic depreciation.

$$Economic\ depreciation\ rate = \left[1-\left(\frac{20,000-6,000}{20,000}\right)^{0.6}\right]\times 100\% = 19\%$$

Economic depreciation amount = (6,000×100)×(1-25%)×(P/A,10%,3) = 1,119,105(Yuan)

In the practice of valuation, there is also a case of <u>economic premium</u>. That means, when the subject property and its products have a good market prospect, or there is a significant policy advantage, the subject property may have an economic premium.

Core Words and Expressions 核心术语

cost approach	成本途径
contemporary appraisal practice	现代评估实践
replacement cost	更新重置成本
reproduction cost	复原重置成本
depreciation/deterioration/obsolescence	折旧，损耗，贬值
replica	复制品
cost-effective	经济的/划算的
physical depreciation/deterioration	实体性贬值
functional depreciation/obsolescence	功能性贬值

economic depreciation/obsolescence	经济性贬值
sustained use	持续使用
potential investors	潜在投资者
historical information and data	历史信息和数据
cost structure	成本构成
incurred cost	实际成本，已发生成本
economic principle	经济原则，经济原理
undue time	不适当的时间
equivalent asset	等价资产
alternative asset	替代资产
lack of market activity	市场活动的缺乏
market transaction	市场交易
comparable property	可比资产，参照物
proposed construction	规划中的建筑
financial reporting	财务报告（会计）
in the context of asset valuation	在资产评估领域
hypothetical exchange	假定的交易
direct sales evidence	直接的相关销售证据
charge made against income	从收入中进行的扣除（额）
systematic allocation	系统提取
depreciable amount	折旧额
particular entity	特定的（会计）主体
accrued depreciation	应计折旧
accounting convention	会计惯例，会计原则

a newly constructed property	全新建造的资产
optimal utility	最佳的功能
replacement cost calculation method	重置核算法
incidental expenses	杂费
book value	账面价值
price level	物价水平
scale economic benefit index method	规模经济效益指数法
empirical data	经验数据
statistical analysis method	统计分析法
statistical principles	统计学原理
observation method	观察法
life-based method	使用年限法
practical service life	实际使用寿命
remaining service life	剩余使用寿命
nominal service life	名义使用寿命
utilization rate	使用率
excess investment cost	超额投资成本
excess operating cost	超额运营成本
economic depreciation rate	经济贬值率
economic depreciation amount	经济贬值额
economic premium	经济性溢价

Questions and Discussion 问题与讨论

1. What are the basic premises and procedures of the cost approach?

2. Please explain how to distinguish the three kinds of depreciation.

3. What is the defect of the cost approach?

4. How to understand the differences in terms of depreciation when it is used in different contexts of valuation and financial reporting?

5. How to estimate the replacement cost and reproduction cost of the subject asset in the application of cost approach.

6. How to estimate the physical depreciation of the subject asset in the application of cost approach.

7. How to estimate the functional depreciation of the subject asset in the application of cost approach.

8. How to estimate the external depreciation of the subject asset in the application of cost approach.

Topic 3: The Income Approach 收益法

Abstract 中文摘要

收益法，又称为收益资本化法，是指通过估算被评估资产未来预期收益的现值来判断资产价值的各种评估方法的总称。其以预期收益原则为基础，采用以利求本的思维方式，通过折现和资本化方法判断和估算资产价值，并认为资产价值的大小从根本上取决于该资产的未来获利能力。预期收益额、折现率（或资本化率）、收益期限是收益法的三个重要参数；三大参数的估测，是应用收益法过程中的重点和难点。

收益法有三个重要的适用前提：一是评估对象所产生的预期收益能够被合理预测并以货币计量；二是评估对象产生预期收益所对应的风险能够度量；三是评估对象取得预期收益的持续时间能够确定或者被合理预测。因此，收益法主要适用于对未来预期收益、实现收益所承担的风险以及收益期限可计量或确认的资产进行估值。

收益法的基本应用步骤如下：（1）明确评估对象，收集与评估对象产生预期收益有关的数据资料；（2）分析测算评估对象的预期收益额；（3）分析测算折现率（或资本化率）；（4）用折现率或资本化率将评估对象的预期收益折算成现值；（5）分析确定评估结果。

收益法实际上是在预期收益还原思路下若干具体方法的集合。收益法中的具体方法可以分为若干类：一是针对评估对象未来预期收益有无限期的情形划分，包括有限期和无限期的评估方法；二是针对评估对象预期收益额的情形划分，包括等额收益评估方法、非等额收益评估方法、收益额按等差级数变化、收益额按等比级数变化等。

在单项资产评估中，收益法常被用于评估无形资产、投资性房地产和其他资产（如非上市交易的股票、债券、长期股权投资等）的价值；在整体资产评估中，收益法的应用通常是对企业价值进行评估。然而，收益法不能适用于无法产生收益或者收益无法用货币形式计量等资产的评估，且其预期收益额、折现率（或资本化率）等参数的测算难度较大，这也会在一定程度上导致收益法的适用性受限。

Text 正文

1. Introduction[*]

From an investor's point of view, earning power is the critical element affecting property value. A basic investment premise holds that the higher the earning, the higher the value, provided the amount of risk remains constant. An investor who purchases income-producing property is essentially trading present money for the expectation of receiving money in the future. This theory forms the basis for the income approach, which also called income capitalization approach.

The income approach provides an indication of value by converting future cash flows to a single current capital value. It considers the income that an asset will generate over its useful life and indicates value through a capitalization process. The income stream may be derived under a contract or contracts, or be non-contractual, eg. the anticipated profit generated from either the use of or holding of the asset. Therefore, in the income approach, the present value of the future benefits of property

---

[*] Partly from: 2010-2011 The Appraisal Foundation (TAF), Uniform Standards of Professional Appraisal Practice, 2009; Wang Chengjun, Professional English, Appraisal Journal of China, 2006.

ownership is measured, and a property's income and resale value upon reversion may be capitalized into a current value.

Capitalization involves the conversion of income into a capital sum through the application of an appropriate discount rate. There are two methods of income capitalization: direct capitalization and yield capitalization. In direct capitalization, the relationship between one year's income and value is reflected in either a capitalization rate or an income multiplier. In yield capitalization, the relationship between several years' stabilized income and a reversionary value at the end of a designated period is reflected in a yield rate. The most common application of yield capitalization is Discounted Cash Flow (DCF) analysis.

Similar to the market and cost approach, the income approach requires extensive market research. Data collection and analysis for this approach are conducted considering supply and demand relationships, which provide information about trends and anticipation of the market. To be specific, the data that an appraiser investigates in the income approach might include a property's expected gross income, the anticipated annual operating expenses, the pattern and duration of the property's income stream, and the anticipated reversionary value. After income and expense are estimated, the income streams are capitalized or discounted into present value by applying an appropriate rate or factor. The rates used for capitalization or discounting are derived from acceptable rates of returns for similar properties.

2. Basic Premises and Procedures

2.1 Basic premises

Application of the income approach focus on three basic elements: the expected income of the subject assets, the discount rate or capitalization rate, and the duration of the expected benefits. Therefore, the availability of the three elements above, either being obtained or estimated, is the application premise of the income approach. Specifically, the following basic premises should be afforded significant weight before application of the income approach:

(a) The future income of the subject asset can be forecasted. The expected income of the subject asset can be reasonably estimated, which requires a predictable relationship between the subject asset and its operating income. At the same time, the main factors, subjective factors and objective factors that affect the expected return of the assets should be relatively clear, so that the expected return can be analysed and calculated;

(b) The risk of gaining returns can be <u>quantified</u>. Risk which is one of the basic parameters in the measurement of the discount rate and capitalization rate should be able to compared and measured. Risks generally come from the industry, region, enterprise, technology, law and so on. High-risk investment requires high rate of return, while low-risk investment may require lower rate of return;

(c) The duration of benefits can be estimated. The accuracy of benefit duration prediction is a vital factor affecting the valuation results.

2.2 Procedures

From the introduction and basic premises of the income approach, it is likely to find that quantifying the future cashflow and risk of the asset is the main work for income approach. The basic procedures of income approach are as follows:

(a) Identify the subject property and collect the information including the asset allocation, capability of production, condition of sales, market situation, state of the industry, future business conditions and so on;

(b) Analyse and forecast the future income of the subject property. Confirm whether the forecast cash flow represents expected cash flows (i.e., probability-weighted scenarios), as opposed to most likely cash flows (i.e., most probable scenario), of the asset, or some other type of cash flow;

(c) Estimate the appropriate capitalization/discount rate;

(d) Convert the future benefits into an indication of present value or apply the discount rate to the forecasted future cash flow, including the terminal value, if any;

(e) Analyse and form the final value estimate.

3. Appraisal Principles

<u>Principle of anticipation</u>: This principle is fundamental to the income approach.

Value is created by the anticipation of benefits to be realized in the future. All income capitalization methods, techniques, and procedures attempt to anticipate future benefits and estimate their present value. This may involve either forecasting the future income or estimating a capitalization rate that implicitly reflects the anticipated pattern of change in income over time.

Principle of supply and demand: This principle and the related concept of competition are particularly useful in forecasting future benefits and estimating rates of return in the income approach. The rents charged by the owners of a motel, a shopping centre, an office building, an apartment building, or any income-producing property usually do not vary greatly from those charged by owners of competing properties. If the demand for a particular type of property exceeds the existing supply, owners intend to increase rents. Thus, the developers may find new constructions are profitable. Property values may increase until the supply satisfies demand. However, if the demand for the property is less than the existing supply, rents may decline, vacancy rates may increase and property values may decrease. Therefore, to estimate rates of return and forecast future benefits, appraisers should consider the demand (both present and anticipated) for a particular type of property and how the demand relates to supply.

4. Applicable Scope

In single-asset valuations, the income approach is often adopted in the valuation of intangible assets, investment real estate and other assets, such as unlisted stocks, bonds, long-term equity investments, etc. In whole-asset valuations, the income approach is usually adopted in business valuation.

However, it is difficult to measure the parameters of income approach, such as the expected returns and discount rates, which will limit the applicability of the income approach. Besides, the income approach cannot be adopted to valuate the assets that cannot generate income or cannot be measured in monetary terms.

5. Concrete Methods

The income approach to value consists of methods, techniques, and mathematical procedures. The concrete methods under the income approach are effectively based on discounting future amounts of cash flow to present value. They are variations of the Discounted Cash Flow (DCF) method and the formulas below apply in part or in full to all income approach methods:

5.1 The income is unchanged

(a) When the asset generates <u>unchanged income</u> and <u>unlimited duration,</u> the following model can be adopted:

$$P = \frac{A}{r}$$

Where P is denoted as the value of subject property; A is denoted as the benefit (cash inflow) that the property can generate in a period of time and this is specifically an <u>annuity</u>; r is denoted as the capitalization rate.

The conditions of the formula include: ① the annual income remains unchanged; ② the capitalization rate is fixed and greater than zero; ③ the duration of benefits is unlimited.

Example 3-1

There is an undisclosed food formula, whose annual income is 100,000 yuan per year with indefinite period. The capitalization rate is 10%. Try to value this formula.

The value of this formula=100,000/10%=1,000,000(Yuan)

(b) When the asset generate income with an unchanged amount and <u>explicit duration,</u> the following model can be adopted:

$$P = \frac{A}{r}\left[1 - \frac{1}{(1+r)^n}\right]$$

Where n denotes the number of period (duration).

The conditions of the formula include: ① the annual income remains unchanged; ② the capitalization rate is fixed and greater than zero; ③ the duration of benefits is n (explicit).

Example 3-2

The subject asset is the franchise of a certain clothing trademark. According to the contract, the remaining service life of the trademark is 5 years. According to the previous business data and market recognition of the trademark, its annual revenue will remain at 150,000 yuan in the future. If the discount rate is assumed to be 15%, try to value this franchise of the trademark.

$$The\ value\ of\ the\ franchise = \frac{150,000}{15\%}\left[1-\frac{1}{(1+15\%)^5}\right] = 502,823 (Yuan)$$

(c) The expected income is unchanged and the discount rate is 0:

$$P = A \times n$$

The conditions of the formula include: ① the annual income remains unchanged; ② the capitalization rate is zero; ③ the duration of benefits is n (explicit).

5.2 The income remains unchanged after several years

(a) When the asset generates <u>volatile incomes</u> with explicit duration, and unchanged income with explicit duration after, the following model can be adopted:

$$P = \sum_{i=1}^{t}\frac{R_i}{(1+r)^i} + \frac{A}{r(1+r)^t}$$

Where R_i denotes the income in year i; i could go from 1 to t.

The conditions of the formula include: ① the annual income is volatile before year t (including year t); ② the annual income remains unchanged after year t (excluding year t); ③ the discount rate is fixed and greater than zero; ④ the duration of benefits is unlimited.

(b) When the asset generates incomes with explicit amount per year and incomes with explicit duration after, the following model can be adopted:

$$P = \sum_{i=1}^{t}\frac{R_i}{(1+r)^i} + \frac{A}{r(1+r)^t}\left[1-\frac{1}{(1+r)^{n-t}}\right]$$

The conditions of the formula include: ① the annual income is volatile before year t (including year t); ② the annual income remains unchanged after year t (excluding year t); ③ the discount rate is fixed and greater than zero; ④ the duration of benefits is n (explicit).

Example 3-3

The income of an asset in the next five years will be 120,000 yuan, 150,000 yuan, 130,000 yuan, 110,000 yuan and 140,000 yuan respectively. It is assumed that from the sixth year, the income of each subsequent year is 140,000 yuan, and the discount rate and capitalization rate are both 10%. Please value this asset with unlimited duration and 50 years' income.

Value with unlimited duration

$$= \frac{120,000}{1+10\%} + \frac{150,000}{(1+10\%)^2} + \frac{130,000}{(1+10\%)^3} + \frac{110,000}{(1+10\%)^4} + \frac{140,000}{(1+10\%)^5} + \frac{140,000}{10\% \times (1+10\%)^5}$$

$$=1,362,037(Yuan)$$

Value with 50 years' income

$$= \frac{120,000}{1+10\%} + \frac{150,000}{(1+10\%)^2} + \frac{130,000}{(1+10\%)^3} + \frac{110,000}{(1+10\%)^4} + \frac{140,000}{(1+10\%)^5}$$
$$+ \frac{140,000}{10\% \times (1+10\%)^5} \times \left[1 - \frac{1}{(1+10\%)^{50-5}}\right]$$

$$=1,350,128(Yuan)$$

5.3 The income is volatile in an explicit duration

When the asset generates <u>volatile incomes with explicit duration</u>, the following model can be adopted:

$$P = \sum_{i=1}^{n} \frac{R_i}{(1+r)^n}$$

This is the most commonly used formula in the application of the income approach. $\sum_{i=1}^{n} \frac{1}{(1+r)^i}$ is also known as <u>present value interest factor</u> *(P/A, r, n)*.

The conditions of the formula include: ① the annual expected income is not equal; ② the duration of benefits is n (explicit); ③ the discount rate is fixed and greater than zero.

Example 3-4

An enterprise can only operate for 3 years. The forecast of the enterprise is as follows:

Year	Expect income	Discount rate
1	300,000	6%
2	400,000	6%
3	200,000	6%

Please try to value the enterprise.

$$\text{The value of the enterprise} = \frac{300,000}{1+6\%} + \frac{400,000}{(1+6\%)^2} + \frac{200,000}{(1+6\%)^3} = 806,941 (Yuan)$$

5.4 The price of assets after several years is explicit

When the asset generates volatile incomes with explicit duration and unchanged income after that, the following model can be adopted:

$$P = \frac{A}{r}\left[1 - \frac{1}{(1+r)^n}\right] + \frac{P_n}{(1+r)^n}$$

The conditions of the formula include: ① the income remains unchanged before the year n (including the year n); ② the price of the asset in year n is predicted to be P_n; ③ the discount rate is fixed and greater than zero.

Example 3-5

The income of the subject asset in the next five years is 70,000 yuan, and the price of the asset after five years is 200,000 yuan. Assuming that the discount rate is 10%, please value the asset.

$$\text{The value of the asset} = \frac{70,000}{10\%}\left[1 - \frac{1}{(1+10\%)^5}\right] + \frac{200,000}{(1+10\%)^5} = 389,539(Yuan)$$

Example 3-6

The subject property which is an intangible asset of a company will generate

120,000 yuan each year in 5 years after the valuation date, and it will be sold at the end of the fifth year. The appraisers anticipate that at the end of the fifth year, this subject's price will be 900,000 yuan, and the discount rate is 20%. Please estimate the market value of the subject property.

The value of the intangible asset $= 120,000 \times (P/A, 20\%, 5) + 900,000/(1+20\%)^5 = 720,561 (Yuan)$

5.5 The income changes according to the arithmetic progression

(a) The income increases by <u>arithmetic progression</u> and the duration is unlimited:

$$P = \frac{A}{r} + \frac{B}{r^2}$$

The conditions of the formula include: ① the expected income increases by arithmetic progression; ② The annual increment of expected income is B; ③ the discount rate is fixed and greater than zero; ④ the duration of benefits is unlimited.

(b) The income increases by arithmetic progression and the duration is explicit:

$$P = \left(\frac{A}{r} + \frac{B}{r^2}\right)\left[1 - \frac{1}{(1+r)^n}\right] - \frac{B}{r} \times \frac{n}{(1+r)^n}$$

The conditions of the formula include: ① the expected income increases by arithmetic progression; ② The annual increment of expected income is B; ③ the discount rate is fixed and greater than zero; ④ the duration of benefits is n (explicit).

(c) The income decreases by arithmetic progression and the duration is unlimited:

$$P = \frac{A}{r} - \frac{B}{r^2}$$

The conditions of the formula include: ① the expected income decreases by arithmetic progression; ② The annual decrease of expected income is B; ③ the discount rate is fixed and greater than 0; ④ the duration of benefits is unlimited; ⑤ The income decreases to zero.

(d) The income decreases by arithmetic progression and the duration is explicit:

$$P = \left(\frac{A}{r} - \frac{B}{r^2}\right)\left[1 - \frac{1}{(1+r)^n}\right] + \frac{B}{r} \times \frac{n}{(1+r)^n}$$

The conditions of the formula include: ① the expected income decreases by arithmetic progression; ② The annual decrease of expected income is B; ③ the discount rate is fixed and greater than zero; ④ the duration of benefits is n (explicit).

Example 3-7

The remaining operation period of an enterprise is 10 years. According to the analysis of professionals, the annual net profit of the enterprise in the next 10 years will maintain an annual decrease of 100,000 yuan, and the current annual income is 1,000,000 yuan. Assuming that the discount rate is 10%, try to value the total shareholders' equity of the enterprise.

Value of the total shareholders' equity

$$= \left(\frac{1,000,000}{10\%} - \frac{100,000}{10\%^2} \right) \left[1 - \frac{1}{(1+10\%)^{10}} \right] + \frac{100,000}{10\%} \times \frac{10}{(1+10\%)^{10}}$$

$=4,174,064$ *(Yuan)*

5.6 The income changes according to the geometric sequence

(a) The income increases by geometric sequence and the duration is unlimited:

$$P = \frac{A}{r-s}$$

The conditions of the formula include: ① the expected income increases by geometric sequence; ② The annual increasing rate of income is s; ③ the discount rate is fixed and greater than zero; ④ the duration of benefits is unlimited; ⑤ $r>s>0$.

(b) The income increases by geometric sequence and the duration is explicit:

$$P = \frac{A}{r-s} \left[1 - \left(\frac{1+s}{1+r} \right)^n \right]$$

The conditions of the formula include: ① the expected income increases by geometric sequence; ② The annual increasing rate of income is s; ③ the discount rate is fixed and greater than zero; ④ the duration of benefits is n (explicit); ⑤ $r>s>0$.

(c) The income decreases by geometric sequence and the duration is unlimited:

$$P = \frac{A}{r+s}$$

The conditions of the formula include: ① the expected income decreases by geometric sequence; ② The annual decreasing rate of income is s; ③ the discount rate is fixed and greater than 0; ④ the duration of benefits is unlimited; ⑤ $r>s>0$.

(d) The income decreases by geometric sequence and the duration is explicit:

$$P = \frac{A}{r+s}\left[1-\left(\frac{1-s}{1+r}\right)^n\right]$$

The conditions of the formula include: ① the expected income decreases by geometric sequence; ② The annual decreasing rate of income is s; ③ the discount rate is fixed and greater than zero; ④ the duration of benefits is n (explicit); ⑤ $0<s\leq 1$.

Core Words and Expressions 核心术语

earning power	盈利能力
income-producing property	具有获利能力的资产
income approach	收益法
income capitalization approach	收益资本化途径
income stream	收益流
present value/current value	现值
future benefits	未来收益
property ownership	资产所有权
resale value upon reversion/reversionary value	终值
direct capitalization	直接资本化
yield capitalization	报酬资本化
capitalization/discount rate	资本化率 / 折现率

income multiplier	收入乘数
yield rate	收益率
discounted cash flow (DCF)	现金流折现
gross income	总收入
annual operating expenses	年运营费用
rates of returns	回报率
capitalization rate	资本化率
quantified	量化
principle of anticipation	预期原则，预期收益原则
anticipation of benefits	收益预期
income capitalization method	收益资本化法
competing properties	竞争性资产
vacancy rate	闲置率，空置率
unchanged income	等额收益
unlimited duration	无限期
annuity	年金
explicit duration	有限期
volatile incomes	不等额收益
mathematical procedure	数学程序
present value interest factor	现值系数
arithmetic progression	等差数列
geometric sequence	等比数列

Questions and Discussion 问题与讨论

1. What are the procedures of the income approach?

2. Please list the important parameters of the income approach.

3. What are the limitations of the income approach?

Topic 4: The Choice of Valuation Approaches/Methods 资产评估方法的选择

Abstract 中文摘要

资产评估方法是确定资产价值的途径和手段及各种技术方法，主要包括市场法、收益法和成本法三种基本方法及其衍生方法。恰当选择评估方法是资产评估程序中必不可少的一个关键步骤，也是影响资产评估结论和资产评估报告质量的重要环节。一般认为，"评估途径"和"评估方法"都是在资产评估中被普遍接受的技术分析途径及方法，即"评估途径"也被直接称作为"评估方法"。但是，二者在具体概念上又略有差异，例如，"评估途径"往往被视为是一种或者多种具体评估方法的集合，与"评估方法"之间存在类似于包含与被包含的关系。

关于评估方法的比较、选择和使用，我们应当认识到，尽管资产评估所涉及的资产类型和评估目的千差万别，但基本评估理论和评估方法是一致的，这是评估行业能成为一个行业的基本出发点。资产评估专业人员的经验以及各国之间的对话也已经证明，除极个别例外的情况，世界各国对于构成评估专业的基本原理有着共识。虽然在一些情况下，当地法律和经济情形可能会要求特殊（如限制性）应用，但评估方法和技术的基本原理在世界各国通常是高度相似。

所有三种评估方法都适用于解决许多评估问题，但某一种或多种评估方法在一个具体评估项目中可能更为重要。资产评估专业人员应当充分理解市场法、成本法、收益法这三种基本评估方法的原理及其局限性，在具体评估项目中应当首先考虑三种基本评估方法的适用性，并根据具体情况决定评估方法的选择和运用。此外，通过不同评估方法得出的不同价值结论，在彼此之间可能相互支持，也可能相互排斥，因此，资产评估专业人员应当尽可能多地采用所有适用的和有数据支持的评估方法及其衍生方法，由此通过比较和综合协调形成最终更为可靠的价值结论。

具体而言，资产评估专业人员在选择评估方法时，应当充分考虑影响评估方法选择的各项因素，例如评估目的、价值类型、评估对象、评估方法的适用前提、数据的质量和数量等等。其中，评估方法的选取应当与评估目的和评估价值类型相适应，应当与评估对象的类型和现实状态相适应，应当与数据资料的收集情况相适应。

Text* 正文

1. Valuation Approach VS Valuation Method

The term <u>valuation approach</u> refers to generally accepted <u>analytical methodologies</u>. In some states, these approaches may be referred to as <u>valuation method</u>s. In general, valuation approach means the way of estimating value that employs one or more specific valuation methods. Depending on the nature and purpose of the property, three valuation approaches may be applied in order to arrive at the valuation defined by the appropriate basis of value. They are the cost approach, the market approach, and the income approach. These approaches help to determine market value or <u>a value other than market value</u>. They are all based on the economic principles of price equilibrium, anticipation of benefits or substitution, etc. Within the valuation approaches, valuation method can be defined as a specific way to estimate a value.

2. The Relationship among Valuation Approaches/Methods

The experiences of professional valuers and dialogues among nations have demonstrated that, with few exceptions, there is worldwide agreement regarding the fundamentals that underpin the <u>valuation discipline</u>. Local laws and economic circumstance may, on occasion, require special (and sometimes limited) applications, but fundamentals of valuation methods and techniques are the same throughout the world.

Valuation approaches generally apply to all types of valuation, including <u>real property</u>, <u>personal property</u>, <u>business</u>, and <u>financial interests</u>. However, valuation of different types of property involves different sources of data that appropriately reflects

---

* *Partly from: The Appraisal Foundation (TAF), 2010-2011 Uniform Standards of Professional Appraisal Practice, 2009; Wang Chengjun, Professional English, Appraisal Journal of China, 2005.*

Chapter 2 Valuation Approaches 资产评估方法

the market in which the property (and/or service or business) is to be valued. For example, individual buildings are commonly sold and valued in the relevant real estate market whereas the values of the shares of stock in the property company that own a number of buildings are reflected by pricing in the relevant shares market.

Each valuation normally employs one or more of the valuation approaches by applying the principle of substitution. The principle holds that a prudent person would pay no more for a good or service than the cost of acquiring an equally satisfactory substitute good or service, in the absence of the complication factors of time, greater risk, or inconvenience. The lowest cost of the best alternative, whether it is a substitute or the original, tends to establish market value. This principle is fundamental to the three approaches to market value.

3. The Choice of Valuation Approaches/Methods

To develop an opinion of value, valuers usually consider three generally accepted approaches: cost, market, and income. Each valuation approach has alternative methods of application. The valuer combines expertise and training, local standards, market requirement, the type of property, the intended use of the appraisal, the identified scope of works, the quality and quantity of data available to determine which approach or approaches are applied.

All three approaches are applicable to many appraisal problems, but one or more of the approaches may have greater significance in a given assignment. For example, the cost approach might not be applicable in valuing old properties that suffer substantial depreciation, a case being difficult to estimate. The market approach might not be applicable to specialized properties such as garbage disposal plants because comparable data may be unavailable. The income approach is rarely used in the valuation of properties that cannot generate income by its nature or for which the owner outbid investors due to some reasons.

Appraisers should apply all the approaches that are applicable and sufficient data is available. The alternative value indications derived through different approaches either support or refute one another. The reason for having alternative approaches and methods is to provide the valuer with a series of analytical procedures which will ultimately be weighed and reconciled into final value estimate, depending upon the particular basis of value involved.

Core Words and Expressions 核心术语

valuation approach	评估途径
analytical methodology	分析方法
valuation method	评估方法
a value other than market value	非市场价值
valuation discipline	评估学科
real property/estate	不动产
personal property	动产，私人财产
business	企业
financial interests	金融权益
local standards	当地准则
intended use	期望用途
scope of work	工作范围
substantial depreciation	大量贬值，实质性贬值
outbid	出价高于
analytical procedure	分析程序
be weighed and reconciled	经过权衡和综合协调

Questions and Discussion 问题与讨论

1. Please describe the difference between valuation approach and valuation method.

2. Which is the best approach among the three basic valuation approaches? Explain the reasons.

3. Please conclude the applicable scope of the three basic valuation approaches.

More Knowledge
知识扩展

Topic: Methods Application in Business Valuation
资产评估方法在企业价值评估中的应用

Abstract 中文摘要

在企业价值评估中，市场法、收益法和成本法（又称为资产基础法）都是较为适用的评估方法，尤其以前两种方法更为常见。

将市场法运用于企业价值评估时，需要通过利用可比企业（相似企业）的所有者权益和销售的有价证券等信息，对其进行适当的调整以求得企业价值。企业价值评估主要有三种信息来源，即股票市场、并购市场和企业以前的交易案例。资产评估专业人员应当重点考虑所选取的与可比企业与被评估企业是否具有可比性。其可比性可以通过两个维度来判断：（1）行业维度：由于处于同一行业的公司通常具有一定的可比性，资产评估专业人员可通过国民经济行业标准分类、证监会上市公司行业分类、国际通用的标准行业代码等确认被评估企业和可比企业的所属行业；（2）财务维度：资产评估专业人员需要通过必要的分析，从业务类型及资本构成、财务指标等方面进行比较，以此体现评估企业和可比企业之间的风险和成长差异。除此之外，资产评估专业人员还应当考虑股权评估的交易背景、交易日期、交易价格、收购股权的比重、影响交易价格的其他重要交易条款等因素。

将收益法运用于企业价值评估时，需要重点考虑企业未来的盈利能力。企业经营的本质是获得收益，所以收益法通过预测企业的盈利能力来判断企业价值，能够更直观地体现企业存在和运营的本质特征。但值得注意的是，这里的企业盈利能力并不是企业当前的实际盈利水平，而是对其未来盈利情况的一种合理预测，所以需要资产评估专业人员进行相应的调整和合理的分析后，据此计算得到企业价值的评估结果。通常情形下，资产评估专业人员依据收益口径的不同，选择股利折现模型、现金流折现模型、经济利润模型等不同的收益法具体方法进行企业价值评估。常见的企业收益额口径有企业净利润、息税前净利润、净现金流量等；

净现金流量指标又包括全投资口径现金流量和股权投资口径企业现金流，即企业自由现金流和股权自由现金流。此外，资产评估专业人员在运用收益法评估企业价值时，还应当注意所使用的收益额与折现率在口径上的匹配和协调。

Text* 正文

1. Market Approach: Application in Business Valuation

The market approach, also called sales comparison approach, is frequently used in business valuation. The market approach compares the subject to similar businesses, business ownership interests, and securities that have been sold in the market. The three most common sources of data used in the market approach are public stock markets in which ownership interests of similar businesses are traded, the acquisition market in which entire businesses are bought and sold, and prior transactions in the ownership of the subject business.

There must be a reasonable basis for comparison with the similar businesses in the market approach. These similar businesses should be in the same industry as the subject or in an industry that responds to the same economic variables. The comparison must be made in a meaningful manner and must be accurate. Factors indicate a reasonable basis for comparison include: similarity to the subject business in terms of qualitative and quantitative business characteristics; amount and verifiability of data on the similar business; whether the price of the similar business represents an arm's-length transaction.

A thorough and unbiased search for similar businesses is necessary to establish the independence and reliability of the valuation. The search should include simple, objective criteria for selecting similar businesses. A comparative analysis of qualitative and quantitative similarities and differences between similar businesses and the subject business must be made.

Through the analysis of publicly traded businesses or acquisitions, a valuer often

---

* Partly from: The International Valuation Standards Council (IVSC), International Valuation Standards 2011 Edition, 2011; Wang Chengjun, Professional English, Appraisal Journal of China, 2007.

computes valuation ratios, which are usually price divided by a measure of income or net assets. Caution must be used in calculating and selecting these ratios.

Valuers should make sure that the ratio provide meaningful information about the value of the business, and the data from similar businesses used to compute the ratio must be accurate. Besides, they should also make clear that the calculation of ratios is accurate. If the data are averaged, the time period considered and averaging method must be appropriate. Meanwhile, all calculations must be done in the same way for both the subject business and the similar businesses, and the price data used in the ratio must be valid as of the valuation date. Wherever appropriate, adjustments may need to be made to render the similar businesses and the subject business more comparable. Moreover, adjustments may need to be made for unusual, non-recurring, and non-operating items; appropriate adjustments for differences in the subject ownership interest and interests in the similar businesses with regard to control or lack of control, or marketability or lack of marketability, must also be made, if applicable.

When prior transactions in the subject business are used to provide valuation guidance, adjustments may need to be made for the passage of time and for changed circumstances in the economy, the industry, and the business.

2. Income Approach: Application in Business Valuation

The income approach, when applied to a business enterprise, begins with a projection of the income-producing capability of the business. It is based on the assumption that the value of the enterprise is dependent on the ability of all the assets to earn a reasonable return. The first step in the income approach, when applied to a business enterprise, is to estimate the level of earnings that an enterprise is capable of producing in normal operation. But we must be aware that the earnings capability, not actual earning, is the key element in income approach. Therefore, the capability is not necessarily what the business actually earns at the time of the appraisal. Adjustments may be made to a current income statement. For a start-up business, one would not immediately assume that the business has no value because it has no earnings at the moment.

In most cases, adjustments to revenues and expenses are minimal or, in the case of a publicly held corporation, may not be made at all. Adjustments of this kind are made when analysing a closely held corporation. The owner of such an enterprise desires to minimize taxes instead of disclosing a profit on the bottom line. Owners' compensation often takes the form of a high salary than dividends, and there are often substantial perks in evidence. In another case, a business can be squeezed for any possible money of earning in order to make it attractive for sale. Purchases of needed equipment or maintenance of existing machinery may have been deferred in order to enhance earnings. So, the appraiser needs to make a proper analysis in order to understand the earnings capability of the business.

Whether the financial statements are audited has no bearing on the need for this analysis. It is not the auditor's responsibility to determine an appropriate salary for the owner, whether equipment maintenance is properly done or not. The appraiser needs to know, however, whether a business gains on a sustainable basis. One cannot simply buy the theory of the most current income statement shows.

For the valuation of a business enterprise, most analysis may use net cash flow as the relevant income stream. Net cash flow is defined as:

Earnings before interest and taxes

Less: income taxes at the statutory rate

Plus: depreciation and other noncash expense

Less: capital expenditures

Less: cash required to increase net working capital

The use of debt-free net cash flow eliminates the effect of how the business is presently financed and taxed. Net cash flow is calculated for a period of the forecast. Obviously, cash flow is not expected to cease at the end of the forecast period, and therefore the value of the ongoing business must be reflected. This is the reversion of the property and is analogous to a landlord regaining possession of a property at the end of a lease. When reversion takes place, it is assumed that the net cash flow in the terminal year of the forecast will continue in perpetuity with depreciation equal to capital needs so that further infusions of cash will not be necessary. The underlying assumption at the reversion year is that product cycles or market shares have matured and the future cash flow growth is expected to be at a steady and sustainable rate.

Chapter 2 Valuation Approaches 资产评估方法

Core Words and Expressions 核心术语

business valuation	企业价值评估
similar businesses	相似企业
business ownership interests	企业所有者权益
securities	证券
public stock market	股票市场
acquisition market	并购市场
prior transactions	以前的交易
economic variables	经济变量
qualitative and quantitative business characteristics	企业的数量和质量特征
independence and reliability of valuation	评估的独立性和可靠性
objective criteria	客观标准
comparative analysis	可比分析
publicly traded businesses	公开交易的企业（上市公司）
measure of income or net assets	收益或净资产指标
if the data are averaged	如果所取的数据是平均数
time period	时间期间
averaging method	平均方法
render …more comparable	使……具有更多的可比性
reasonable return	合理回报
level of earnings	盈利水平
in normal operation	在正常经营情况下
earnings capability	获利能力

income statement	损益表，利润表
start-up business	新开张的企业
publicly held corporation	公共持股公司
closely held corporation	内部持股公司
on the bottom line	在（账表）底栏
minimize taxes	减少税收
owners' compensation	所有者的报酬
substantial perks	大量的津贴
maintenance of existing machinery	对现有设备进行的维护
financial statement	财务报表
audit	审计
net cash flow	净现金流
income taxes at the statutory rate	依法定税率征收的所得税
depreciation and other noncash expense	折旧和其他非现金费用
capital expenditures	资本性支出
net working capital	净营运资本
debt-free net cash flow	无负债现金流
at the end of the forecast period	在预测期末
ongoing business	持续经营的企业
reversion of the property	财产的复归
at the end of a lease	租赁到期时
in the terminal year of the forecast	在预测期最后一年
infusions of cash	现金的投入
underlying assumption	基本假设

product cycles	产品周期
market share	市场份额

Questions and Discussion 问题与讨论

1. Please explain the precautions to be taken when considering the profitability of the corporation in the process of business valuation with income approach.

2. When the economy is unstable, which valuation approach will have a more reasonable outcome?

Information Extension

思政微课堂

资产作为生产要素，其价格实质上是其获利能力的价值表现。资产受到市场环境、资源配置等因素的影响，因而在实践中不能简单地按照其原值或账面价值进行定价，否则可能出现价格无法体现资产价值的情况，在交易中往往也会损害某一方的利益，影响交易活动的进行。只有合理选择和使用评估方法，才能够科学有效地反映资产价值，保障产权有序流转，保证市场公平交易。党的二十大报告强调，"实践没有止境，理论创新也没有止境。"资产评估是市场经济中不可或缺的专业服务行业，资产评估专业人员在选择和使用评估方法时应当首先做到：(1) 坚持问题导向，在评估过程当中增强问题意识，聚焦实践遇到的新问题；(2) 坚持系统观念，把握好全局和局部的关系，不断提高辩证思维、系统思维、创新思维等能力；(3) 拥有进步理念，在先进评估方法的应用和评估执业准则的遵循层面保持与国际接轨。以此为基础，规范资产评估方法的选择、运用和披露，引导资产评估专业人员在执业实践中合理选择和使用评估方法，有利于资产评估行业提升执业质量，更好助力我国经济社会高质量发展。

现阶段，我国资产评估专业人员恰当选择资产评估方法的要求已上升至法律层面。《中华人民共和国资产评估法》第二十六条规定："评估专业人员应当恰当选择评估方法，除依据评估执业准则只能选择一种评估方法的外，应当选择两种以上评估方法，经综合分析，形成评估结论，编制评估报告。"据此，《资产评估基本准则》（财资〔2017〕43号）对资产评估方法的选择和运用作出了原则性规定，资产评估执业准则进一步细化和落实了《中华人民共和国资产评估法》的相关规定和要求。为规范资产评估机构及其资产评估专业人员在执行评估业务时使用评估方法的行为，中国资产评估协会于2020年3月1日正式施行《资产评估执业准则——资产评估方法》（中评协〔2019〕35号），对资产评估专业人员有关评估方法的理解和应用作出具体要求，并对不同情形下评估方法的使用和披露进行规范。

根据《资产评估执业准则——资产评估方法》（中评协〔2019〕35号）规定，在有相关法律、行政法规和财政部部门规章的规定，或评估对象仅满足一种评估方法的适用条件，或者存在资产评估行业通常的执业方式普遍无法排除的操作条件限制只能采用一种评估方法时，可以采用一种评估方法。资产评估专业人员应当在资产评估报告中对资产评估方法的选择及其理由进行披露。因适用性受限而选择一种评估方法的，应当在资产评估报告中披露其他基本评估方法不适用的原因；因操作条件受限而选择一种评估方法的，应当对所受的操作条件限制进行分析、说明和披露。

Chapter 3
Plant and Equipment Valuation
机器设备评估

Wisdom
名人名言

工欲善其事,必先利其器。

——孔子

物之不齐,物之情也。

——孟子

Give me a place to stand and with a lever I will move the whole world.

—Archimedes

One's real value first lies in to what degree and what sense he set himself.

—Albert Einstein

Rudimentary Knowledge
基本知识

Abstract 中文摘要

机器设备评估是指资产评估专业人员依据相关法律、法规和评估准则，对机器设备的价值进行分析、估算并发表专业意见的行为和过程。其中，机器设备是指人类利用机械原理以及其他科学原理制造的、特定主体拥有或者控制的有形资产，包括机器、仪器、装置、附属的特殊建筑物等。本章在对机器设备进行定义的基础上，列举并解释了部分不属于机器设备的有形资产，如房地产、矿产、自然资源、原材料、消耗品、库存和存货、私人财产、农业资产等。

机器设备评估的目的通常有两类：一是机器设备是企业价值或者其他整体资产组合评估的组成部分，此种情况下机器设备评估的目的需要服从于企业价值评估的目的；二是机器设备或者机器设备组合出资、抵押、转让、保险、涉讼、涉税，以财务报告为目的的公允价值计量、资产减值测试等。资产评估专业人员在机器设备评估过程中，需要考虑资产自身状态、环境影响及经济用途等因素。自身因素包括机器设备的技术规范、使用寿命、资产状况、维护历史纪录等；环境因素包括机器设备的原材料来源、产品所处的市场、限制使用的法律规制等；经济因素包括机器设备的实际或潜在盈利能力、产品的市场需求等。

在很多情况下，机器设备是与房屋、土地等资产结合在一起使用的，并且流水线等整体设备还需要在不同设备同时运转时才能进行生产和发挥效用。因此，资产评估专业人员在对机器设备进行评估时，需要注意明确评估范围和合理设定评估假设。例如，机器设备评估中常见的评估假设包括：（1）持续使用假设和变现假设：持续使用假设指的是机器设备未来将按照某种特定用途继续使用；变现假设指的是机器设备将在未来以二手设备或其他设备的方式出售；（2）现行用途使用假设与改变用途使用假设：现行用途假设是指被评估的机器设备按照目前的用途持续使用；改变用途使用假设是指被评估的机器设备未来将改变用途使用；（3）原地使用假设与移地使用假设：原地使用假设是指被评估的机器设备未来将在原来的使用地点使用；移地使用假设是指被评估的机器设备未来将改变使用地点持续使用。

在机器设备评估中，成本法、市场法和收益法都具有不同程度的适用性。成本法通过估算机器设备的重置成本并扣减其在使用过程中的贬值得到评估结果，适用于评估绝大多数的机器设备；市场法根据目前公开市场上与机器设备相似或可比的参照物的价格来调整确定评估对象的价值，适用于评估市场交易活跃的机器设备；收益法通过将机器设备的未来预期收益按一定的折现率和收益期限折算为现值得到评估结果，适用于具有独立获利能力或者获利能力可以量化的机器设备。

Text* 正文

1. Introduction of Plant and Equipment

Items of plant and equipment are tangible assets that are held by an entity for use in the production or supply of goods, or services, for rental by others, or for administrative purposes; and are expected to be used over a period of time. However, real property, mineral or natural resources, raw materials and consumables, stock and inventory, personal property, agricultural assets, etc., are not classed as plant and equipment.

A valuation of plant and equipment normally requires the consideration of a range of factors relating to the asset itself, such as the environment the asset lives in and its economic potential. Factors that may need to be considered under each of these headings include the following:

The first part consists of asset-related factors, such as the asset's technical specification, the remaining physical life, and the asset's condition, including maintenance history. If an asset is not valued in its current location, we also need to consider the costs of decommissioning and removal. Furthermore, other potential loss of a complementary asset also needs to be considered.

The second part consists of environment-related factors, including the location in relation to source of raw material and market for product as well as the impact of any

---

* Partly from: The International Valuation Standards Council (IVSC), International Valuation Standards, 2011 Edition, 2011.

environmental or other legislation that either restricts utilization or imposes additional operating or decommissioning costs.

The third part consists of economic-related factors, such as the actual or potential profitability of an asset, the demand for the product from the plant and equipment with regard to both macro and micro economic factors, and the potential that an asset becomes more valuable in the future.

Other than these three main parts, an intangible asset may have an impact on the value of plant and equipment assets though it <u>falls outside</u> the classification of plant and equipment assets. For example, the value of patterns and dies is often inextricably linked to associated <u>intellectual property</u> rights. Operating software, technical data, production records and patents are further examples of intangible assets that can have an impact on the value of plant and equipment assets. In such cases, the valuation process will involve consideration of the inclusion of intangible assets and their impact on the valuation of the plant and equipment assets.

2. Financing Arrangements

An item of plant and equipment may be subject to a financing arrangement. Accordingly, the asset must be sold with the lender or <u>lessor</u> being paid any balance outstanding under the financing arrangement. The payment may or may not exceed the <u>unencumbered</u> value of the item. Depending upon the purpose of the valuation, it may be appropriate to identify any encumbered assets and to report their values separately from the unencumbered assets.

Items of plant and equipment that are subject to operating leases are the properties of the third parties and therefore excluded from a valuation of the assets of the <u>lessee</u>. However, such assets may need to be recorded as their presence may impact on the value of owned assets used in association.

3. Forced Sale

Plant and equipment assets can be particularly susceptible to sale conditions. An example is that the assets have to be removed from a property in a time frame that precludes proper marketing because the lease of the property is being terminated.

The impact of such circumstances on value needs careful consideration. In order to advise on the value likely to be realized, it is necessary to consider any alternatives to a sale from the current location, such as the practicality and cost of removing the items to another location for <u>disposal</u> within the available time limit.

4. Valuation Approaches

All the three principal valuation approaches can be applied to the valuation of plant and equipment assets.

4.1 Market Approach

For <u>homogenous</u> plant and equipment, e.g., motor vehicles and certain types of office equipment or industrial machinery, the market approach is commonly used because of sufficient data of recent sales of similar assets. However, many types of plant and equipment are specialized so that the direct sales evidence for such items may be unavailable. This scenario calling for either the income approach or the cost approach.

4.2 Income Approach

The income approach to the valuation of plant and equipment can be used if specific cash flows can be identified for the asset or a group of complementary assets, e.g., where a group of assets forming a process plant produces a marketable product. However, some of the cash flows may be attributable to intangible assets and difficult to separate from the cash flow contribution of the plant and equipment. Therefore, the income approach is not normally practical for many individual items of plant or equipment.

4.3 Cost Approach

The cost approach is commonly adopted for plant and equipment particularly in the case of individual assets that are specialized. This is done by calculating the depreciated replacement cost of the asset. The cost of replacing the subject asset to a market participant needs to be estimated. The replacement cost is the cost of obtaining an alternative asset of equivalent utility, which can either be a modern equivalent providing the same functionality or the cost of reproducing an exact replica of the subject asset. The latter is only appropriate to the cost of a replica less than the cost of a modern equivalent or the utility offered by the subject asset being provided by a replica rather than a modern equivalent.

Having established the replacement cost, <u>deduction</u>s are then made to reflect the physical, functional, and economic obsolescence of the subject asset compared to the alternative asset that could be acquired at the replacement cost.

Core Words and Expressions 核心术语

plant and equipment	厂房和设备，机器设备
raw material	原材料
consumable	消耗品
inventory	存货
technical specification	技术规范
physical life	使用寿命
decommission	拆卸，退役
complementary asset	辅助性资产，互补性资产
fall outside	超出，超越
intellectual property	知识产权
lessor	出租人
unencumbered	没有阻碍的，不受妨碍的
lessee	承租人
disposal	清理，处置
homogenous	同质的
deduction	扣除，减除

Questions and Discussion 问题与讨论

1. We need proper assumptions for a given circumstance. How many kinds of assumptions have been mentioned in the text? And how will these assumptions affect the process of valuation?

2. How will environmental factors affect the value of plant and equipment?

3. Among the three approaches, which is the best one for the valuation of plant and equipment?

More Knowledge
知识扩展

Topic: Fair Value Measures of Plant and Equipment 机器设备的公允价值计量

Abstract 中文摘要

一般认为，会计准则规定的计量属性可以理解为相对应的资产评估价值类型。在现行国际会计准则框架下，机器设备（厂房和设备）的计量允许采用历史成本计量模式和公允价值计量模式。历史成本计量模式下，机器设备的价值是用历史成本减去累计折旧和任何累计减值损失；公允价值计量模式下，机器设备的价值是用重估日的公允价值减去随后发生的折旧。若经常对机器设备进行公允价值重估，则其账面价值不会与资产负债表当日的公允价值产生过大差异。

通过对历史成本计量模式和公允价值计量模式的可靠性进行比较分析，一般认为对机器设备使用公允价值计量模式相较于历史成本计量模式更加科学。虽然在可验证性方面，历史成本计量模式在自行构建资产的情况下比公允价值计量模式更具优势，但这一优势并不十分显著，并且历史成本计量模式忽略了机器设备的可比性特征，而公允价值计量模式则可以在可比性基础上对不同期间报告的机器设备进行估值。

本节重点讨论采用公允价值计量机器设备以及当前一些观点所面临的挑战。

对公允价值的重估是国际和各国会计制度所普遍接受的做法。例如，英国、澳大利亚、新西兰等许多国家都允许以公允价值报告机器设备；在美国，只要资产的可收回金额低于其账面价值，就应当确认减值损失；在其他一些国家或地区，资产的可收回金额是其净售价和使用价值中的较高者，两者均基于现值计算。

Text* 正文

1. The Valuation of Plant and Equipment Across Countries

1.1 International Financial Reporting Standards (IFRS)

The current rules for the measurement of property, plant, and equipment are provided in International Accounting Standards (IAS). Separate rules for the accounting of <u>investment property</u> and agriculture are outlined in IAS respectively. IAS permits two accounting models for the measurement of property, plant, and equipment subsequent to initial recognition. Under the cost model, property, plant, and equipment are carried at historical cost less accumulated depreciation and any accumulated <u>impairment loss</u>es. Under the <u>revaluation</u> model, property, plant, and equipment are carried at fair value at the date of revaluation less subsequent depreciation. Revaluations are to be made often enough so that the carrying amount does not significantly differ from fair value at the <u>balance sheet</u> date. The practice of upward asset revaluations for firms reporting in accordance with international standards appears to be common.

Under the revaluation model, fair value is normally determined by appraisal. When property, plant, and equipment are revalued, the entire class to which that asset belongs should be revalued as well. This is to avoid the selective revaluation of certain property, plant, and equipment and to avoid reporting a mixture of historical costs and fair values for the same asset class in the financial statements. Initial <u>upward revaluations</u> are credited to a <u>revaluation surplus</u> in <u>stockholders' equity</u> and initial <u>downward revaluations</u> are recognized as an expense. The revaluation surplus in stockholders' equity may be transferred to retained earnings when the surplus is

---

* Partly from: Herrmann D, Thomas W B, Saudagaran S M. The quality of fair value measures for property, plant, and equipment. Accounting Forum, 2006: 43-59; International Accounting Standards Board (IASB), The International Accounting Standards, 2003 Edition, 2003.

realized (i.e., through sale, disposal, or as the asset is used). Upward revalued amounts do not affect income except for the subsequent increase in depreciation expense as depreciation is based on the revalued amount.

Requirements for measuring impaired assets are outlined in IAS. For example, in the United States, an impairment loss should be recognized whenever the recoverable amount of an asset is less than its carrying amount. However, in some other countries or region, the recoverable amount of an asset is the higher one of its net selling prices and its value in use both of which based on present value calculations. Net selling price is the amount obtainable from the sale of the asset in an arm's length transaction. Value in use is calculated as the present value of estimated pre-tax future cash flows over the asset's useful life and subsequent disposal. An impairment loss should be recognized as an expense in the income statement for assets carried at cost and treated as a revaluation decrease for assets carried at revalued amounts. An impairment loss should be reversed (and income recognized), once an increase in the estimates used to determine an asset's recoverable amount exists since the last impairment loss was recognized. For assets carried at revalued amounts, a reversal of an impairment loss should be recognized as a revaluation increase up to what the current carrying value would have been, had the asset never been impaired.

1.2 Generally Accepted Accounting Principles (GAAP)

Revaluations have not always been a violation of U.S. GAAP. Prior to about 1940, upward valuations of property, plant, and equipment were an acceptable accounting alternative in the United States. Montgomery's 1940 edition of *Auditing* makes reference to the write-ups or footnote disclosures of appraisal values for property, plant, and equipment as though, from an auditing perspective, these practices were clearly acceptable accounting alternatives. After 1940, accounting academics in the United States continued to support for either the upward valuation of property, plant, and equipment or the footnote disclosure of current market values. The demise of fair value measures for property, plant, and equipment in the United States can be linked to the early years of the Securities and Exchange Commission (SEC). Neither the SEC nor the earliest private accounting standard setting body in the United States (i.e., the Committee on Accounting Procedures) produced explicit rules addressing the issue of upward asset valuations. Rather, the removal of fair value measures and/or fair value disclosures of property, plant, and equipment in financial reporting were imposed through progressively more stringent informal administrative procedures by the SEC. The SEC began discouraging fair value accounting for property, plant, and equipment in response to unsubstantiated asset revaluations by corporations made in the 1920s, prior to the establishment of the SEC.

In the mid to late 1930s, the SEC discouraged, but did not restrict, asset write-ups to fair value in the filing of financial information leading to the registration of securities for public offering. By the 1940s, the SEC had essentially removed the option of upward revaluation of property, plant, and equipment through the enforcement of financial statement information filed with SEC registration statements. By the 1950s, this ban had been extended to the disclosure of fair values in the footnotes to the financial statements. All was accomplished indirectly through internal enforcement procedures within the SEC without ever issuing a formal statement disallowing the practice of fair value accounting for property, plant, and equipment.

An exception to reporting property, plant, and equipment at historical cost is made for impairments under the guidelines of <u>Statement of Financial Accounting Standard (SFAS)</u>. SFAS states that impairment exists when the sum of the undiscounted expected future net cash flows of an asset is less than its carrying amount. The asset is written down from its current carrying amount to either fair value or present value of expected future net cash flows if no active market exists for the asset, and a loss is recognized in the income statement. The reported asset impairments can have a significant impact on a company's financial statements and empirical research documents evidence of their usefulness to decision makers.

2. Summary and Conclusions

This topic overviews the valuation of property, plant, and equipment internationally and discusses the use of fair value measures for property, plant, and equipment.

Recording property, plant, and equipment at fair value is not a new idea. IAS includes the option to revalue property, plant, and equipment to fair value. Many countries including Australia, the United Kingdom, and New Zealand permit the reporting of property, plant, and equipment at fair value.

Fair values for property, plant, and equipment are more relevant to decision makers. Academic research has shown that upward revaluations of property, plant, and equipment are correlated with stock prices and are helpful in predicting future earnings. Fair values also provide relevant information regarding dividend restrictions. In addition to improved predictive value, fair values provide more valuable feedback and more timely financial information than historical cost measures.

Core Words and Expressions 核心术语

impairment loss	减值损失
investment property	投资性房地产
revaluation	资产重估
upward revaluations	向上重估
balance sheet	资产负债表
revaluation surplus	重估盈余
stockholders' equity	股东权益
downward revaluations	向下重估
impaired assets	减值资产
the recoverable amount of an asset	资产可收回金额
net selling price	净售价
pre-tax	税前
Generally Accepted Accounting Principles (GAAP)	美国一般公认会计准则
footnote	财务报表附注
Securities and Exchange Commission (SEC)	美国证券交易委员会
Statement of Financial Accounting Standard (SFAS)	美国财务会计准则

Questions and Discussion 问题与讨论

1. About the valuation of property, plant and equipment, what is the difference between International Financial Reporting Standards and U.S. GAAP?

2. Why is fair value measure for property, plant, and equipment superior to historical cost?

Information Extension
思政微课堂

机器设备是制造业企业的重要实物资产。中国改革开放的伟大实践，催生了大量的机器设备评估需求，使其逐渐发展成为我国资产评估行业的传统业务板块。为规范机器设备评估行为，保护资产评估当事人合法权益和公共利益，中国资产评估协会于2017年9月修订发布了《资产评估执业准则——机器设备》（中评协〔2017〕39号），对资产评估机构执行机器设备评估业务时所须遵循的基本准则、操作要求、评估方法和披露要求作了详尽的规定。根据该准则，机器设备，是指人类利用机械原理以及其他科学原理制造的、特定主体拥有或者控制的有形资产，包括机器、仪器、器械、装置、附属的特殊建筑物等；机器设备评估是指资产评估机构及其资产评估专业人员遵守法律、行政法规和资产评估准则，根据委托对评估基准日特定目的下单独的机器设备、资产组合或者作为企业资产组成部分的机器设备价值进行评定和估算，并出具资产评估报告的专业服务行为；资产评估专业人员执行机器设备评估业务，应当根据评估目的、评估对象、价值类型、资料收集等情况，分析成本法、市场法和收益法三种资产评估基本方法的适用性，选择评估方法。

党的二十大报告强调，"坚持把发展经济的着力点放在实体经济上，推进新型工业化，加快建设制造强国、质量强国、航天强国、交通强国、网络强国、数字中国"。数据显示，2022年，我国高技术制造业、装备制造业的增加值年均分别增长10.6%、7.9%。可以预计，我国机器设备评估的业务领域还会进一步扩大，并将在我国推进新型工业化、加快建设制造强国、实施产业基础再造工程和重大技术装备攻关工程的过程中继续发挥重要的专业服务作用。

Chapter 4
Real Property Interests Valuation
不动产权益评估

Wisdom
名人名言

横看成岭侧成峰,远近高低各不同。

——苏轼

不务天时则财不生,不务地利则仓廪不盈。

——管仲

Boundless risk must pay for boundless gain.

William Morris

Wide diversification is only required when investors do not understand what they are doing.

—Warren Buffett

Rudimentary Knowledge
基本知识

Abstract 中文摘要

不动产权益评估是指资产评估专业人员依据相关法律、法规和评估准则,对不动产权益的价值进行分析、估算并发表专业意见的行为和过程。其中,不动产权益是指对土地和建筑物拥有、控制、使用或者占有的权益。需要注意,不动产权益与不动产实体在概念上存在一定差异:不动产权益在法律意义上是一种寓含于不动产实体中的各种经济利益以及由此形成的各种财产权利,包括对土地和建筑物的所有权、控制权、使用权或占用权;而不动产实物指的是土地和土地上的建筑物以及其他永久附着物。

在不动产权益评估中,资产评估专业人员应当首先明确评估对象并特别关注不动产权益的层级差异,通常涉及三种基本类型:一是不动产的优先权益,即权益所有者对土地和附着其上的建筑物拥有永久的绝对的占有权和控制权,仅受一些次级权益和法定的或其他法律的强制性约束;二是不动产的次级权益,即给予其拥有者在指定期限内(例如在租赁合同期限内)独家占有和控制特定土地区域或建筑物的权利;三是不动产的使用权益,即能够使用但不是独家占有或控制一项土地或建筑物的权利,如一项土地通行权利或者用于特定活动的权利。不同类型的不动产权益并不相互排斥,优先权益也可能受制于一个或多个次级权益。

在不动产权益评估中,市场法、收益法和成本法都具有不同程度的适用性:

(1)市场法通过对与评估对象可比的不动产权益的交易价格进行修正调整,以求得评估对象在评估基准日的价值,其重点在于寻找相似的交易案例并对差异项进行调整。市场法的适用前提包括:具有充分、活跃的不动产交易市场;可以搜集到被评估不动产的可比参照物及其可比因素、技术参数等资料。因此,市场法一般适用于评估居住类、商业类、工业类、综合类等不动产权益的价值;对于图书馆、体育馆等市场交易不活跃的不动产以及古建筑、名胜风景区等特殊类型的不动产,市场法的适用性相对受限。

(2)收益法通过对不动产权益能够产生的未来预期收益进行折现计算得到

评估结果。收益法的适用前提包括三点：一是不动产权益产生的未来收益可以预测并能够通过货币衡量；二是不动产权益拥有者获得未来收益所承担的风险可以预测；三是不动产权益的未来获利年限可以预测。因此，收益法更加适用于评估可以产生租金收益的不动产权益价值，如商场、写字楼、旅馆、公寓等；对于政府机关、学校、公园等非经营性的不动产权益，收益法一般不适用。

（3）成本法通过计算不动产权益的重置成本，并对已发生的实体性、功能性和经济性贬值进行适当调整，以求得评估对象在评估基准日的价值。成本法对于评估缺乏活跃的市场交易或者不具备可衡量的实际或名义现金流的不动产权益尤其适用，如政府办公楼、学校、医院、图书馆、机场、博物馆等。

Text* 正文

1. Types of Real Property Interest

A real property interest is a right of ownership, of control, use or occupation of land and buildings. There are three basic types of interests:

(a) The superior interest in any defined area of land. The interest owner has an absolute control of the land and any buildings upon it in perpetuity subject only to any subordinate interests and any statutory constraints.

(b) A subordinate interest that gives the holder rights of exclusive possession and control of a defined area of land or buildings for a defined period, e.g., under the terms of a lease contract.

(c) A right to use lands or buildings without an exclusive possession or control, e.g., a right to pass over land or to use it only for a specified activity.

Although different words and terms are used to describe these types of real property interest in different states, the concepts of an unlimited ownership, an exclusive interest for a limited period or a non-exclusive right for a specified purpose are common to most of the jurisdictions. The immovability of land and buildings means that it is the right, which transferred in an exchange, that a party holds, not the physical

---

* Partly from: The International Valuation Standards Council (IVSC), International Valuation Standards, 2011 Edition, 2011.

land and buildings. The value, therefore, attaches to the property interest rather than to the physical land and buildings.

2. The Hierarchy of Interests and Valuation

The different types of real property interest are not mutually exclusive. A superior interest may be subject to one or more subordinate interests. The owner of the <u>absolute interest</u> may grant a <u>lease interest</u> in respect of part or all of his/her interest. Lease interests which granted directly by the owner of the absolute interest are "<u>head lease</u>" interests. Unless prohibited by the terms of the lease contract, the holder of a head lease interest can grant a lease of part or all of that interest to a third party, which is known as a <u>sub-lease interest</u>. A sub-lease interest is always shorter than the head lease from which it is created, even if only by a single day.

These property interests have their own characteristics, as illustrated in the following examples:

(a) Although an absolute interest provides outright ownership in perpetuity, it may be subject to the effect of subordinate interests. These subordinate interests could include leases, restrictions imposed by a previous owner or restriction imposed by statute.

(b) A lease interest is for a defined period, at the end of which the property reverts to the holder of the superior interest. The lease contract normally imposes obligations on the lessee, e.g., the payment of rent and other expenses. It may also impose conditions or restrictions, such as in the way the property may be used or on any transfer of the interest to a third party.

(c) A right of use may be held in perpetuity or may be for a defined period. The right may be dependent on the holder making payments or <u>complying with</u> certain other conditions.

When valuing a real property interest, it is therefore necessary to identify <u>the nature of the rights</u> accruing to the holder of that interest and reflect any constraints or <u>encumbrance</u>s imposed by the existence of other interests in the same property. It is important that the description of the real property interest provided in the report should be in sufficient detail of the physical assets to which the rights relate.

Furthermore, care is required where a non-physical asset, i.e., an intangible asset, is associated with the real estate or a business operated from it. Some intangible assets may have an impact on the cash flows generated by the holder of the real property interest, and therefore it will be necessary to clarify whether or not these assets are included in the valuation of that interest. It is also important to note that the sum of the individual values of various different interests in the same property differ from the value of the unencumbered superior interest. Property interests are normally defined by law and often regulated by national or local legislation so that an understanding of the relevant legal framework before undertaking a valuation is quite essential.

An interest in real property may be held for the physical benefit that ownership provides, for the benefit of any income or <u>capital appreciation</u> that it provides or a combination of both. For certain valuation purposes, classification as either owner-occupied property or investment property may have an impact on the valuation approach required or on the matters that need to be addressed in the report. In addition to describing the real property interest to be valued, it is therefore often appropriate to also describe the purpose for which it is held by the current owner or <u>prospective owner</u>.

Besides, it is necessary to consider the <u>contract rent</u> and the <u>market rent</u> when valuing either a superior interest that is subject to a lease or an interest created by a lease. Contract rent is the rent payable under the terms of an actual lease. It may be fixed for the duration of the lease or variable. The frequency and basis of calculating variations in the rent may be set out in the lease and must be identified and understood in order to establish the total benefits accruing to the lessor and the liability of the lessee. Market rent is the estimated amount for which a property would be leased on the valuation date between a willing lessor and a willing lessee on appropriate lease terms in an arm's length transaction, after proper marketing and knowledgeable, prudent and voluntary actions of both parties. In particular, the estimated amount excludes the rent inflated or deflated by special terms, considerations or concessions. The "appropriate lease terms" are terms that would typically be agreed in the market for the type of property on the valuation date between market participants. A valuation of market rent should only be provided in conjunction with an indication of the principal lease terms that have been assumed.

3. Valuation Approaches

All the three principal valuation approaches can be applicable for the valuation of a real property interest.

3.1 Market Approach

Property interests are not homogeneous. Even if the land and buildings to which the interest being valued relates have identical physical characteristics to others being exchanged in the market, the location will be different. Notwithstanding these dissimilarities, the market approach is commonly applied for the valuation of real property interests.

In order to compare the subject of the valuation with the price of other real property interests that have been recently exchanged or that may be currently available in the market, it is usual to adopt a suitable unit of comparison. Units of comparison that are commonly used include analysing sale prices by calculating the price per square meter of a building or per hectare for land. Other units used for price comparison where sufficient homogeneity between the physical characteristics includes a price per room or a price per unit of output, e.g., crop yields. A unit of comparison is only useful when it is consistently selected and applied to the subject property and the comparable properties in each analysis. If possible, any unit of comparison should be common in the relevant market.

The reliance that can be applied to any comparable price data in the valuation process is determined by comparing various characteristics of the property and transaction from which the data is derived with the property being valued. Differences between the following should be considered:

(a) the interest providing the price evidence and the interest being valued;

(b) the respective locations;

(c) the respective quality of the land or the age and specification of the buildings;

(d) the permitted use or zoning at each property;

(e) the circumstances under which the price was determined and the basis of value required;

(f) the effective date of the price evidence and the required valuation date.

It is also important to establish that the transaction being used to provide comparable data is on the same terms as the basis of value required.

3.2 Income Approach

Various methods are used to derive value under the general heading of the income approach, all of which share the common principle that value is based upon an actual or estimated income that either is or could be generated by an owner of the interest. In the case of an investment property, whose income could be in the form of rent. In an owner-occupied building, an assumed rent (or rent saved) could be based on how much it would cost the owner to lease equivalent space. Where a building is suitable for only a particular type of trading activity, the income is often related to the actual or potential cash flows that would to the owner of that building from the trading activity. The use of a property's trading potential to suggest its value is often referred to as the "profits method".

The income stream is then used to indicate the value by a process of capitalization. An income stream that is likely to remain constant can be capitalized using a single multiplier, often known as the capitalization rate. This figure represents the return that an investor, or the notional return in the case of an owner-occupier, would expect to reflect the time cost of money and the risks and rewards of ownership. The method, often known as the all risks yield method, is quick and simple but cannot be reliably used for an income expected to change in future periods to an extent greater than that generally expected in the market or a requirement of a more sophisticated analysis of risk.

In such cases, various forms of discounted cash flow models can be used. These vary significantly in detail but share the basic characteristic that the net income for a defined future period is adjusted to a present day value using a discount rate. The sum of the present day values for the individual periods represents the capital value. As in the case of the all risks yield method, the discount rate in a discounted cash flow model is based on the time cost of money and the risks and rewards attaching to the income stream.

The yield or discount rate discussed above is determined by the objective of the valuation. The rate used may reflect their required rate of return or the weighted average cost of capital when valuers aim at establishing the value to a particular owner or potential owner based on their own investment criteria. The rate can be derived from observation of the returns implicit in the price paid for real property interests traded in the market between market participants when valuers target at market value.

The appropriate discount rate should be determined from analysis of the rates implicit in transactions in the market. Wherever this is not possible, an appropriate discount rate may be determined from other methods such as building up from a typical "risk free" return adjusted for the additional risks and opportunities specific to the particular real property interest. The appropriate yield or discount rate might also depend on whether the income inputs or cash flows used are based on current levels or projections have been made to reflect anticipated future inflation or deflation.

3.3 Cost Approach

This approach is generally applied to the valuation of real property interests through the depreciated replacement cost method. It is normally used when evidence of transaction prices for similar property, identifiable actual or notional income stream that would accrue to the owner of the relevant interest is absent. It is principally used for valuing specialized property that is rarely if ever sold in the market, except by way of sale of the business or entity of which it is a part.

The first step requires a replacement cost to be calculated, which is normally the cost of replacing the property with a modern equivalent at the relevant valuation date. An exception is when an equivalent property would need to be a replica of the subject property in order to provide a market participant with the same utility, in which case the replacement cost would be that of reproducing or replicating the subject building rather than replacing it with a modern equivalent. The replacement cost needs to reflect all incidental costs such as the value of the land, infrastructure, design fees and finance costs that would be incurred by a market participant in creating an equivalent asset.

The cost of the modern equivalent is then subject to adjustment for obsolescence. The objective of the adjustment for obsolescence is to estimate how much the subject property of less valuable would be to a potential buyer than the modern equivalent. Obsolescence considers the physical condition, functionality and economic utility of the subject property compared to the modern equivalent.

4. Other affected factors

4.1 Transaction Costs

In general, market value is the estimated exchange price regardless of the seller's costs of sale or the buyer's cost of purchase and without adjustment for any taxes payable by either party as a direct result of the transaction. This does not mean that the effect of such costs and taxes on market participants and their decision to buy or sell has to be ignored, only that the market value reported is the price that would be agreed in the transaction, not the gross cost that would be incurred by the buyer or the net receipt that would be received by the seller. The transaction costs for real property can be significant. The costs do affect the pricing decisions of market participants and should be reflected when analysing market data and in the valuation methods adopted.

4.2 Special Purpose Companies

In some jurisdictions, high taxes on real property transfers lead to higher real property interests being held in special purpose companies or other legal vehicles, and transfers take place of the shares in the company or vehicle rather than of the property because the tax on share transactions is lower.

The value of the company or vehicle may include assets or liabilities other than the property interest, that may affect its value or the price paid in a transaction. However, subject to the foregoing, if most participants in the market for real property of the type being valued hold and transact using special purpose companies or vehicles, the price evidence in the market may be for similar transactions and therefore be a relevant indicator of the market value of the subject interest.

5. Valuation of Historic Property

A historic property is real property that publicly recognized or officially designated by a government body as of cultural or historic importance because of its association with a historic event or period, with an architectural style or with a nation's heritage. The common characteristics of historic property include the following:

(a) it is historic, architectural and/or cultural importance;

(b) the statutory or legal protection to which it may be subject;

(c) restraints and limitations placed upon its use, alteration and disposal;

(d) a frequent obligation in some jurisdictions that it be accessible to the public.

Historic property is a broad term, encompassing many property types. Some historic properties are restored to its original condition, and some are partially restored. Historic property also includes properties partially adapted to current standards, e.g., the interior space, and properties that have been extensively modernized.

Historic property may have legal or statutory protection because of its cultural and economic importance. Many governments have enacted measures to safeguard specific historic property or to protect whole areas of special architectural or historic interest. However, not all historic property is necessarily recorded in registers of officially designated historic properties. Many properties with cultural and historic importance also qualify as historic property.

Under certain premises, all the three principal valuation approaches can be applied to the valuation of a historic property. However, the valuation of historic property requires consideration of a variety of factors associated with the importance of these properties, including the legal and statutory protections to which they are subject, the various restraints upon their use, alteration and disposal, and possible financial grants, tax rate or tax exemptions to the owners of such properties in some jurisdictions.

When undertaking a valuation of a historic property, the following matters should be considered depending on the nature of the historic property and the purpose of the valuation. For example, the costs of restoration and maintenance may be considerable for historic property and these costs, in turn, affect the value of the property. Legal measures to safeguard historic property may limit or restrict the use, intensity of use or alteration of a historic property.

The valuation of historic property involves special considerations dealing with the nature of older construction methods and materials, the current efficiency and performance of such properties in terms of modern equivalent assets, the appropriateness of methods used to repair, restore, refurbish or rehabilitate the properties, and the character and extent of legal and statutory protections affecting the properties. The land or site upon which a historic property stands may be subject to constraints upon its use. In turn, any such constraints may affect the <u>overall value</u> of the historic property.

In some cases, historic property may lack reliable valuation because relevant market evidence, potential for generating income and demand to warrant replacement are unavailable. An example would be a partially ruined building with no income generating potential, despite its potential historic significance, which could not be replicated or replaced.

Core Words and Expressions 核心术语

real property interest	不动产权益
superior interest	最高权益
subordinate interest	次级权益
exclusive possession	独占，独有使用权
non-exclusive right	非独占权益
jurisdiction	行政辖区，管辖权
absolute interest	绝对权益
lease interest	租赁权
head lease	开头租赁，原始租赁
sub-lease interest	转租权，分租权
comply with	遵从
the nature of the rights	权利的性质
encumbrance	财产留置权，产权负担

capital appreciation	资本增值
prospective owner	准业主
contract rent	合同租金
market rent	市场租金
subject property	标的资产
comparable data	参照数据
time cost	时间成本
net income	净收益
incidental costs	附加成本
finance cost	融资费用
net receipt	净收入
share transaction	股份交易
historic property	历史建筑
financial grants	财政拨款
tax exemptions	免税
construction methods	施工方法
overall value	整体价值

Questions and Discussion 问题与讨论

1. How many types of real property interests are there? What are they?

2. What is the hierarchy of interests? Use your own words to describe it.

3. Please choose one of the three methods and show how to valuate a real property.

More Knowledge
知识扩展

Topic: The Diversity of Real Estate Valuation
不动产评估的多样性

Abstract 中文摘要

不动产可以根据不同的划分标准进行分类。按照不同的物质形态，不动产可以划分为土地、房屋构筑物、土地定着物、在建工程、不动产开发项目等不同类型；按照不同的用途，不动产可以划分居住、商业、工业、农业、综合、特殊不动产等不同类型；按照不同的经济行为，不动产价格可以包括买卖价格、租赁价格、抵押价格、保险价格、计税价格、征收价格等不同类型。

不动产评估是对不动产交换价值和交易价格的最佳估计。现实中对不动产评估的需求亦来自多个方面，包括房产中介、代理商、抵押放贷者、房屋建造者等。资产评估专业人员在执行不动产评估时，首先应当对不动产的实物状态、权力状态、区位和交易状况、会计核算等方面进行清查核实；其次应当根据评估目的、评估对象的具体情况、资料收集情况和数据来源等相关条件，恰当地选择评估方法。不同国家由于具有不同的法律和文化背景，评估方法可能不完全相同，但大多数传统评估方法都可以用于评估不动产权益的市场价值。例如，可以通过寻找参照物或者对不动产的观测数据进行回归分析，以获得评估值；也可以通过分析市场并直接模拟市场参与者的思维过程来试图估计房地产的交换价值。一般认为，后者具有更强的定量性，通常也被称为更为高级的评估方法。

Text* 正文

1. Introduction

Real property is defined as all the interests, benefits, rights and encumbrances

---

* Partly from: Pagourtzi E, French N, Hatzichristos T, etal. Real Estate Appraisal: A Review of Valuation Methods. Journal of Property Investment & Finance, 2003, 21(4):383-401.

inherent in the ownership of physical real estate, where real estate is the land together with all improvements that are permanently affixed to it and all <u>appurtenances</u> associated thereto.

The valuation of real estate therefore requires a <u>quantitative</u> measure of the benefit and liabilities accruing from the ownership of the real estate. Valuations are required, and often carried out, by various players in the marketplace. These may include:

(a) real estate agents;

(b) appraisers;

(c) assessors;

(d) mortgage lenders;

(e) brokers;

(f) property developers;

(g) investors and fund managers;

(h) lenders;

(i) market researchers and analysts;

(j) shopping centre owners and operators;

(k) other specialists and consultants.

We aim to examine the valuation of real estate prices, using <u>prediction</u> strategy based on selection of the <u>best fitting model</u> for use. The objective of the part is to review various methods used in real estate valuation.

2. The role of valuation

For any valuation to have validity, it must produce an accurate estimate of the market price of the property. The model should therefore reflect the market culture and conditions at the time of the valuation. The model should represent the <u>underlying fundamentals</u> of the market. Thus, in the <u>property market</u>, what is often called a valuation is the best estimate of the <u>trading price</u> of the building.

In this context, the following convention is adopted: price is the actual exchange price in the marketplace; market value is an estimation of that price if the property is to be sold in the market; and calculation of worth is used to assess the inherent worth to the individual or group of individuals.

In many property markets, it is commonplace for the ownership of property to be separate from its use. The price of exchange is the same whether the purchaser has investment or occupation in mind, but the view of the two groups of bidders can be different. An investor can view worth as the discounted value of the rental stream produced by the asset, whereas the owner-occupier may see the asset as a factor of production and assign to it a worth derived from the property's contribution to the profits of the business. There is no doubt that both groups of bidders might be mindful of its potential resale price to a purchaser from the other group.

The concept of the worth of a property is the most important in markets that are underdeveloped in terms of liquidity and the separation of ownership and use rights. Here most transactions are based on owner-occupiers' views of the worth of the property, i.e., the contribution it will make to business profit, as well as subjective issues such as status and feelings of security. Valuers, with hardly any transaction evidence, can only attempt to replicate these calculations of worth for an estimate of exchange price.

One of the paramount concerns of the valuation profession is the need to ensure that information presented to a client is clear and unambiguous. Not only should all parties understand the terminology used, but it is also important that the client receives all other information that might be required to make a rational financial or investment decision. The latter point not only concerns the semantics of definitions of exchange price, but must also address the issue of valuation methodology. Given that clients are becoming more sophisticated in the way they make the buy or sell decisions, the pricing model used to assess the most likely exchange price should reflect their thought processes. Therefore, the valuer needs to better understand the client's requirements and adopt more advanced valuation models that can reflect the increased amount of data and information.

3. Market value

A definition of value is an attempt to clarify the assumptions made in estimating the exchange price of a property if it were to be sold in the open market. These assumptions may include the nature of the legal interest, the physical condition of the building, the nature and timing of the market, and assumptions about possible purchasers in that market. Given that a compelling reason for using market value definitions is to ensure consistency in the process of valuation, it is important that a consistency of definition in all countries exists. For this reason, the International Valuation Standards Council (IVSC) has set a standard to provide a common definition of market value.

Market value is a representation of value in exchange, or the amount a property would bring if offered for sale in the open market at the date of valuation under circumstances that meet the requirements of the market value definition. In order to estimate market value, a valuer must first estimate the highest and best use, the most probable use, a continuation of a property's existing use or some alternative. These conclusions are made from market evidence.

Market value is estimated through the application of valuation methods and procedures that reflect the nature of property and the circumstances under which the given property would most likely be traded in the open market. Market value is defined for the purpose of the standards as follows:

Market value is the estimated amount for which an asset should exchange on the date of valuation between a willing buyer and a willing seller in an arm's length transaction after proper marketing wherein the parties had each acted knowledgeably, prudently and without compulsion.

4. Methods

Each country has a distinct culture and experience, which will determine the methods adopted for any particular valuation. The majority of all methods will rely on comparison to assess market value. This may be done, in its simplest form, by direct capital comparison or may rely on a number of observations that allow the valuer to determine a regression model. Any such method is referred to as traditional.

Other models and methods try to analyse the market by directly mimicking the thought processes of the players in the market in an attempt to estimate the point of exchange. These models tend to be more qualitative in method and will be referred to as advanced. Methods can be grouped as follows:

4.1 Traditional valuation methods:

(a) Comparable method;

(b) Investment/income method;

(c) Profit method;

(d) Development/residual method;

(e) Contractor's method/cost method;

(f) Multiple regression method;

(g) Stepwise regression method.

4.2 Advanced valuation methods:

(a) Artificial neural networks (ANNs);

(b) Hedonic pricing method;

(c) Spatial analysis methods;

(d) Fuzzy logic;

(e) Autoregressive integrated moving average (ARIMA).

Core Words and Expressions 核心术语

appurtenance	附属物
quantitative	定量的
prediction	预报，预测
best fitting model	最佳拟合模型
underlying fundamentals	基本原理

property market	房地产市场
trading price	交易价格
resale price	转售价格
replicate	复制
paramount	最重要的
thought process	思维过程
International Valuation Standards Council (IVSC)	国际评估准则理事会
legal interest	法定利率
regression model	回归模型
multiple regression	多元回归
stepwise regression	逐步回归

Questions and Discussion 问题与讨论

1. Why the valuation of real property will be required by a number of different players in the marketplace?

2. What are the differences between traditional valuation methods and the advanced ones?

Information Extension

思政微课堂

随着经济快速发展和改革开放不断深入，我国房地产评估行业从无到有，并伴随着房地产市场的迅猛发展而逐渐成长起来，其业务范围也由单一的房地产交易评估扩展至如今所涉及的融资、司法鉴定、拆迁、课税、企业合并、资产重组等各项经济活动。房地产评估已经成为我国民生住房保障体系建设中不可或缺的专业支撑力量。

《中华人民共和国民法典》第一百一十五条规定，"物包括不动产和动产。对动产与不动产的划分通常是依据其自然性质是否可以自由移动为标准的。凡是不能够自行移动或者用外力不能够推动的财产，如土地、房屋等不可移动的财产，属于不动产"。为规范房地产估价活动，统一房地产估价程序和方法，保证房地产估价质量，住房城乡建设部于2015年发布了国家标准《房地产估价规范》（GB/T 50291-2015）。为规范不动产评估行为，保护资产评估当事人合法权益和公共利益，中国资产评估协会于2017年10月1日修订发布了《资产评估执业准则——不动产》（中评协〔2017〕38号）。根据该准则，不动产是指土地、建筑物及其他附着于土地上的定着物，包括物质实体及其相关权益；不动产评估是指资产评估机构及其资产评估专业人员遵守法律、行政法规和资产评估准则，根据委托对评估基准日特定目的下的不动产价值进行评定和估算，并出具资产评估报告的专业服务行为；不动产评估包括单独的不动产评估和企业价值评估中的不动产评估；执行不动产评估业务，应当根据评估目的、评估对象、价值类型、资料收集等情况，分析市场法、收益法和成本法三种资产评估基本方法以及假设开发法、基准地价修正法等衍生方法的适用性，选择评估方法。

现阶段，党的二十大报告指出，我国"改造棚户区住房四千二百多万套，改造农村危房二千四百多万户，城乡居民住房条件明显改善"；要"坚持房子是用来住的、不是用来炒的定位，加快建立多主体供给、多渠道保障、租购并举的住房制度。"对于住房和房地产这一世界性的难题，以上部署为我国住房和房地产发展提供了根本遵循，确立了行动指南，也为房地产评估业务转型发展指明了方向。随着住房的民生属性凸显，从"有的住"迈向"住得好"，房地产市场的量价正向平稳回归。可以预见，作为经济发展重要引擎的房地产业，将迎来广阔的发展空间。评估机构应制定具有可持续性的专业战略规划来引导自身的长远发展，做到坚守底线、坚持创新、敢于试错，在技术服务方面要不断精益求精，以求在新赛道开创新局面，更好助力房地产市场的平稳发展和经济社会的和谐稳定。

Chapter 5
Intangible Assets Valuation
无形资产评估

Wisdom
名人名言

凡事预则立，不预则废。

——子思

安居不用架高堂，书中自有黄金屋。

——赵恒

Intangible asset valuation is not a science in the same sense that chemistry and physics are sciences. However, intangible asset valuation is a science in the sense that mathematics and economics are sciences.

—Robert Reilly & Robert Schwaihs

If a man empties his purse into his head, no man can take it away from him, an investment in knowledge always pays the best interest.

—Benjamin Franklin

The real measure of our wealth is how much we'd be worth if we lost all our money.

—John Jowett

Rudimentary Knowledge
基本知识

Abstract 中文摘要

无形资产评估是指资产评估专业人员依据相关法律、法规和评估准则，对无形资产的价值进行分析、估算并发表专业意见的行为和过程。其中，无形资产是指特定主体拥有或者控制的，不具有实物形态，能持续发挥作用并且能带来经济利益的资源。

无形资产有许多类型，可以根据不同的划分标准进行分类。以是否能够独立存在为分类标准，无形资产可以划分为可辨认无形资产和不可辨认无形资产。可辨认无形资产又进一步划分为市场相关类、客户相关类、技术相关类、艺术相关类等不同类型，如专利权、商标权、著作权、专有技术、销售网络、客户关系、特许经营权、合同权益、域名等；不可辨认无形资产一般是指商誉。以性质为划分标准，无形资产还可以划分为权利型无形资产、关系型无形资产、知识型无形资产和组合型无形资产。权利型无形资产是指特定当事人经由他人授权，并通常会通过书面（或非书面）契约的形式，以特定当事人付费（或不付费）为代价，获得能给特定当事人带来超额收益的相关权利；关系型无形资产是指特定主体通过提高企业经营管理水平、商品质量、服务质量和商业信誉方面逐渐建立起来的经济资源，如销售网络、客户关系；知识型无形资产是指通过人类通过智力劳动创造形成的知识成果，如工业产权、著作权；组合型无形资产则是由多种因素综合形成的无形资产，如商誉。

无形资产评估的应用领域非常广泛，涉及出资、交易、质押、法律诉讼、财务报告、税收、保险、管理、租赁等多种评估目的。在无形资产评估中，资产评估专业人员应当对无形资产的具体类型、法律权属和经济利益进行明确界定，并对无形资产的产权因素、获利能力、成本因素、市场因素、有效期限、法律保护、风险因素等相关因素给予重点关注；当无形资产与其他资产共同发挥作用时，应当分析这些资产对无形资产价值的影响。此外，资产评估专业人员还应当关注宏观经济政策、行业政策、经营条件、生产能力、市场状况等各项因素对无形资产效能发挥的制约，关注其对无形资产价值产生的影响。

在无形资产评估中，收益法、市场法和成本法都具有不同程度的适用性。其中，收益法是无形资产评估中最常用以及被优先采用的评估方法。收益法通过测算该项无形资产所产生的未来预期收益并折算成现值，以求得被评估无形资产的价值，包括超额收益法、许可费使用节省法、增量收益法等具体方法。超额收益法的思路是测算无形资产与其他资产共同产生的收益，扣除其他资产的收益贡献，将剩余收益作为该无形资产的超额收益，并将每期的超额收益折现到评估基准日，作为该项无形资产的价值；许可费使用节省法的思路是测算由于拥有该无形资产而节省的向第三方支付的许可使用费，并将每年支付的许可使用费折现到评估基准日，作为该项无形资产的价值；增量收益法的思路是通过对比企业使用标的无形资产和不使用标的无形资产（但其他因素保持不变）这两种情景下的收益差异（即增量收益），并将每一时期的增量收益折现到评估基准日，作为该项无形资产的价值。

Text* 正文

1. Introduction

An intangible asset is a non-monetary asset that manifests itself by its economic properties. It lacks physical substance but grants rights and economic benefits to its owner.

Valuations of intangible assets are required for many different purposes including acquisitions, mergers and sales of businesses or parts of businesses, purchases and sales of intangible assets, reporting to tax authorities, litigation and insolvency proceedings, and financial reporting.

To comply with the requirement to identify the asset or liability, the intangible asset shall be clearly defined by reference to its type and the legal right or interest in that asset. The scope of work should identify any contributory assets and confirm whether or not these are to be included in the valuation. A contributory asset is one

---

* Partly from: Zhonghe Appraisal Company Ltd, BMI Appraisals Limited Company, *Business Valuation and Case Studies*, China Financial&Economic Publishing House, 2010: 17-21; Zabihollah Rezaee, *Financial Services Firms: Governance, Regulations, Valuations, Mergers, and Acquisitions*, 3rd Edition, Wiley Online Library, 2012: chapter10.

that is used in conjunction with the subject asset to generate the cash flows associated with the subject asset. If contributory assets are to be excluded, it will be necessary to clarify whether the subject intangible asset is to be valued on the assumption that the contributory assets are available to a buyer or on the assumption that they are not, i.e., the subject asset is valued on a stand-alone basis.

2. Principal Types of Intangible Assets

Specific intangible assets are defined and described by characteristics such as their ownership, function, market position and image. These characteristics differentiate intangible assets from one another.

2.1 According to Independent Existing Forms

An intangible asset can be either identifiable or unidentifiable.

2.1.1 Identifiable Assets

An intangible asset is identifiable if it is separable, which means it can be separated or divided from the entity and sold, transferred, licensed, rented or exchanged, either individually or together with a related contract, identifiable asset or liability, regardless of whether the entity intends to do so. Or it arises from contractual or other legal rights, regardless of whether those rights are transferable or separable from the entity or from other rights and obligations.

The principal classes of identifiable intangible assets are marketing related, customer-or supplier-related, technology related and artistic related. Within each class, assets may be either contractual or non-contractual.

Marketing related intangible assets are used primarily in the marketing or promotion of products or services. Examples include trademarks, trade names, unique trade design, internet domain names and non-compete agreements.

Customer-or supplier-related intangible assets arise from relationships with or knowledge of customers or suppliers. Examples include service or supply agreements, licensing or royalty agreements, order books, employment agreements and customer relationships.

Technology-related intangible assets arise from contractual or non-contractual rights to use patented technology, unpatented technology, databases, formulae, designs, software, processes or recipes.

Artistic-related intangible assets arise from the right to benefits, for example, royalties from artistic works such as plays, books, films and music, and from non-contractual copyright protection.

2.1.2 Goodwill

Any unidentifiable intangible asset associated with a business or group of assets is generally termed goodwill. Goodwill is any future economic benefit arising from a business, an interest in a business or from the use of a group of assets non-separable. Different definitions of goodwill apply under specific financial reporting or tax regimes; these may need to be noted where valuations are being undertaken for these purposes.

Examples of benefits reflected in goodwill include company specific synergies following a business combination like a reduction in operating costs or economies of scale which not reflected in the value of other assets; and growth opportunities like expansion into different markets, and organisational capital like the benefits accruing from an assembled network.

In general terms, the value of goodwill is the residual amount remained after the values of all identifiable tangible, intangible and monetary assets, which adjusted for actual or potential liabilities, have been deducted from the value of a business.

2.2 According to the Nature of Intangible Assets

The following describes the four categories of Intangible assets, including Rights, Relationships, Intellectual Property and Grouped Intangibles:

(a) Rights – They exist according to the terms of a contract, written or unwritten, that is of economic benefit to the parties. Examples are supply contracts, distribution contracts, licensing permits and so on.

(b) Relationship – It is normally non-contractual, short-lived and can have great value to the parties. Examples include assembled workforce, customer relationship, supplier relationship, etc.

(c) Intellectual Property – It is a special classification of intangible assets because it is usually protected by law from <u>unauthorized use</u> by others. For example, <u>brand</u> names, trademarks, copyrights, <u>patents, know-how</u> and so on.

(d) Grouped Intangibles – They are residual intangible asset value left after all identifiable intangible assets have been valued and deducted from total intangible asset value. Grouped intangibles are also called Goodwill.

3. Valuation Approaches

All the three principal valuation approaches can be applied to the valuation of intangible assets.

All methods of valuing intangible assets require an estimation of the remaining useful life, which may be a finite period limited by either contract or typical life cycles in the sector for some assets. Other assets may have an indefinite life. Estimating the remaining useful life include consideration of legal, technological, functional and economic factors. As an example, an asset comprising a drug patent may have a remaining legal life of five years until <u>expiry</u>. But a competitor drug with expected improved efficacy may be expected to reach the market in three years, this might cause the remaining useful life of the first product to be assessed as only three years.

3.1 Income Approach

Under the income approach, the value of an intangible asset is determined by reference to the present value of income, cash flows or cost savings generated by the intangible asset. The principal valuation methods under the income approach used in the valuation of intangible assets are <u>excess earnings method, relief-from-royalty method</u> and <u>premium profits method</u>.

All of these methods involve converting forecast cash flows to an indication of value using either discounted cash flow techniques or, in simple cases, the application of a capitalization multiple to a representative single period cash flow.

3.1.1 Excess Earnings Method

The excess earning method is a modified capitalization method. The basic concept is to estimate the value of intangible assets by capitalizing the amount of earnings over and above a reasonable return on tangible assets.

The excess earnings method defines the value of an intangible asset as the present value of the cash flows attributable to the subject intangible asset after excluding the proportion of the cash flows that are attributable to contributory assets. The method is typically used in the valuation of customer contracts, customer relationships and in-process research and development projects.

The method can either be applied by using a single period of forecast cash flows, referred to as "the single period excess earnings method", or by using several periods of forecast cash flows, referred to as "the multi period excess earnings method". "The multi period excess earnings method" is more commonly used as intangible assets normally bring monetary benefits over an extended period.

The method involves allocating the expected cash flows to the smallest business or group of assets of the entity that includes all the income derivable from the subject asset.

From this forecast of cash flows, a deduction is made in respect of the share of the cash flows attributable to contributory tangible, intangible and financial assets. The deduction process is done by calculating an appropriate charge or economic rent for the contributory assets and deducting this from the cash flows. To arrive at a reliable valuation of the subject asset, it may also be appropriate to make an additional deduction to reflect any additional value attributable to the fact that all the assets are utilized together as a going concern. The above process typically reflects the benefit of the cash flows attributable to the asset of an assembled workforce that would not be available to a buyer of the individual asset.

Actually, under this method, net tangible asset value, usually at market values, should firstly be estimated. Then a required rate of return is assessed to support the net tangible assets. Multiplying the assessed required rate of return by the net tangible asset value yields the required amount of return on the tangible assets. Subtract it from the estimated normalized level income and the result is the amount of excess earnings. An appropriate capitalization rate is then estimated based on the characteristics of the intangible assets. Finally, dividing the amount of excess earnings by the capitalization rate yields the estimated value of the intangible assets.

The following presents an example of the excess earnings method:

Assumptions:	
Net tangible asset value	$100,000
Normalized annual economic income	$25,000
Required return to support tangible assets	15%
Capitalization rate for excess earnings	25%
Calculations:	
Net tangible asset value	$100,000
Required return on tangible assets	15% × $100,000 = $15,000
Excess earnings	$25,000 − $15,000 = $10,000
Value of excess earnings (the intangible assets)	$10,000/25% = $40,000

The major difficulty associated with this method is the estimation of the <u>incremental effect</u> of the brand on sales or profits. In addition, similar to income capitalization method, this method is generally inapplicable for a company with <u>fluctuating</u> expected future earnings.

3.1.2 Relief-from-Royalty Method

Relief-from-royalty method is a modified DCF method which is referred to as royalty savings method sometimes. The principle is that if an intangible asset is not owned by the company using it, the company may have to pay a royalty to a third party owning it. By owning the intangible asset, the company avoids paying such royalty. Therefore, the value of an intangible asset is determined by reference to the value of the hypothetical royalty payments that would be saved through owning the asset. The hypothetical royalty payments over the life of the intangible asset are adjusted for tax and discounted to present value at the valuation date.

A critical consideration in this methodology is the determination of an appropriate <u>notional royalty rate</u> which is referred to as hypothetical royalty rate in some literature. It is applied to the estimated future sales of the company over the useful life of the intangible asset to derive gross notional royalty incomes over the period. In terms of profitability, the notional royalty rate must enable the <u>hypothetical licensee</u> to derive, after allowance for notional royalty expenses, an adequate return on its net assets other than the intangible asset. Depending on the terms of the notional <u>licensing arrangements</u> assumed, the expenses may include trademark registration, <u>public relations</u>, <u>quality control</u> and <u>legal expenses</u>. These expenses are deducted from the gross notional royalty incomes to derive net notional royalty incomes.

Net notional royalty incomes are then discounted back to a net present value, the value of the intangible asset, using a rate of return incorporating all related risks and growth prospects.

As mentioned above, the determination of an appropriate notional royalty rate is a challenging task and can be critical to the accuracy of the valuation. Two methods can be used to derive a notional royalty rate. The first is based on market royalty rates for comparable or similar transactions. A prerequisite for this method is the existence of comparable intangible assets that are licensed at arm's length on a regular basis. The second method is based on a split of profits that would hypothetically be paid in an arm's length transaction by a willing licensee to a willing licensor for the rights to use the subject intangible asset.

Some or all of the following valuation inputs are considered in the relief-from-royalty method:

(a) projections for the financial <u>parameter</u>, e.g., revenues that the royalty rate would be applied to over the life of the intangible asset together with an estimate of the life of the intangible asset;

(b) rate at which tax relief would be obtainable on hypothetical royalty payments;

(c) the cost of marketing and any other costs that would be borne by a licensee in utilizing the asset;

(d) an appropriate discount rate or capitalization rate to convert the asset's hypothetical royalty payments to a present value.

Actually, we can conclude that the value is equal to the cost savings over the life of the asset, discounted to present value. We could give an example about a favourable lease using this method. Suppose that a bank has a 3,000 square foot branch in the lobby of an office building leased at a rate of $20 per square foot per year, but market rates for comparable space are $30 per square foot each year. Also, suppose the lease has seven years remaining before the bank must renew it at market rates. The value of the intangible asset created by a below-market rate leasehold interest is about $95,070 and the following presents calculation:

Year	Market Rent	Lease Rent	Cost Saving	Discount Factor	Present Value
1	$90,000	$60,000	$30,000	0.909	$27,270
2	90,000	60,000	30,000	0.826	$24,780
3	90,000	60,000	30,000	0.751	$22,530
4	90,000	60,000	30,000	0.683	$20,490
Net Present Value					$95,070

All in all, royalty rates can often vary significantly in the market for apparently similar assets. It is therefore prudent to benchmark the assumed royalty input by reference to the operating margin that a typical operator would require from sales generated from use of the asset.

3.1.3 Premium Profits Method

The premium profits method which is referred to incremental income method, involves comparing the forecasted profits or cash flows that would be earned by a business using an intangible asset with those that would be earned by a business without using an intangible asset. It is often used when market-based royalty rates are unavailable or unreliable.

Having established the difference in the profits that may be generated, an appropriate discount rate is applied to convert forecasted incremental periodic profits or cash flows to a present value or a capitalization multiple to capitalize constant incremental profits or cash flows.

The premium profits method can be used to value both intangible assets whose use may either save costs or generate additional profits or cash flows.

3.2 Market Approach

Under the market approach, the value of an intangible asset is determined by reference to market activity, e.g., transaction bids or offers identical or similar assets.

The heterogeneous nature of intangible assets means that it is rarely possible to find market evidence of transactions involving identical assets. If there is any market evidence at all, it is usually in respect of assets that are similar, but not identical. As an alternative, or in addition to, comparison with the prices in any relevant transactions involving identical or similar assets through analysis of sale transactions may provide evidence of valuation multiples, e.g., it may be possible to determine a typical price to earnings ratio or rate of return for a class of similar intangible assets.

Wherever evidence of either prices or valuation multiples is available, it is necessary to make adjustments to reflect differences between the subject asset and those involved in the transactions.

These adjustments are necessary to reflect the differentiating characteristics of the subject intangible asset and the assets involved in the transactions. Such adjustments may only be determinable at a qualitative rather than quantitative level. Situations giving rise to qualitative adjustments include the following examples:

(a) The brand being valued may be considered to command a more dominant position in the market than those involved in the transactions.

(b) A drug patent being valued may have greater efficacy and fewer side effects than those involved in the transactions.

3.3 Cost Approach

The cost approach is mainly used for internally generated intangible assets that have unidentifiable income streams. Under the cost approach, the replacement cost of either a similar asset or one providing similar service potential or utility is estimated.

Examples of intangible assets for which the cost approach may be used include the following:

(a) self-developed software, as the price of software with the same or similar service capacity can sometimes be obtained in the market;

(b) websites, as it may be possible to estimate the cost of constructing the website;

(c) an <u>assembled workforce</u> through determining the cost of building up the workforce.

The inputs that are considered when applying the cost approach include the following:

(a) the cost of developing or purchasing an identical asset;

(b) the cost of developing or purchasing an asset offering the same utility or service potential;

(c) any adjustments required to the cost of developing or purchasing to reflect the specific characteristics of the subject asset, such as economic or functional obsolescence;

(d) any opportunity cost incurred by the developer of the asset.

Core Words and Expressions 核心术语

intangible asset	无形资产
non-monetary	非货币的
litigation	官司，诉讼
insolvency proceeding	破产程序
contributory asset	贡献资产
stand-alone	独立的
licensed	得到许可的
contractual	合同性的，契约性的
identifiable intangible asset	可辨认无形资产
trademark	商标
trade name	商号
unique trade design	专有设计
internet domain name	互联网域名

non-compete agreement	非竞争协议
licensing	许可证
royalty agreement	特许经营协议
order book	订货清单
employment agreements	雇佣协议
customer relationship	客户关系
patented technology	专利技术
unpatented technology	非专利技术
formulae	配方
recipe	食谱，处方
copyright	版权，著作权
goodwill	商誉
organisational capital	组织资本
residual amount	余额
supply contract	供应合同
distribution contract	分销合同
assembled workforce	集合劳动力
supplier relationship	供应商关系
unauthorized use	未经授权使用
brand	品牌
patent	专利，专利权
know-how	专有技术
expiry	终止满期，届期
excess earnings method	超额收益法

relief-from-royalty method	许可费使用节省法
premium profits method	增量收益法
normalized annual economic income	标准化年经济收益
incremental effect	递增效应
fluctuating	波动的，不稳定的
notional royalty rate	名义提成率
hypothetical licensee	假设的被许可方
licensing arrangement	许可协议
public relation	公共关系
quality control	质量控制
legal expense	法律费用
parameter	参量，参数
benchmark	基准，以……为基准
incremental income method	增量收益法
taxable income	应纳税所得额

Questions and Discussion 问题与讨论

1. What is a contributory asset? Why should it be considered in the valuation of intangible assets?

2. What is the difference between the identifiable intangible assets and unidentifiable intangible assets? What are the principal classes of identifiable intangible assets?

3. What are the methods of income approach？ And what are the differences between them?

More Knowledge
知识扩展

Topic 1: Intellectual Property Valuation 知识产权评估

Abstract 中文摘要

知识产权是无形资产中的一个重要子集，同样满足无形资产的定义。知识在企业中表现为智力资本，包括人力资本、结构资本、知识资产和知识产权。知识产权是获得了法律保护的知识资产，具体包括专利权、商标权、著作权、商业秘密等。

在知识产权评估中，资产评估专业人员应当至少关注以下几点：确定公司可用的智力资本；衡量组成智力资本部分的价值；与公司内部其他潜在智力资本构建交付手段和增加杠杆；管理智力资本的现金流和分销渠道；通过将知识资本转化为知识产权以保护知识资本；在全球范围内管理知识产权的注册；管理者是否向第三方和从第三方获取知识产权的许可；管理者是否遵守所有知识产权相关的协议。

此外，对知识产权和许可协议谈判的估值而言，一个重要的难点在于如何确定市场特许权使用费率。一般主要依靠三种传统的渠道予以解决，即来自客户、来自调查或者来自司法意见。

Text* 正文

Today's business press is constantly full of articles about companies and their competitive advantages resulting from their intellectual property or intellectual capital. Even our business processes are being patented today as highlighted in major business magazines. New industries, based on technologies like genetic engineering, are emerging, which are totally based on intellectual properties of the new companies.

---

* Partly from: Mard M J, Hyden S D, RigbyJS, Intellectual Property Valuation. Financial Valuation group, 2000-4-20.

Chapter 5 Intangible Assets Valuation 无形资产评估

Business managers with basic intellectual property knowledge and intellectual property professionals are becoming increasingly influential leaders in the information age. This article will provide management with an overview of the key concepts that must be carefully considered when valuing or computing <u>infringement damages</u> for any intellectual property.

1. Intellectual Capital and Intellectual Property

Knowledge underlies how value is created. Successful utilizing that knowledge contributes to the progress of society. The knowledge in business is manifested as intellectual capital which includes <u>human capital</u>, <u>structural capital</u>, <u>intellectual assets</u> and intellectual property.

Human capital is a collection of experience, skill and education of a company's employees. Structural capital, which includes intangible assets such as <u>process documentation</u> and the <u>organisational structure</u>, is the supportive infrastructure provided to human capital. Structural capital encourages human capital to create and <u>leverage</u> its knowledge. Intellectual assets are the codified physical descriptions of specific knowledge that can be owned and readily traded. Intellectual assets receiving legal protection become intellectual property. There are five forms of intellectual property: patents, copyrights, trademarks, trade secrets, and know-how. Companies often fail to <u>capitalize on</u> the opportunities offered by their intellectual properties because they fail to identify all the intellectual properties they own.

2. Challenges in Valuing Intellectual Property

One of the major difficulties in valuing intellectual property or negotiating licensing agreements is determining the market royalty rates that should be used. Most consultants traditionally develop royalty rates based on three traditional sources: firstly, from the client, if the client has its own negotiated licensing agreements; secondly, from surveys performed by various professionals, generally in cooperation with <u>trade associations</u>; and thirdly, from judicial opinions which vary greatly depending on individual fact patterns. The valuer should augment the three traditional tools through a search of public documents for licensing agreements, which makes the valuation more complicated.

3. Managing the Millennium

Intellectual capital is the value generator of the future. To sustain growth, companies in the future have to:

(a) identify the intellectual capital available to them;

(b) measure the value of the intellectual capital components;

(c) structure the means of delivery and potential leverage with other potential intellectual capital within the company;

(d) manage the cash flow and the distribution channels of the intellectual capital;

(e) protect the intellectual capital by converting it to intellectual property;

(f) manage the intellectual property registrations on a worldwide basis;

(g) license intellectual property to and from third parties;

(h) assure compliance with all agreements.

4. Distinction between Intellectual Property and Intangible Assets

Intellectual property is a <u>subset</u> of intangible assets. Intellectual properties, specifically patents, copyrights, trademarks and identifiable know-how, satisfy the definitional requirements of intangible assets. As can be seen below, valuation methodologies applicable to intangible assets also apply to intellectual property.

Intangible assets are <u>long-lived assets</u> used in the production of goods and services that, unlike fixed or tangible assets, lack physical properties. Intangible assets represent certain long-lived legal rights or competitive advantages developed or acquired by a business enterprise. Intangible assets differ considerably in their characteristics and useful lives and are classified in the <u>Financial Accounting Standards Board (FASB)</u> as follows:

(a) Identifiability – Patents, copyrights, franchises, trademarks, and other similar intangible assets that can be specifically identified with reasonably descriptive names;

(b) Manner of Acquisition – Intangible assets that may be purchased or developed internally;

(c) Determinate or Indeterminate Life – Many intangible assets that have a determinate life established by law or by contract or economic behaviour;

(d) Transferability – The right to a patent, copyright or franchise that can be identified separately and bought or sold.

In terms of valuation, the intangible assets must be readily identifiable and separated from the other assets employed in the business. An intangible asset can be defined by practical considerations such as whether it is supported by a contract, or can be economically measured objectively with a determinate life. Intangible assets that exist but cannot be specifically identified are included in goodwill.

5. Attributes of Intangible Assets

5.1 Attributes of Identifiable Intangible Assets

For an identifiable intangible asset to exist from a valuation or economic perspective, it should possess certain attributes. The common attributes include the following:

(a) It should be subject to specific identification and a recognizable description.

(b) It should be subject to the right of a private ownership, and the private ownership must be legally transferable.

(c) There should be some tangible evidence or manifestation of the existence of the intangible asset (e.g., a contract, a license, a registration document, a computer diskette, a set of procedural documentation, a listing of customers, recorded on a set of financial statements, etc.).

(d) It should have been created or have come into existence at an identifiable time (or time period) or as the result of an identifiable event.

(e) It can be destroyed or subject to a termination of existence at an identifiable time (or time period) or as the result of an identifiable event.

In other words, there should be a specific bundle of rights (legal and otherwise) associated with the existence of any intangible asset.

For an identifiable intangible asset to have a quantifiable value from an economic analysis or appraisal perspective, it should possess certain additional attributes. Additional attributes include the following:

(a) The intangible asset should generate some measurable amount of economic benefits to its owner; these economic benefits could be in the form of an income increment or of a cost savings and are measured by comparison to the amount of income otherwise available to the intangible asset owner if the subject intangible asset did not exist.

(b) This economic benefit may be measured in a number of ways, such as net income, net operating income or net cash flow.

(c) The intangible asset should be able to enhance the value of other assets associated; these assets may encompass all other assets of the business, including tangible personal property, tangible real estate, or other intangible assets.

Commonly valued intangible assets are:

(a) Patents - product or process;

(b) Brands - consumer goods' brands, trademarks, corporate names;

(c) Publishing Rights - magazines, books, mastheads, film and music rights;

(d) Intellectual Property - patents, copyrights, technology, know-how.

5.2 Attributes of Unidentifiable Intangible Assets

Economic phenomena that lack above attribute tests typically fail to be identifiable intangible assets. Some economic phenomena may describe conditions that contribute to the existence and value of identifiable intangible assets. But these phenomena lack the requisite elements to distinguish themselves as intangible assets.

For a typical business, descriptive economic phenomena that fail to be identifiable intangible assets include high market share, high profitability, general positive reputation, monopoly position, market potential and other economic phenomena.

However, while these descriptive conditions fail to be identifiable intangible assets, they may indicate the existence of identifiable intangible assets that do have substantial economic value. The intangible asset is often referred to as goodwill.

Chapter 5 Intangible Assets Valuation 无形资产评估

Core Words and Expressions 核心术语

intellectual capital	智力资本
infringement damages	侵权损害赔偿
human capital	人力资本
structural capital	结构资本
intellectual assets	知识资产
process documentation	进程性文件
organisational structure	组织结构
leverage	杠杆
capitalize on	利用
trade association	行业协会
subset	子集
long-lived asset	长期资产
Financial Accounting Standards Board (FASB)	财务会计准则委员会
determinate life	确定寿命
quantifiable value	可量化的价值
requisite element	必要的因素

Questions and Discussion 问题与讨论

1. What is the intellectual capital?

2. Please describe the distinction between intellectual property and intangible assets.

3. Please conclude the attributes of identifiable intangible assets. Which is the biggest different attribute between identifiable assets and unidentifiable ones?

Topic 2: Intangible Assets Valuation Process
无形资产评估程序

Abstract 中文摘要

无形资产评估程序是指资产评估专业人员执行无形资产评估业务所履行的系统性工作步骤。其中，对与无形资产价值相关的信息资料进行收集、归纳、整理和分析，尤其是对无形资产预期经济表现的预测，属于无形资产评估程序中的核心环节。无形资产评估的基本程序如下：

（1）明确评估业务基本事项。在受理无形资产评估业务前，资产评估专业人员应当与委托方就各项基本问题达成一致，包括对评估目的、评估对象和评估范围、价值类型、评估基准日、评估报告的使用范围等问题给予充分考虑。

（2）信息资料收集与分析。资产评估专业人员需要收集有关无形资产的特性、权属、历史经济资料、市场情况、宏观经济等多种数据，并对数据进行分析调整，使其有效服务于资产评估过程。具体而言，可能涉及与无形资产权利相关的法律权属资料、反映其获利能力的数据资料、反映其性质和特征以及发展状况的数据资料、反映其剩余经济寿命和法定寿命的数据资料、关于其实施范围和限制条件的信息资料、既往交易（质押、出资情况）的信息资料等。

（3）选用评估方法进行评定估算。无形资产评估方法的选择主要取决于无形资产的类型以及可用于分析的数据的质量和数量。收益法、市场法、成本法都可以不同程度地适用于评估无形资产的价值。资产评估专业人员应当根据评估目的、评估对象、价值类型、资料收集等具体情况，尽可能选用多种方法对其进行评估，并根据所采用的评估方法，选取相应的公式和参数进行分析、计算和判断，形成测算结果。

（4）确定评估结论。资产评估专业人员在得出评估结论前，应当对评估过程进行回顾和思考，并对采取不同评估方法得到的结果进行合理分析和选择；同时，资产评估专业人员在确定评估结论后，应当对特别事项说明、限制使用条件等问题在评估报告中进行恰当披露。

Chapter 5 Intangible Assets Valuation 无形资产评估

Text* 正文

1. Introduction

The appraisal process is a systematic approach to answering a client's specific question about property value. The appraisal process begins with the identification of the specific question, and ends when an answer is reported to all interested parties.

Each intangible asset appraisal assignment is unique, and many different types of value can be estimated for a particular intangible asset. Even under unique circumstances, the appraisal process provides the <u>analytical framework</u> for estimating the value of an intangible asset.

The appraisal process provides a pattern that can be used in any appraisal assignment to perform market research and data analysis, to apply appraisal methods and procedures, and to integrate the result of these analyses into an estimate of a specifically defined value.

2. The Nature of the Appraisal Process

The appraisal of intangible assets is an evolving discipline. The intangible asset appraisal process provides a structure for the analysis of the value of intangible assets so that the analytical discipline can improve over time.

As with most properties, the value of an intangible asset is a reflection of the present value of the future economic income that the intangible asset is expected to generate. One immediate purpose of an intangible asset appraisal assignment is to make reasonable projections of future events.

The predictable economic performance of an intangible asset adds greatly to the understanding and acceptance of its estimated valuation. In many ways, the appraisal of intangible asset is the culmination of <u>exploratory research</u> into the predictable economic performance of an intangible asset.

The intangible asset appraisal process follows four similar steps:

---

* *Partly from: Robert F. Reilly, Robert P. Schweihs. Valuing Intangible Assets, Library of Congress Cataloging-in-Publication Data, 1998.*

(a) identification of the intangible asset appraisal problem;

(b) data collection and analysis;

(c) application of the three approaches to value;

(d) estimation of the value conclusion.

When results of the process are unexpected, a new cycle begins. As with any exploratory research, the new postulates associated with each intangible asset appraisal assignment are subject to testing, sometimes leading to dozens of subsequent investigations.

If the intangible asset appraisal process were perfect, then it would determine at one stroke which model or theory is correct. The determination would be made by simply comparing the values observed with those predicted. A perfect appraisal process could also precisely detect the slightest flaw in the agreement between the predicted value and the actual value. Thus, the perfect appraisal process would point to a refinement of the model.

But the intangible asset appraisal process is imperfect. Since the estimate of the value of any property is sensitive to prevailing economic conditions during the time period in question, actual economic events that have taken place subsequent to the valuation date are only relevant to the extent that they were predictable as of the valuation date. An analyst estimates value without the benefit of knowing with certainty about future events. In fact, the analyst performs the appraisal by only considering the events one could reasonably expect to occur after the valuation date. In many intangible asset appraisal assignments, this perspective becomes the most important one.

The main purpose of the intangible asset appraisal process is to make reliable predictions. If the predictions are reasonably accurate, the appraisal is successful. If not, the appraisal model is replaced or adjusted until an accurate predictions result is made. Analysts do not expect a model to be constantly successful, because more extensive or more accurate experimental measurements are likely to be made.

The purpose of the intangible asset appraisal process is to postulate a conceptual valuation model from which the observable behaviour of the marketplace may be predicted with reasonable accuracy. The validation of the valuation model follows the appraisal method:

(a) Postulate a model based upon existing experimental observations or measurements.

(b) Check the predictions of this model against further observations or measurements.

(c) Adjust or replace the model as required by the new observations or measurements.

The third step leads back to the first step, and the process continues as a loop. No claim can be made about the reality of the model. The sole criterion for assessing the quality of the model is the reasonable prediction of economic performance from the simplest, most convenient, or most satisfying model.

Prediction of the future behaviour of the marketplace is neither perfectly accurate nor certain. Analysts should always be prepared to observe experimental results that necessitate the adjustment or replacement of the model. Models should not only predict with reasonable accuracy, but also conform to the prevailing analytical standards of the times.

The construction of a valuation model for a particular intangible asset appraisal assignment is a creative act that somewhat defies the standard-lows a regular process called the appraisal process. Models are subject to revision, but each new model keeps the advantages of old ones. Thus, appraisal knowledge is cumulative.

Valuation models are not proved, they are validated. The validated process means that the model has made reasonably accurate predictions. In considering the continued application of an already validated model, the model is expected to continuously predict as accurately in the future as it did in the past. However, there is no guarantee of any model's continued predictive ability.

The appraisal process is merely a formalization of learning by experience. Analysts who learn by experience implicitly use the appraisal process. The basic postulate of value analysis and estimation is that the marketplace is predictable. The critical analysis of the intangible asset appraisal process has a lofty final objective: to evoke new thinking or to reveal new approaches to old problems. Critical analysis presents an analyst with an unending task. Analysts rarely achieve a final, perfect valuation model. Rather, they begin with the question, "How do we estimate value?" and they conclude with the question, "How can we estimate value more accurately?"

3. Identification of the Appraisal Problem

Posing a right question is sometimes more difficult than finding a correct answer. When presented with an intangible asset appraisal assignment, an analyst first identifies the central issues plans a strategy for complicating the assignment. The inability to complete an intangible asset appraisal assignment is usually the result of poor communication between the analyst and his/her client about the objectives of the appraisal. The clients who are unfamiliar with the appraisal process may not understand how the implementation of the value methods may affect the valuation conclusion. Different <u>property types</u>, <u>ownership interests</u>, <u>legal rights</u> and privileges, and uses of the appraisal conclusion can significantly affect the appraisal process and the appraisal conclusion.

The client and the analyst should fully understand and reach an agreement on the assignment, preferably in writing, before the valuation analysis begins.

Many ownership interests and potential value conclusions exist for an intangible asset. Any change in the applicable standard of value, premise of value, or valuation data can radically change the value conclusion for the very same intangible asset.

The statement of the intangible asset appraisal problem should include:

(a) identification of the subject intangible asset;

(b) identification of the subject intangible asset property rights to be valued;

(c) objective of the intangible asset appraisal assignment;

(d) purpose of the intangible asset appraisal assignment;

(e) definition of the appropriate standard of value;

(f) date of the value estimate;

(g) a listing of limiting conclusions, if any.

The intangible asset property rights to be valued include the rights that are legally held, or may be held, by the owner of the intangible asset. An analyst may estimate the fee simple interest or partial ownership interests created by the severance or division of ownership rights. Information regarding the specific rights to be valued and the financing involved may be critical at the start of the assignment, because the complexity of these rights and terms may affect the procedures, skills, and time required to complete the assignment.

Also, the sum of the partial interests in a particular intangible asset may not equal its fee simple value. To estimate the value of a partial interest in a particular intangible asset, direct evidence of the attitude of the market to such a partial interest is usually preferred by analysts. A clear identification of the intangible asset appraisal assignment helps the analyst directly toward the essential information and avoids unnecessary and expensive tangible analysis.

4. Highest and Best Use

Through the highest and best use analysis, an analyst interprets the market factors that influence the subject property and identifies the use upon which the final value estimate is based. The highest and best use analysis helps an analyst to identify comparable properties and to identify obsolescence factors that may affect the value or the life of the subject intangible asset.

Critical valuation factors are identified during the highest and best use analysis including: systematic and non-systematic risk, economic income estimates, and economic income capitalization rates. During the course of the appraisal, the analyst may test the sensitivity of the valuation. In this manner, a reasonable range of values for the intangible asset may be established.

The identification of various operating scenarios may be uncovered during the highest and best use analysis. Interrelationships between several of the critical valuation factors and their probability of occurrence in the future may be analysed, helping to establish the reasonable range of values for the subject intangible asset.

5. Data Collection

After defining the appraisal problem, the next step is a <u>preliminary data</u> analysis. During this step, an analyst develops the analytical work plan. The analyst gathers, analyses, and adjusts data, as appropriate, when performing the appraisal assignment. Such data and information include:

(a) characteristics of the intangible asset: ownership interest to be valued, rights, privileges, conditions, and factors affecting ownership or operational control;

(b) nature, history, and outlook of the business and industry in which the intangible asset operates;

(c) historical financial information for the intangible asset;

(d) related assets and liabilities required for economic operation of the subject intangible asset;

(e) the nature and conditions of the relevant industries that have an impact on the intangible asset;

(f) local, national, and international economic factors affecting the intangible asset;

(g) available rates of return on alternative investment and a description of relevant market transactions;

(h) prior transactions involving the subject intangible asset;

(i) other relevant information.

The work plan includes an analysis of the market for the intangible asset and its supply and demand relationships. To complete an intangible asset appraisal assignment quickly and efficiently, an analyst schedules the primary steps in the appraisal process. Time and personnel requirements vary with the complexity of the appraisal objective and the available data. Some assignments can be completed in a few days and others require months to gather and analyse the appropriate data.

Some assignments need the assistance of specialists of other fields. For example, the valuation of the contract rights associated with the distribution of a particular entertainer's work product may benefit from the opinion of a professional agent.

The analyst is responsible for the work product and should, therefore, have a clear understanding of the responsibilities of each member of the appraisal assignment team. Taking a comprehensive view, the assignment's primary analyst recognizes the type, volume, and sequence of work to be done.

The amount and type of data collected for an appraisal depend on how the assignment has been defined. For example, the appraisal problem may require that one valuation approach emphasize more on the final value estimate. Ultimately, the analyst's expertise and professional judgment and the quality and quantity of available data determine the applicability of the valuation approaches. The collected and analysed data affect the judgments made in the valuation analysis; therefore, the appraisal report usually includes a description of the information considered by the analyst.

6. Three Approaches to Value

The appraisal process is applied to develop a well-supported estimate of a defined value based on consideration of all pertinent data. The intangible asset property value is estimated after considering three distinct approaches to value: cost, market, and income. One or more of these approaches are used in estimations of value. Which of the three approaches is the most applicable in the particular analysis depends upon the type of property, the use of the appraisal, and the quality and quantity of data available for analysis.

All three approaches are applicable to many appraisal problems. Depending on the specific assignment, one or more of the approaches may have greater significance. Wherever possible, the analyst should apply more than one approach. Alternative value indications can serve as useful comparisons for assessing the reasonableness of the results of the principal approach.

7. Contingent and Limiting Conditions

It is important to realize that it is necessary for an analyst to make general assumptions in order to carry out an appraisal assignment in an efficient manner. General assumptions deal with issues such as legal and title considerations, liens and encumbrances, information furnished by others (e.g., engineering studies, market studies), hidden conditions and environmental hazards, and compliance with laws and regulations.

The analyst should make it clear that possession and use of the report is limited to the specific purpose and the specific audience for which it was prepared. Typically, no updating of the report or further consultation or expert testimony is required as part of a particular appraisal assignment.

The report is based on all the information available to the analyst as of the date of the report. The analyst typically assumes the information to be accurate. Projections used as part of the analysis are based on information effective as of the valuation date and are subject to changes of future economic and market conditions.

Independent appraisals certify that the analyst has personally conducted the appraisal and has no present or prospective interest in the property that is the subject of the appraisal report. The analyst declares no personal interest or bias with respect to the parties involved. With regard to independent appraisals, the fee for performing the analysis is not contingent upon the value reported or the attainment of a stipulated event. Also, with regard to independent appraisals, multiple analysts are required to conduct their professional appraisal activities in compliance with valuation Standards.

8. Valuation Conclusion

The intangible asset appraisal assignment is performed to investigate the value of an intangible asset. Even within the same valuation approach, different methods might typically result in different indications of value. For example, using the capitalized economic income methods would likely yields an indicated value different from the result of the discounted economic income method.

The process of reconciliation involves the analysis of the alternative valuation conclusions in order to arrive at a final value estimate for the subject intangible asset. Before reaching a final value estimate, the analyst should review the entire intangible asset appraisal for appropriateness and for accuracy. It is noteworthy that the definition of value estimated, and its relationship to each step in the valuation process, should be carefully considered throughout the reconciliation process.

9. Reporting the Valuation Conclusion

The results of the intangible asset appraisal process are presented in an appraisal report. Appraisal reports may be oral (e.g., <u>expert testimony</u>) or written.

If the report is prepared in a manner consistent with valuation standards, it should clearly and accurately set forth the appraisal. It should contain sufficient information to enable the audience to understand it properly, and it should clearly disclose an extraordinary contingent or limiting condition that impacts the appraisal.

The analyst's professional qualifications and experience are included in an independent appraisal report as evidence of the analyst's competence to perform the assignment.

Understanding the basic steps in the appraisal process and the reasons for the basic steps are essential to the successful conduct of an intangible asset valuation or economic analysis. The appraisal process provides a general analytical structure that assists the analyst in the collection, assessment, manipulation, and interpretation of market-derived valuation evidence. These steps provide a logical framework that allows the analyst to synthesize and conclude a reasonable estimate of value. They also assist the analyst in communicating the results of the appraisal in a well-reasoned and adequately documented report. The most complex appraisal problem can be more easily understood and more effectively solved if the analyst perceives it in terms of the appraisal process.

Core Words and Expressions 核心术语

analytical framework	分析框架
exploratory research	探索性研究
postulate	假设
refinement	细化，精化
validation	确认
property types	资产类型
ownership interests	所有者权益
legal rights	法定权利
preliminary data	初始数据
expert testimony	专家作证，专家证词

Questions and Discussion 问题与讨论

1. What should be included in the statement of the intangible asset appraisal problem?

2. What kind of data should be collected in the process?

3. Please summarizes the basic steps in the appraisal process.

Topic 3: Amortization and Impairment of Intangible Assets
无形资产的摊销和减值

Abstract 中文摘要

无形资产虽不具有实物形态，却是企业整体价值的重要组成部分。在基于税收和会计的目的下，一项资产要成为无形资产应当满足两个特征，即非物质性和不可分离性。非物质性是指无形资产属于非实体性、非流动资产，且公司并不打算将其出售；不可分离性是指无形资产应当与企业的活跃业务密不可分。

无形资产包括可辨认无形资产和不可辨认无形资产，可辨认无形资产又可以划分为可摊销无形资产和不可摊销无形资产。因此，企业价值的总和也可被视为是有形资产、可摊销无形资产、不可摊销无形资产以及商誉的总和减去负债的数值。

无形资产摊销可以实现一定数量的税收节省，潜在的节省税额等于摊销金额乘以边际税率。然而，对无形资产进行摊销需要满足诸多要求。例如，美国国税局（IRS）关于对无形资产摊销的要求包括：其必须能够与商誉相分离，其使用寿命必须是有限的，且有限的寿命必须能够以合理的精度进行测量。因此，确定资产有限的使用寿命对于无形资产的摊销是非常重要的，一般在实践中要经过深入综合的分析。

在企业合并情形下，不可辨认无形资产即商誉，也被认为是一种不应当进行摊销的资产，但应当定期进行减值测试，即，在每年的减值测试中，需要测试商誉等无形资产是否存在减值。如果其账面价值超过其隐含的公允价值，则被视为存在减值，需要对商誉等无形资产的账面价值进行调整。减值一经确认，不得转回。

Chapter 5 Intangible Assets Valuation 无形资产评估

Text* 正文

1. Criteria for Defining Intangible Assets

Intangible assets lack physical substance but are nonetheless integral to the overall value of a business. The value of an intangible asset is usually the result of economic benefits that accrue to the owner. By standards of common law, assets such as stocks, bonds, and loans are considered intangible. For tax and accounting purposes in acquisitions, however, these types of assets are not considered intangible. For tax and accounting purposes, an asset is intangible if it has two key characteristics.

The first one is immateriality. This criterion distinguishes an intangible asset from a non-tangible asset. Intangible assets are considered immaterial noncurrent assets, which means they have a relatively permanent nature and are not intended for sale. Non-tangible assets, however, are claims against other parties, such as notes and receivables, and could be sold individually. It is for this reason that the loans of a bank are not considered intangible assets even though they are incorporeal property.

The second one is inseparability. Assets are considered intangible if they are inseparable from the active business. In other words, the intangible asset, separated from the business, is usually worthless or meaningless.

Under most circumstances, it is necessary to identify and value intangible assets only for tax and accounting reasons. Substantial tax benefits can be derived from valuing the intangible assets, and financial reporting requirements. Part of these can be amortizable for tax purposes. Nonetheless, it is useful to consider their value when analysing an acquisition.

2. Amortizable Versus Non-amortizable Intangible Assets

The total value of a business is the sum of the tangible and intangible asset values less liabilities assumed. The intangible assets can be identified as intangibles or unidentified intangibles. Moreover, the identified intangibles can be either amortizable, enabling a depreciation like deduction against taxable income to be taken, or non-

---

* Partly from: Zabihollah Rezaee, Financial Services Firms: Governance, Regulations, Valuations, Mergers, and Acquisitions, 3rd Edition, Wiley Online Library, 2012: chapter 10.

amortizable. Consequently, the total value of a business is the sum of tangible asset value, amortizable intangible asset value, non-amortizable intangible asset value and goodwill less liabilities assumed.

The ability to first identify an intangible asset and then prove it amortizable can yield significant tax savings and result in increased post-acquisition cash flow.

2.1 Benefits of Amortization

Amortization refers to the depreciation of an intangible asset. It is based on the concept of the wasting or exhaustible asset, although an intangible asset does not waste away as a physical asset does. The wasting away of an intangible asset is legal fiction but is necessary to consider in order to spread the recovery of a payment for that intangible asset over its fixed or useful life.

If an intangible asset can be amortized, significant tax savings can be realized. The potential tax savings is equal to the amortization amount multiplied by the marginal tax rate. For example, if an intangible asset valued at $100 million is amortizable over ten years, the annual amortization is $10 million. If the marginal tax rate is 25 percent, an annual tax saving of $2,500,000 to the acquirer is possible.

2.2 Requirements for Amortization

The Internal Revenue Service (IRS) issued several rulings that relate to intangible assets amortization. The two most significant are Revenue Ruling 68-483 and Revenue Ruling 74-456. In general, these rulings hold that in order for an intangible asset to be amortizable for income tax purposes, it must meet three tests. Firstly, it must be separately identifiable from goodwill. Secondly, it must have a limited useful life. Thirdly, the limited life must be measurable with reasonable accuracy.

Separating intangible assets from non-amortizable goodwill is never considered easy. In general, the IRS has been very aggressive in its interpretation of goodwill and tends to allocate as many intangible assets as possible to that category. However, historically, separating identification of intangible assets is not the main cause for denial of the amortization deduction. The reason for disallowance is the inability to establish and measure a limited useful life. Consequently, it may be possible to identify an intangible asset but not be able to life it. Therefore, non-amortizable identified intangible assets are defined and treated identically from goodwill for tax purposes.

The ability to life an intangible asset depends on proving and then measuring that limited life. In determining whether an intangible has a limited life, it is useful to ask two questions. One is whether the asset's value to the business diminishes progressively over time, which applies to intangible assets that do not regenerate naturally. The other is whether or not the availability of the asset to the business is limited, regardless of that asset's current or future value. An example of the second question is the intangible asset created by a below-market lease rate on a branch. The value actually may increase if market lease rates escalate, but if the lease is in effect for only five years, its availability to the bank is limited and so it has a limited useful life.

The second key aspect is how to measure the length of a useful life. Unless the intangible asset has a clear duration, estimating the life is usually the most difficult aspect of proving amortizable. The courts have indicated in numerous cases that the life need only be determined with reasonable, not perfect, accuracy. In practice, the most supportable lives are based on in-depth, comprehensive analyses of the experiences of the business owning the asset.

2.3 Measuring the Useful Life of an Intangible Asset

Measuring the life of an intangible asset is relatively straightforward if there is a contractual life without renewal possibilities.

Intangibles without a stated contractual life are the most vulnerable to attack and potential disallowance of amortization deduction. Consequently, it is essential that the life of intangible assets to be amortized be established from thorough, objective analysis. Two factors appear to improve the supportability of a useful life calculation:

(a) Using the unique experience of the business being acquired relative to the intangible asset being lived–in other words, not using industry averages or other businesses' experiences as the basis for the life.

(b) Wherever possible, lifting each component of the intangible asset base or a component as small as possible, for example, with loan servicing contracts, estimating the average life of each contract based on its characteristics rather than an overall average.

2.4 Individual Component Analysis

Tax law surrounding intangible assets involves a concept known as the <u>mass asset</u> rule. The courts have defined a mass asset to be a group of intangible assets grouped together for the convenience of the owner of the business. If a mass asset is acquired and not a group of individual intangible assets, the amortization deduction will not be allowed. The courts have reasoned that a mass asset does not have a determinable or measurable useful life, even though some of the individual components do. Consequently, to support an amortization deduction, it is necessary to prevent intangible assets from being classified as mass assets. In general, it is best to have a detailed analysis of the individual intangible assets when estimate the useful life.

3. Intangible Asset Valuation and Amortization

Intangible asset valuation should an integral part of the negotiations and acquisition agreement rather than an afterthought. To improve the supportability of intangible asset amortization, it is beneficial to follow these seven key guidelines:

(a) Be familiar with the latest IRS rulings. The acquiring bank and its counsel should become familiar with cases involving intangible assets, especially cases related to financial institution related. Understanding the reasoning of the courts and the IRS positions is helpful in designing a more supportable acquisition tax plan.

(b) Include intangible asset value in acquisition agreement. The binding acquisition agreement should state the classes of tangible and intangible assets being acquired and the allocation of the purchase price among them. This will help support the separation of amortizable intangible assets from goodwill and non-amortizable intangible assets.

(c) Avoid the temptation to eliminate goodwill completely. A bank acquisition without some element of goodwill is rare. Consequently, a portion of the purchase price should be allocated to goodwill and included in the contract.

(d) Be meticulous when establishing useful lives. The establishment of a useful life is the area the IRS is likely to find fault. Consequently, the best techniques, using the bank's own unique data and experiences when possible, should be employed. Perfect accuracy is not required, only reasonable accuracy. In general, however, the closer to perfect, the better the argument can be supported.

(e) Establish intangible asset values professionally. The supportability of value is strengthened when independent, qualified valuation professionals are used. Their experience and objectivity strengthen the taxpayer's evidence if valuation professionals called on to defend the amortization deduction. Moreover, professionals are aware of the best techniques to use in a given situation.

(f) Maintain good records. From the first step in the acquisition process, the buyer should maintain complete records, especially related to the assets purchased and their value. Consequently, it is often beneficial to have preliminary valuations of major intangible assets early in the process.

(g) Be reasonable and logical. All the research and analysis should be checked for reasonableness and logic upon completion.

By following these seven guidelines, the likelihood that intangible asset amortization will be supportable increases.

4. Impairment

4.1 Intangible Assets Impairment

Intangible assets impairment is a rather complex issue. To better reflect the underlying market value of the intangible assets, the Financial Accounting Standards Board (FASB) issued Statement of Financial Accounting Standard (SFAS), which provides a clear path to measure intangible asset impairments. Intangible assets should be tested annually according to the guidelines using a two-step process that begins with an estimate of the fair value of a reporting unit. The first step is a screen for potential impairment, and the second step measures the amount of impairment, if any. However, if certain criteria are met, the requirement to test intangibles for impairment annually can be satisfied without a measurement of the fair value of a reporting unit.

4.2 Goodwill Impairment

In a business combination, goodwill is considered an asset and should not be amortized. Instead, annual impairment tests should be conducted to determine whether an indication of goodwill impairment exists.

4.2.1 Impairment Test

Goodwill should be assigned to reporting units and test for impairment periodically. Two procedures are involved. Step one is comparing a reporting unit's fair value to its carrying amount, which is used as a screening process to identify potential goodwill impairment. Step two is to measure the amount of the reporting unit's goodwill impairment loss, if the carrying amount of a reporting unit is more than the reporting unit's fair value. To perform step 1 of the goodwill impairment test, an entity must:

(a) Identify its reporting units. The unit of accounting for goodwill is at a level of the entity referred to as a reporting unit. For the annual or event-driven impairment assessment, it is important to identify the reporting units.

(b) Assign assets and liabilities to its reporting units. An entity should be assigned the appropriate assets and liabilities to the respective reporting units in a goodwill impairment test, if both of these criteria are met. The asset is employed in or the liability related to the operations of a reporting unit. Meanwhile, the asset or liability is in determining the fair value of the reporting unit.

(c) Assign all goodwill to one or more of its reporting units. Goodwill must be assigned to one or more reporting units as of the acquisition date, no matter whether other assets or liabilities of the acquired entity are assigned to those reporting units.

An entity might follow one of two approaches when assigning goodwill to reporting units: an acquisition method approach and a with-and-without approach.

(d) Determine the fair value of those reporting units to which goodwill has been assigned.

4.2.2 Impairment Model

Goodwill is deemed impaired if its carrying amount exceeds its implied fair value. To identify a potential impairment and measure an impairment loss, a two-step impairment test is performed:

Step1. Compare the fair value of the reporting unit with the reporting unit's carrying amount including goodwill, to identify any potential impairment.

(a) If the reporting unit's fair value is more than its carrying amount, the reporting unit's goodwill is considered not impaired, and step 2 is not needed.

(b) If the reporting unit's fair value is less than its carrying amount, the reporting unit's goodwill may be impaired, and step 2 must be applied to detect the amount of the goodwill impairment loss.

Step2. Compare the implied fair value of the reporting unit's goodwill with the carrying amount of the reporting unit's goodwill.

(a) If the carrying amount of the reporting unit's goodwill is more than the implied fair value of the reporting unit's goodwill, an impairment loss should be recognized for the excess.

(b) After a goodwill impairment loss for a reporting unit is measured and recognized, the adjusted carrying amount of the reporting unit's goodwill becomes the new accounting basis for that goodwill. A subsequent reversal of previously recognized goodwill impairment losses is prohibited if the measurement of that impairment loss is recognized.

Core Words and Expressions 核心术语

Immateriality	非物质性
Criterion	准则
non-tangible asset	非有形资产
inseparability	不可分离性
tax benefit	税收优惠
amortizable	可摊销的，可分批偿还的
tax savings	税收节约
waste away	日渐消耗
Internal Revenue Service	国内税务局

contractual life	合约期
renewal possibility	续约的可能性
mass asset	大规模资产
reporting unit	报告单位
periodically	定期地，周期性地
carrying amount	账面值，维持费用

Questions and Discussion 问题与讨论

1. For tax and accounting purposes, what are the two key characteristics of intangible assets? Please explain.

2. Why do intangible assets need amortization?

3. How do we know whether there exists an impairment of goodwill?

Information Extension

思政微课堂

无形资产是企业的重要组成部分。尤其对于高新技术企业，知识产权作为无形资产的重要子集，更是其创造价值的核心资产。《中华人民共和国民法典》第一百二十三条规定，"民事主体依法享有知识产权"，确立了知识产权保护的重大法律原则。数据显示，2022年，我国发明专利授权数达79.8万件，是2017年的1.9倍，每万人口高价值发明专利拥有量达9.4件，较上年增长了1/4，全国专利密集型产业增加值达到14.3万亿元；专利密集型产业增加值占国内生产总值（GDP）比重超过11.6%，版权产业增加值占GDP比重超过7.39%。

随着我国科技创新的快速发展，科学合理地评估无形资产的价值，构建无形资产评估方法体系，可以助推无形资产交易的顺利进行，盘活知识产权资产、优化资源配置，有利于维护知识产权权利人的合法权益，激发创新动力。为规范无形资产评估执业行为，保护资产评估当事人合法权益和公共利益，中国资产评估协会先后发布《资产评估执业准则——无形资产》（中评协〔2017〕37号）、《资产评估执业准则——知识产权》（中评协〔2023〕14号）、《专利资产评估指导意见》（中评协〔2017〕49号）、《著作权资产评估指导意见》（中评协〔2017〕50号）、《商标资产评估指导意见》（中评协〔2017〕51号）等准则，对不同类别无形资产的评估对象、操作要求、评估方法、相关披露等作出说明和要求。

2021年，中共中央、国务院印发了《知识产权强国建设纲要（2021—2035年）》，要求"提高知识产权代理、法律、信息、咨询等服务水平，支持开展知识产权资产评估、交易、转化、托管、投融资等增值服务""完善无形资产评估制度，形成激励与监管相协调的管理机制""健全版权交易和服务平台，加强作品资产评估、登记认证、质押融资等服务"。随后，中共中央 国务院印发的《"十四五"国家知识产权保护和运用规划》（国发〔2021〕20号）也提出，要"完善无形资产评估制度""健全知识产权价值评估体系，鼓励开发智能化知识产权评估工具"。资产评估行业本身作为技术密集、知识密集的现代高端服务业，也属于该项规划的培育对象。

2022年，党的二十大报告进一步强调，要"加强知识产权法治保障，形成支持全面创新的基础制度"。这一部署对我国推进建设知识产权强国意义重大，也为资产评估行业自身的发展提供重大机遇。资产评估行业需要站在新的战略高度，继续开拓创新，不断完善知识产权价值评估体系，健全知识产权评估市场化运作机制。

Chapter 6
Business Valuation
企业价值评估

Wisdom
名人名言

苟日新，日日新，又日新。

——曾子

富其家者资之国，富其国者资之天下，欲富天下，则资之天地。

——王安石

Buyers and sellers can create substantial value through merger and acquisition (M&A). Both can win from a transaction. That is the beauty of deal making.

—Chris Mellen & Frank Evans

The single most important decision in evaluating a business is pricing power. If you've got the power to raise prices without losing business to a competitor, you've got a very good business. And if you have to have a prayer session before raising the price by 10 percent, then you've got a terrible business.

—Warren Buffett

Rudimentary Knowledge
基本知识

Abstract 中文摘要

企业价值评估是指资产评估专业人员对评估基准日特定目的下的企业整体价值、股东全部权益价值或股东部分权益价值进行分析、估算并发表专业意见以及撰写评估报告的行为和过程。其中，企业价值是企业获利能力的货币化体现，即：企业在遵循价值规律的基础上，通过以价值为核心的管理，使企业利益相关者均能获得满意回报的能力。

有关企业价值评估的需求通常源自多种评估目的，包括企业收购与兼并、企业改制、企业上市、股权转让、税收、法律诉讼、破产清算以及财务报告等。在企业价值评估中，资产评估专业人员应当将企业作为一个有机整体，依据其拥有或占有的全部资产状况和整体获利能力，充分考虑影响企业获利能力的各种因素，结合企业所处的宏观经济环境及行业背景，对企业价值进行综合性评估。资产评估专业人员应当根据评估业务的具体情况，确定所需资料的清单并收集相关资料，并注意企业信息的来源和质量。企业的信息质量高低，会直接影响到资产评估专业人员的判断。信息的收集、整理和归纳需要满足可靠性原则、相关性原则、有效性原则、客观性原则和经济性原则。

执行企业价值评估业务，资产评估专业人员应当充分考虑评估目的、市场条件、评估对象自身条件等因素，恰当选择价值类型，并应当根据评估目的、评估对象、价值类型、资料收集等情况，分析收益法、市场法、资产基础法这三种基本方法的适用性，恰当选择评估方法。其中，资产基础法是以被评估单位评估基准日的资产负债表为基础，通过评估企业表内以及表外可识别的各项资产、负债的价值，并以资产扣减负债后的净额确定评估对象价值的评估方法；市场法是将评估对象与可比上市公司或者可比交易案例进行比较并通过适当调整来确定评估对象价值的评估方法，包括上市公司比较法、交易案例比较法等常用方法；收益法是通过将预期收益资本化或者折现以确定评估对象价值的评估方法，包括股利折现法、现金流量折现法等常用方法。此外，资产评估专业人员在企业价值评估过程中，还应当关注企业价值的溢价或折价调整问题，包括缺乏市场流动性折价、少数股权折价、控制权溢价、规模溢价、关键人物折价等。

Text* 正文

1. Business Valuation Overviews

1.1 Business and Business Valuation

A business is a commercial, industrial, service or investment activity. Business valuation is generally defined as the act or process of arriving at an opinion or estimation of the value of a business or enterprise/entity or an interest therein. Business valuation is usually equal to the total value of the equity in a business, which is the value of a business to all of its shareholders, plus the value of its debt or debt-related liabilities, minus any cash or cash equivalents available to meet those liabilities. Nowadays, business valuation has also been expanded to cover valuation of assets, including both tangible assets and intangible assets.

A valuation of a business may either comprise the whole of the activity of an entity or a part of the activity. It is important to distinguish between the value of a business entity and the value of the individual assets or liabilities of that entity. If the purpose of the valuation requires individual assets or liabilities to be valued and those assets are separable from the business and transferable independently, those assets or liabilities should be valued in isolation and not by apportionment of the value of the entire business. Therefore, it is important to establish whether the valuation is of the entire entity, shares or a shareholding in the entity, a specific business activity of the entity or of specific assets or liabilities before undertaking a valuation of a business.

Nowadays, valuations of businesses are required for different purposes including loans, acquisitions, mergers and sales of businesses, taxation, litigation, insolvency proceedings and financial reporting. For example, a company may want to know the true value of another company before deciding whether to acquire it. Business valuation is also frequently involved in <u>divorce disputes</u>, <u>fraud cases</u> and insurance

---

* *Partly from:* The International Valuation Standards Council (IVSC), International Valuation Standards, 2011 Edition: IVS 200, 2011; Zhonghe Appraisal Company Ltd, BMI Appraisals Limited Company, Business Valuation and Case Studies, China Financial &Economic Publishing House, 2010: 7-15; 22-23.

investigations. In China, the demand for business valuation has been surging over the past few years. The increase is attributed to increasing activities in the equity capital market such as merger & acquisitions (M&A), initial public offerings (IPO) and so on.

1.2 Bases of Valuation

While the majority of business valuations use market value, other bases should be adopted under some circumstances. It is important that both valuers and users of valuations clearly understand the distinctions between market value and non-market value-based valuations, and how these differences may affect the applicability of the valuation. The following presents commonly used bases of valuation for business valuation:

(a) Market Value – The estimated amount for which an asset should exchange on the date of valuation between a willing buyer and a willing seller in an arm's length transaction after proper marketing wherein the parties each acted knowledgeably, prudently, and without compulsion.

(b) Value in Use – The value a specific asset has for a specific use to a specific user and therefore non-market related. This value type focuses on the value that specific asset contributes to the entity of which it is a part, regardless of the asset's highest and best use or the monetary amount that might be realized upon its sales.

(c) Investment Value – The value of an asset to a particular investor, or a class of investors, for identified investment objectives. The investment value of an asset may be higher or lower than the market value of the asset.

(d) Going Concern Value – The value of a business or of an interest therein, as a going concern. The intangible elements of going concern value in an operating business result from factors such as: having a trained work force; an operational plant; the necessary licenses, systems, and procedures in place.

(e) Insurable Value – The value of an asset provided by definitions contained in an insurance contractor policy.

(f) Liquidation or Forced Sale Value – The amount that may reasonably be received from the sale of an asset within a time frame too short to meet the marketing time frame required by the market value definition. Forced sale value may also involve an unwilling seller and a buyer or buyers who know the disadvantage of the seller.

1.3 Business Information

The valuation of a business entity or interest frequently replies on information from management, representatives of the management or other experts. Significant care should be taken to specify what information can be verified, and the extent of verification required, during the valuation process at settlement of the work scope.

Although the value on a given date reflects the anticipated benefits of future ownership, the history of a business is useful in giving guidance as to the expectations for the future. Also, awareness of relevant economic developments and specific industry trends is essential for business valuation. Matters such as political outlook, government policy, exchange rates, inflation, interest rates and market activity may affect businesses that operate in different sectors of the economy quite differently.

The valuation of an ownership interest in a business is only relevant in the context of the financial position of the business at a point in time. It is important to understand the nature of assets and liabilities of the business and to determine which items are required for use in the income-producing process and the ones redundant to the business at the valuation date.

Businesses may have unrecorded assets or liabilities not reflected on the balance sheet. Such assets could include patents, trademarks, copyrights, brands, know-how and proprietary databases. Goodwill is a residual value after all tangible and identifiable intangible assets have been taken into account.

2. Business Valuation Approaches

For business valuation, the asset-based approach is commonly adopted in three ways: cost approach, market approach and income approach. The market and the income approaches can be applied to the valuation of a business or business interest. Generally, the <u>asset-based approach</u> is seldom applied except in the case of early stage or start-up businesses where profits and/or cash flow cannot be reliably determined and adequate market information is available on the entity's assets.

Since not one approach can be universally appropriate for every valuation, determining an appropriate one becomes a critical part of business valuation. In addition, given multiple applicable approaches, different approaches may produce significantly different values. Therefore, based on available information, good valuers need to make frequent professional judgments to determine which approach to use. Besides that, the value of certain types of businesses, e.g., an investment or holding business, can be derived from a summation of the assets and liabilities. This is sometimes called the net asset approach or asset approach. This is not a valuation approach in its own right, because the values of the individual assets and liabilities are derived using one or more of the principal valuation approaches before being aggregated.

2.1 The Asset-based Approach

The asset-based approach is based on the principle of substitution, i.e., an asset is worth no more than it would cost to replace all of its constituent part. In this approach, the cost values of all assets, both tangible and intangible, and all liabilities on the balance sheet are replaced with market values. If market or liquidation values apply, costs of sale may need to be considered. Taxes may also need to be taken into consideration.

2.1.1 Valuation Procedures

The first step is to review all the assets and liabilities on the balance sheet. Add assets and liabilities, if any, that influence the financial or operation aspect of the company but not presented on the balance sheet, such as non-cancelable operating leases, contingent liabilities, etc. Eliminate assets and liabilities that have no influence on the financial or operation aspect of the company, for example, unidentified aging accounts receivable. Then, revalue all the concerned assets and liabilities to their market values. So, the value of the company is equal to the total market values of all the concerned assets subtracted by the total market values of all the concerned liabilities.

In general, a valuer can obtain most of the assets and liabilities from the balance sheet. If the company lacks a balance sheet, the valuer needs to request the management of the company for details of the assets and liabilities. The valuer may also need to conduct site visits for verification purposes.

As mentioned, the valuer needs to pay attention to assets and liabilities not shown on the balance sheet, because those items could constitute a significant part of the company's total assets. Unidentified assets and liabilities may include intangible assets generated internally by the company, contracts related to either assets or liabilities and non-cancelable, and the fully-depreciated assets in use.

Some assets and/or liabilities need to be eliminated, such as <u>obsolete</u> or aging inventories. Moreover, if the company did not record sufficient <u>bad debt</u> expenses for its accounts receivable, some accounts receivable needs to be eliminated accordingly.

Under the asset-based approach, the calculated value is the market value of 100% interest in the subject company.

2.1.2 Application of the Asset-based Approach

The asset-based approach should be considered in valuations of <u>controlling interest</u>s in business entities that involve an investment or holding business, such as a property business or a farming business. Besides, it is applicable to a business valued on a basis other than as a going concern.

This approach is easy to understand and use because people are usually familiar with financial statements, especially balance sheets. Also, this approach is particularly adequate if the company lacks intangible assets.

But asset-based approach is not suitable for the company with significant intangible assets and contingent items. And it is inappropriate for valuing going-concern businesses. Moreover, it may be expensive and difficult to obtain reliable market-derived data for valuation of many assets and liabilities.

The asset-based approach should not be the sole valuation approach used in the valuation of going concerns unless it is customarily used by the seller and the buyer. If the valuation is not conducted on a going concern basis, the assets should be valued on a market value basis or on a basis that assumes a shortened time period for exposure in the market. All costs associated with the sale of the assets or the closing of the business need to be taken into account for the valuation. Intangible assets such as goodwill may not have value under these circumstances, although other intangible assets such as patents or brands may retain their value.

2.2 The Market Approach

The market approach compares the subject business to similar ones, business ownership interests and securities that have been exchanged in the market and any relevant transactions of shares in the same business. Prior transactions or offers for any component of the business may be indicative of value.

2.2.1 Valuation Procedures

Because no companies are identical, a comparative analysis of qualitative and quantitative similarities and differences between comparable businesses and the subject business should be made.

Firstly, we should identify recent transactions of similar companies, and then compare the identified similar companies with the subject company trying to make adjustments to the purchase prices to reflect differences. Next, we need to calculate a price multiple of each of the similar companies using EBITDA, net profit, etc. as the denominator. Average the price multiple and then apply the "average" multiple to the subject company to determine its market value.

Under this approach, data collection is very important. The three most common sources of data used in this approach are public stock markets in which ownership interests of similar companies are traded, the acquisition market in which entire companies are bought and sold, and prior transactions in the ownership of the subject company.

When using similar company's comparison, the similar companies should be in the same industry as the subject company or in an industry that responds to the same economic variables. Factors to be considered in this comparison method include:

(a) Whether the market has sufficient amount of recent transactions on the similar companies. Besides, the data of the transactions should be verifiably available from the market;

(b) How similar are the identified companies to the subject company with respect to both qualitative and quantitative company characteristics? For example, similar companies have a size comparable to that of the subject company;

(c) Whether the price of the similar company represents an arm's-length transaction. The purchase price cannot be used as a reference if it was a compelling transaction and the purchase price was either higher or lower than the market value of the company.

When valuers adjust the purchase price of similar companies, conditions that require adjustments include the existence of non-recurrent revenue or expenses on the financial statements of the similar companies, differences in terms of the quantity of the similar companies, such as market capitalization, earnings growth rate, etc., different market conditions between the date of valuation and the dates of identified transactions for similar companies.

Under the market approach, the calculated value is the market value of the company. If the company has debts, the market value of the equity (100% interest) is the calculated value minus the market value of all the debts.

2.2.2 Application of the Market Approach

Market approach is considered the most preferred approach for valuation because it is based on real historical data. In other words, it involves much less estimations and assumptions compared with the other approaches. It is also a preferred approach to value publicly listed companies, because excellent comparative financial data of these companies are usually available. If valuing a controlling ownership interest, no premium for control is needed. Actually, this approach has been generally understood and accepted by courts and widely used for merger and acquisitions transactions.

However, the biggest problem of this approach is data. Generally speaking, it is inapplicable to most intangible assets, as there may be very limited transaction data for intangible assets in the market. And it cannot value the acquired company private before acquisition because the financial data are limited. Moreover, if valuing a minority interest, discounts for minority ownership interest or lack of marketability may be controversial and hard to quantify

2.3 The Income Approach

The income approach estimates the market value of the company by summing up the present values of all expected income generated by the company in the future. While both the asset-based approach and the market approach focus on assets to determine a value, the income approach focuses on income, which is based on an assumption that the market value of any company is equal to the present value of its future expected income.

There are three different types of income that can be used under the income approach, i.e., dividends, net income and <u>free cash flows</u>. Among them, free cash flows are the most commonly adopted. Regardless of which type of income to be used, the accuracy of valuation under this approach strongly depends on the accuracy of forecasting the income in the future. Therefore, all the estimations and assumptions of the future income made by the valuer should be as reasonable as possible. The two more common methods under the income approach are income capitalization method and Discounted Cash Flow (DCF) method.

2.3.1 Income Capitalization Method

This method is a <u>mathematical simplification</u> of DCF method which is described later. Income method permits the value of the company to be calculated by dividing a company's income by a capitalization rate which takes into account the business <u>specific risk</u>s and expected future <u>annual growth rate</u>.

2.3.1.1 Valuation Procedures

The first step is to determine an appropriate income. The next step is to estimate future expected income by <u>referring to</u> the actual historical income with adequate adjustments made to take into account expected changes in terms of the economy, the market and the strategy of the business affecting the business profitability. The following procedure is to estimate a discount rate incorporating all the risks the company is and will be exposed to, and determine a long-term stable annual growth rate for the company. The discount rate minus the annual growth rate is the capitalization rate. The market value of the company is calculated by dividing the estimated annual income by the capitalization rate. Using this method, the calculated value is the market value of either the company or the 100% equity, depending on the differences in treatments of the expected income.

2.3.1.2 Estimation of Future Annual Income

The type of income that is most frequently adopted in this method is net profit, although other type of income such as pre-tax earnings, earnings before interest and tax (EBIT), free cash flows, or even dividends can also be used. When estimating the future annual income, the following factors need to be considered:

(a) income from gains on selling <u>fixed assets</u>;

(b) income from gains on selling <u>investment securities</u>;

(c) unexpected higher or lower <u>dividends distribution</u>;

(d) non-recurring expenses such as restructuring expenses;

(e) contingent liabilities or litigations that could significantly affect the future income of business.

2.3.1.3 Determination of the Capitalization Rate

Determination of an appropriate capitalization rate is probably the most challenging task in this method, since the rate must be able to reflect all the risks associated with the company and its expected future annual growth. An appropriate capitalization rate must satisfy the following two important criteria.

First, the required rate of return of the investor should be <u>incorporated</u>. Meanwhile, the capitalization rate and the income are determined under the same conditions, for example, after-tax conditions.

Other factors to be considered in determining the capitalization rate include the nature, scale, financial conditions, general conditions and the market conditions of this company, etc. even the experience and expertise of the management.

2.3.1.4 Application of Income Capitalization Method

Income capitalization method is preferred to value closely held companies or intangible assets with stable growth rates in the future. It is simple to understand and use, especially by investors, and does not require long-term forecast of future income.

However, it is not suitable for valuing start-up or high-growth companies. Moreover, it is hard work to estimate these parameters including the long-term future annual income and the capitalization rate.

2.3.2 Discounted Cash Flow Method (DCF)

Discounted cash flow method is based on the concept that the value of any asset is the present value of its expected future cash flows. This method involves discounting all future expected cash flows generated by a company back to the present values by a discount rate. The market value of the company is the sum of all of the present values.

Under DCF method, the future near-term growth is not expected to be slow-growing or stable. This is a major difference between discounted cash flow method and capitalization of value method. Another major difference is a terminal value represents the estimated value of the sale of the company at the final projection year. The terminal value of discounted cash flow is based on the capitalized value of the company's future income stream from that point onward.

2.3.2.1 Valuation procedures

The first step of valuation is to obtain the future earnings forecast from the client. If the client lacks the information, the valuer needs to do the forecast based on information provided by the client. Afterwards, the valuer may adjust the forecast to eliminate historical non-recurring activities affecting the financial results of the company and to reflect its expected future performance. The valuer also needs to consider other factors that may affect the company's cash flows in the future, for example, tax benefits.

Moreover, some parameters need to be determined, such as the long-term annual growth rate for the forecast period, the expected cash flow for each of year, a discount rate which incorporates all risks associated with the company.

Then, we could discount all future expected cash flows and the terminal value back to present values using the estimated discount rate. The sum of all the present values is the value of the company after considering other adjustments, e.g., lack of marketability discount. Same as income capitalization method, the calculated value under DCF method can be the market value of either the company or the 100% equity, depending on the differences in treatments of the expected cash flows.

2.3.2.2 Estimation of Future Cash Flows

A valuer can use net income, EBIT or even EBITDA to calculate free cash flows.

Take net income as an example, the formula is as follows:

Free cash flow = Net Income + *Non-cash Expenses* + *After-tax Interest Expense* - *Capital Expenditure* - *Increase in Working Capital*,

here the non-cash expenses are the expenses such as the depreciation and amortization.

2.3.2.3 Determination of Discount Rate

Similar to the capitalization rate in income capitalization method, determining an appropriate discount rate is both challenging and critical in DCF method. If the discount rate is larger than adequate one, the company may be undervalued significantly, and vice versa.

Either the <u>Weighted Average Cost of Capital (WACC)</u> or the <u>cost of equity</u> can be used as the discount rate, depending on the financial structure of the company under valuation. For example, if the company has debts, the WACC is the right candidate for determining the discount rate, otherwise, the cost of equity should be used. In general, WACC and CAPM are the two common methods that the valuer usually uses to determine the discount rate.

(a) The Capital Asset Pricing Method (CAPM)

Investors usually require a higher rate of return on an investment involving more risks. Risks can be divided into <u>systematic risk</u>s and non-systematic risks. Non-systematic risks include company-specific risks can be eliminated by <u>diversification</u>, while systematic risks include those cannot.

The <u>Capital Asset Pricing Method (CAPM)</u> is commonly used to estimate the systematic risks involved in an investment. It states that the expected return on a company can be written as a function of the <u>risk-free rate</u> and the beta of the company:

$E(R) = R_f + \beta [E(R_m) - R_f]$

$E(R)$: Expected return on the company

R_f: Risk-free rate

$E(R_m)$: Expected return on market portfolio

$E(R_m)$: Market risk premium

$[E(R_m) - R_f]$: Market risk premium

β: Beta of the company

A risk-free rate is defined as the rate of return available on a security free of default risk. The U.S. Treasury securities are widely accepted as risk-free assets. The valuations of most Hong Kong companies use Hong Kong Exchange Fund Notes (HKEFN). For valuing companies in mainland China, treasury bonds can be preferable risk-free assets. Various HKEFN and treasury bonds with different maturities, such as two years, three years, ten years, etc., are available for the valuer. The valuer should match the maturity of the HKEFN and treasury bonds to be adopted in the CAPM with the forecast period of the company.

Market risk premium is the premium demanded by investors for investing in the market portfolio, which includes all risky assets in the market, instead of investing in a riskless asset. Under the CAPM, market risk is a systematic risk, hence an additional rate of return is required to compensate for it.

Beta is a measure of systematic risk in the CAPM. It reflects the sensitivity of returns over the risk-free rate for a security to that for a market. If a company bears the same risks as the market does, the company's beta is 1.0. If investing in a company is riskier than investing in the market, the company's beta should be larger than 1.0, and vice versa.

Betas of public companies can be easily obtained from financial information providers such as Bloomberg or Reuters. Betas of closely held companies are usually derived from the average beta of public companies in the same industry. Adjustments, however, frequently need to be made to take into account differences among the peer companies before averaging. The differences may include market capitalization and proportion of revenue generated from the same business as the subject company.

After proper adjustments, an average beta is calculated and can be applied to the CAPM. Please be aware that the average beta has incorporated industry-specific risks.

Beta can be classified into levered beta and unlevered beta. W0ich beta to be used in the CAPM depends on whether the subject company has debts. If the company has debts, levered beta should be used, and vice versa. The relationship between levered beta and unlevered beta can be explained by the following equation:

$$B_L = B_u [1 + (1-t)(D/E)]$$

B_L: Levered beta

B_u: Unlevered beta

t: Tax rate for the company

D/E: Debt-to-equity ratio (market value)

In determining the discount rate, a valuer also consider non-systematic risks, which is also called company-specific risks, and add additional required rate of return arising from the non-systematic risks in terms of premiums to the expected rate of return calculated under the CAPM. Company-specific risks may be generated by:

- smaller company size compared to the peer group;
- concentration of customer base;
- key person dependence or small management base;
- key supplier dependence;
- abnormal present or <u>pending competition</u>;
- <u>pending lawsuits</u>;
- relatively undiversified operations in terms of product or location;
- unrecorded liabilities;
- <u>pending regulatory changes</u>;
- industry risks not fully reflected in beta.

(b) The Weighted Average Cost of Capital (WACC)

The other way to determine the discount rate is using Weighted Average Cost of Capital. The WACC is the minimum return that a company must earn on an existing asset base to satisfy its creditors, owners, and other providers of capital, persuading them from invest elsewhere. Companies raise money from a number of sources: common equity, preferred stock, straight debt, convertible debt, exchangeable debt, warrants, options, pension liabilities, executive stock options, governmental subsidies, and so on. Different securities, which represent different sources of finance, are expected to generate different returns. The WACC takes is calculated taking into account the relative weights of each component of the capital structure. The more complex the company's capital structure, the more laborious it is to calculate the WACC.

$WACC=(E/V)*Re+(D/V)*Rd*(1-Tc)$

Re: cost of equity

Rd: cost of debt

E: market value of the firm's equity

D: market value of the firm's debt

$V = E + D$

E/V: percentage of financing that is equity

D/V: percentage of financing that is debt

Tc: corporate tax rate

By taking a weighted average, we can see how much interest the company has to pay for amount of money it finances. Companies can use WACC to see if the investment projects available to them are worthwhile to undertake.

2.3.2.4 Application of DCF Method

DCF method is preferred to value closely held companies or intangible assets with unstable expected annual growth rates and expected cash flow, for example, fast growing companies. It can capture the future benefits generated by the company and increasingly accepted in the courts.

However, DCF method may be difficult to understand and explain, especially to those without sufficient financial background. Besides that, it is also a hard to estimate future economic benefits for an appropriate discount rate.

3. Discount and Premium Adjustments

When valuing the company using either the market approach or the income approach, discount and premium adjustments need to be frequently made to reflect company-related characteristics. Among various discounts and premiums, a discount for lack of marketability is probably the most common in valuation. Valuers should consider other discounts and premiums such as discounts for minority interest (premiums for control), size premium, key person discounts, etc.

3.1 Discounted for Lack of Marketability

Marketability is defined as the ability to quickly convert assets to cash at the minimal cost. The existence of a discount for lack of marketability is due to the difficulty of selling an interest in a closely held company compared with an interest in a publicly traded company where investors can sell shares and receive cash easily. Therefore, investors are willing to buy an interest in a closely held company only at a significant discount compared with others to compensate for the lack of marketability or illiquidity risk. Empirical studies reveal that discounts for lack of marketability can range from 15.6% to 40.5%.

The following factors affecting discounts for lack of marketability:

(a) Dividends or Withdrawals–A smaller discount for lack of marketability is required for higher amount of dividends or withdrawals, because investors rely less on the easiness of selling their investments to realize their return;

(b) Put Rights–An option to sell can greatly reduce a discount for lack of marketability;

(c) Potential Pool of Buyers–A smaller discount for lack of marketability is required if a wider pool of realistic potential buyers is present;

(d) Size of Block–Ignoring control premium that will be discussed later in this section, the larger the size of an interest in a closely held company, the higher the discount for lack of marketability would be;

(e) Prospect of IPO or Buyout–A smaller discount for lack of marketability is required if a closely held company has a potential for an IPO or a buyout;

(f) Restrictive Transfer Provisions–Restrictions that constrain the ability to transfer the interest usually give rise to a higher discount for lack of marketability;

(g) Information Access and Reliability–A higher discount for lack of marketability would be required for poorer information access and reliability.

3.2 Discounted for Minority Interest (Premium for Control)

A discount for minority interest is defined as the discount for lack of control applicable to a minority interest, which means having an ownership position less than 50% of the voting interest in a company. It can be one of the critical adjustments in valuation if the investor is acquiring less than half of the total interest in a company, while it is unnecessary when an investor is acquiring 100% interest in a company. Empirical studies indicate that the average range of the discount is 14% to 25%.

Ownership rights are usually defined within a jurisdiction by legal documents such as articles of association, clauses in the memorandum of the business, articles of incorporation, bylaws, partnership agreements and shareholder agreements, etc. It may be of part, or share, of a business or of the entire business.

In general, some documents, such as articles of incorporation, bylaws, etc., may contain restrictions on the transfer of the interest and may contain provisions governing the basis of valuation that has to be adopted in the event of transfer of the interest. For example, the documents may stipulate that the interest should be valued as a pro rata fraction of the entire issued share capital regardless of it is a controlling or minority interest or not. In each case, the rights of the interest being valued and the rights attaching to any other class of interest need to be considered at the outset.

Meanwhile, a non-controlling interest may have a lower value than a controlling interest. A majority interest is not necessarily a controlling interest. The voting and other rights attaching to the interest will be determined by the legal framework under which the entity is established. There are often different classes of equity in business, each having different rights. Where this is the case, it is therefore possible that a minority interest may still have control or an effective veto over certain actions.

Moreover, another thing needs to be considered is swing vote. For example, a 2% block would have some value as a swing vote block if there were two 49% blocks.

3.3 Size Premium

Size premium is defined as an additional expected return required for incurring additional risk of investing in companies smaller than the "market index". Therefore, the smaller the size of a company, the larger the size premium is. While it is literally called size premium, it is in fact a discount that reduces the value of a company under valuation. Size premium is usually included in the cost of equity. For example, if the required rate of return for an investment in the company calculated using the CAPM is 10% and the size premium due to the small company size is 3%, the cost of equity will be 13%.

3.4 Key Person Discount

Key person discount is defined as a discount rate that takes into account risks associated with death of a key person in the company, such as the CEO or the chairman, which substantially impact the operations of the company. Key person discount may not be a big issue if the company is well established and its operations and/or decision making are not heavily relied on a few people.

Core Words and Expressions 核心术语

divorce dispute	离婚争议
fraud case	欺诈案件
equity capital market	权益资本市场，股票资本市场
merger & acquisitions (M&A)	兼并与收购
initial public offerings (IPO)	首次公开募股
a class of investors	某一类投资者
identified investment objectives	特定的投资目标
operational plant	运作有效的工厂
insurance contract	保险合同

time frame	时段，期限
asset-based approach	资产基础法
operating leases	经营租赁，营业租赁
contingent liabilities	或有债务
aging	老化，陈化
accounts receivable	应收账款
obsolete	废弃的，淘汰的
bad debt	坏账
controlling interest	控股权益
price multiple	价格乘数
non-recurrent revenue	非经常收入
market capitalization	市值，市场资本总额
earnings growth rate	收入增长率
premium for control	控制权溢价
free cash flow	自由现金流
mathematical simplification	数学上的简化
specific risk	特定风险
annual growth rate	年度增长率
referring to	参照
fixed assets	固定资产
investment securities	投资证券，有价证券
dividends distribution	股息分配

incorporate	合并，包含
near-term growth	近期增长
non-recurring activities	非经常项目
undervalue	低估
Weighted Average Cost of Capital (WACC)	加权平均资本成本
cost of equity	股权资本成本
systematic risk	系统性风险
diversification	多样化，分散投资
Capital Asset Pricing Method (CAPM)	资本资产定价模型
risk-free rate	无风险报酬率
default risk	违约风险
exchange fund note	外汇基金债券
maturity	到期（期限）
market risk premium	市场风险溢价
market portfolio	市场投资组合
Bloomberg	彭博社，彭博资讯
Reuters	路透社
industry-specific risk	行业特有风险
levered/unlevered beta	使用/未使用财务杠杆的 β
pending competition/lawsuits	胜负未定的竞争/诉讼
pending regulatory changes	尚未确定的法规变化
company-related characteristics	公司特征

discount for lack of marketability	缺乏市场流动性折价
illiquidity	非流动性
withdrawal	退股
put rights	卖权，看跌权
potential pool of buyers	潜在的买方群体
size of block	股份规模
buyout	买断
restrictive transfer provisions	限制转让的规定
minority interest	少数股权
voting interest	表决权
articles of incorporation	公司章程
bylaw	规章制度，制度
swing vote	关键选票，决定性选票
block	股票
market index	市价指数，市场指数
key person discount	关键人物折价

Questions and Discussion 问题与讨论

1. What is the definition of business valuation?

2. How many kinds of value standards are there?

3. Please describe the difference between the discount rate and the capitalization rate.

More Knowledge
知识扩展

Topic1: Business Information Collection and Analysis
企业信息收集与分析

Abstract 中文摘要

在资产评估过程中，信息的收集至关重要。根据信息来源，企业价值评估中需要收集的信息可以分为内部来源和外部来源。内部来源主要指企业的财务数据和运营数据，包括：评估对象相关权属资料，企业经营管理结构和产权架构资料，企业资产、财务和管理资料，企业发展规划和经营计划资料以及以往相关评估及交易资料。其中，财务数据可以通过历史财务报表、历史纳税申报、财务预测等获得，运营数据可以通过企业网站、实地考察、立法文件等获得。外部来源主要包括国家、地区以及行业的经济运行数据。国家、地区的宏观数据可以通过政府、数据服务机构、专业研究机构、高等院校机构在网站、刊物、书籍等出版物中发布的信息获得。行业的经济运行数据则可以通过行业协会网站、商业化行业分析报告、证券公司行业分析报告、行业期刊获得。

在分析企业价值时，资产评估专业人员通常会采用一种自上而下的分析方法，即首先考虑企业运行的国家和地区的经济大环境，然后考虑行业环境，再考虑企业自身的特征。这里通常涉及三个层次的常用分析工具，即国家和地区经济分析、波特五力模型和SWOT分析方法。其中，国家和地区经济分析方法要求资产评估专业人员根据评估对象的具体情况，如规模大小、营业范围等，合理地估计国家的经济状况或者区域性的经济状况对评估对象所在行业产生的潜在影响；波特五力模型主要用于分析行业的经济环境，"五力"分别代表供应商的议价能力、购买者的议价能力、潜在竞争者进入的能力、替代品的替代能力、行业内竞争者现在的竞争能力，五种力量的不同组合最终影响行业利润潜力和企业的价值；SWOT分析法，又称为态势分析法或优劣势分析法，具体通过确定企业自身的竞争优势、竞争劣势、机会和威胁，将公司的战略与公司内部资源、外部环境有机地结合起来，是一种分析企业特征的常用方法。

Text* 正文

1. Information collection

Information collection is one of the critical steps in valuation. Source of information can be divided into <u>internal source</u> and <u>external source</u>.

1.1 Internal Source (From the Company)

1.1.1 Financial Data

We could obtain the financial data from the following ways. The first one is historical financial statements. In fact, a valuer usually requests from the company for its historical financial statements, including both annual and half-year financial statements, over the past five years. While, under certain circumstances including substantial changes in technology, products or the business environment related to the company, the valuer may need to examine additional previous financial statements. On the other hand, fewer financial statements may be acceptable if the company has made significant changes in the operational structure such as merger and acquisitions. Also, by examine the company's historical tax returns, the valuer may get a better picture of the financial conditions of the company, such as the taxation strategy of the company and the impact of tax expenses on its net income.

Moreover, it is a good indication of the company's view on its operations and the economic environment affecting it in the future if there is a projection provided by the company. Besides that, other financial information including <u>sales and purchase agreement</u>s, patents, trademarks, <u>share placement</u>, <u>pending litigation</u>s, contingent liabilities, etc. are also need to be considered.

1.1.2 Operating Data

Generally, a valuer can obtain plenty of information of the company from its website, such as the management members, products, subsidiaries, etc. Moreover, the valuer could have an <u>on-site visit</u> to the company to better understand the company's

---

* *Partly from: Zhonghe Appraisal Company Ltd, BMI Appraisals Limited Company, Business Valuation and Case Studies, China Financial &Economic Publishing House, 2010: 15-18.*

operations or meet the management to obtain additional financial and operational information, such as the strategies, futures planning and new products.

In addition, the valuer could check the company's legal documents to verify ownership of the company's assets, existence of contracts and other interests. The legal documents may include the business license, partnership agreements, sales and purchase agreements, <u>loan agreements</u>, <u>lease contracts</u>, etc.

1.2 External Source

1.2.1 The Country's Economy

The domestic economy usually has substantial impact on the performance of the company. Good economic conditions are associated with lower unemployment rate and higher wage. Under this situation, people tend to spend more money and as a result companies usually can make more profits. Reverse results will happen for a recession. In addition to domestic economy, the economy of foreign countries could have a significant impact on domestic companies, particularly for companies targeting at foreign markets.

The valuer usually can keep track of the economic conditions by study the key economic indicators including GDP, inflation rate, unemployment rate, <u>consumer price index</u>, interest rate, etc.

1.2.2 Local's Economic Conditions

For smaller companies, the impact of local economic conditions is more influential, especially if most of their customers are limited in that area. Therefore, when valuing a small company, a valuer should pay more attention to the economic data specifically for that area. Examples include demography, <u>income per capita</u>, local government planning, etc.

1.2.3 Industry Information

Industry information plays a critical role in estimating the future performance of the company, since this type of information is the closest and most influential external source of information for the company. For example, although both the country and the local area are in good economic conditions, a poor prospect of the industry in which a company operates can more than offset the good business environment provided by the country and the local area and thus seriously affect the business of the company. A valuer may easily obtain industry information from government departments, business chambers, trade associations, etc.

2. Analytical Techniques

To value the company, a valuer needs to make reasonable estimation of the company's future cash flows. In general, the valuer adopts an "up-down" approach, i.e., firstly look at the economy of the country in which the company operates, followed by the local economy, the industry, and lastly the characteristics of the company. Three analytical techniques corresponding to the above approach include Country and Local Economies Analysis, Porter's Five Force Analysis, and SWOT Analysis.

2.1 Country and Local Economies Analysis

2.1.1 Analysis of the Country's Economy

The economy of a country generally has a significant impact on most of the industries within the country. Therefore, a valuer should pay attention to both the current conditions and the future development of the economy to reasonably estimate its potential impact on the industry in which the company operates. The common economic indicators that the valuer is concerned with include GDP, inflation rate, interest rates, unemployment rate, etc.

2.1.2 Analysis of Local Economy

If a company is local and small, the local economy may have more direct influence on the prospects of the company than the country's economy. Therefore, the valuer should, in the initial stages of the valuation, pay attention to the scale of the business and its geographic coverage.

2.2 Porter's Five Forces Analysis

A valuer needs to closely study the subject industry to valuate the business environment, in particular, the competitiveness of the industry, as it can significantly affect the profitability of the company. Porter's Five Forces model is a commonly used models for that purpose. The model comprises of the following five components as shown in the Figure 6-1.

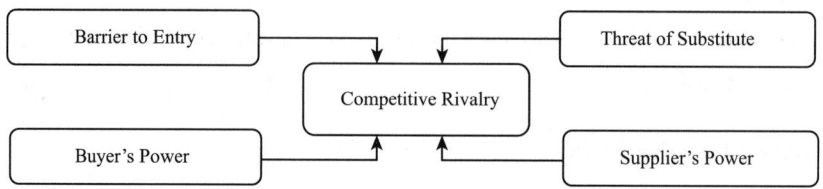

Figure 6-1　Porter's Five Forces Model

2.2.1 Barriers to Entry

Economies of scale, e.g., the benefits associated with bulk purchasing.

(a) The high or low cost of entry, e.g., how much will it cost for the latest technology?

(b) Ease of access to <u>distribution channels,</u> e.g. Do our competitors have the distribution channels sewn up?

(c) <u>Cost advantages</u> not related to the size of the company, e.g., personal contacts or knowledge that larger companies do not own or <u>learning curve effects</u>.

(d) Will competitors retaliate?

(e) Government action, e.g., will new laws be introduced that will weaken our competitive position?

(f) How important is differentiation? For instance, the Champagne brand cannot be copied. This desensitizes the influence of the environment.

2.2.2 Buyer's Power

(a) Large volume of a company's business (High Buyer Concentration);

(b) Availability of information;

(c) Buyer's low cost of switching products;

(d) High number of <u>alternate suppliers</u>.

2.2.3 Supplier's Power

(a) The power of suppliers tends to be a reversal of the power of buyers;

(b) The switching costs are high e.g., switching from one software supplier to another;

(c) Power is concentrated if the brand is powerful e.g., Cadillac, Pizza Hut, and Microsoft;

(d) There is a possibility of the supplier integrating forward e.g., Brewers buying bars;

(e) Customers are fragmented (not in clusters) so that they have little bargaining power e.g., Gas/Petrol stations in remote places;

(f) Reputation of Supplier and Demand for its Goods.

2.2.4 Competitive Rivalry

(a) Ability of rival companies to respond to change;

(b) Advertising of rival companies;

(c) Research and development of rival companies;

(d) Alliances of rival companies and suppliers;

(e) Increase in competition.

2.2.5 Threat of Substitutes

(a) There is a product-for-product substitution e.g., email for fax;

(b) There is a substitution of need e.g., better toothpaste reduces the need for dentists;

(c) There is generic substitution (competing for the currency in your pocket) e.g., Video suppliers compete with travel companies.

2.3 SWOT Analysis

When assessing a company's characteristics, a valuer can use SWOT analysis including strengths, weaknesses, opportunities and threats to investigate the company, especially its competitive advantages. The analysis includes:

2.3.1 Strengths

(a) the ownership of patents and/or trademarks;

(b) Strong brand;

(c) Innovation of product lines;

(d) Leadership in research and development;

(e) Marketing effectiveness;

(f) Core competencies (outstanding skills that are better than those of the competitors).

2.3.2 Weaknesses

(a) Lack of marketing expertise;

(b) Undifferentiated products or services (i.e., in relation to the competitors);

(c) Poor quality goods or services;

(d) Damaged reputation;

(e) Poor access to distribution channels;

(f) High-cost structure;

(g) Weak bargaining power for suppliers and buyers;

2.3.3 Opportunities

(a) A developing market such as the internet;

(b) Mergers, joint ventures or strategic alliances;

(c) Moving into new market segments that offer improved profits;

(d) A new international market;

(e) A market vacated by an ineffective competitor.

2.3.4 Threats

(a) A new competitor in your home market;

(b) Price wars with competitors;

(c) A competitor has a new, innovative product or service;

(d) Competitors have superior access to channels of distribution;

(e) New taxation is introduced on your product or service.

Core Words and Expressions 核心术语

internal source	内部来源
external source	外部来源
sales and purchase agreement	买卖协议
share placement	股份处置
pending litigation	未决诉讼
on-site visit	实地勘查
loan agreement	贷款协议
lease contract	租赁合约
consumer price index (CPI)	消费者物价指数
income per capita	人均收入
offset	抵消
business chamber	商会
analytical technique	分析技术
profitability	盈利能力
Porter's Five Forces Model	波特五力模型
distribution channels	分销渠道
cost advantage	成本优势
learning curve effect	学习曲线效应
alternate supplier	备用供应商
switching cost	转换成本
integrating forward	前向一体化
bargaining power	议价能力
competitive advantage	竞争优势

product line	生产线
marketing effectiveness	市场营销效果
cost structure	成本结构
joint venture	合资企业
strategic alliance	战略联盟
price war	价格战

Questions and Discussion 问题与讨论

1. Please sketch the macro-economic factors you can learn from this part.

2. Please explain the Potter's five forces model. What role does it play in valuation?

3. Why does a valuer use SWOT analysis during business valuation process?

Topic2: M&A Valuation Process 企业并购估值流程

Abstract 中文摘要

企业价值评估程序是指资产评估专业人员执行企业价值评估业务所履行的系统性工作步骤。本节重点以并购这一企业价值评估的常见评估目的为例，介绍企业并购估值的基本流程。企业并购是将两个或两个以上单独的企业合并形成一个报告主体的交易或事项，被认为是短期内改变公司战略的途径之一，但其本身也存在着并购成本。企业并购估值的基本步骤如下：

（1）确定并购动机及基本策略。常见的并购动机包括收购价值被低估的公司、归类合并以实现规模经济和降低风险、获得协同效应、接管有管理漏洞的公司并改善管理水平、迎合管理层自身的利益需求等。

（2）确定目标公司并对其进行估值。一旦并购动机及基本策略形成，即需要确定两个关键事项：一是如何识别最优的潜在目标公司；二是如何对目标公司进行估值。其中，协同效应是企业并购估值的一个重要方面，具体包括经营协同效应、财务协同效应、管理协同效应等类型。本节将重点介绍前两种协同效应。

（3）确定交易结构并为合约支付成本。在目标公司及其估值结果明确以后，则需要进一步确认最终收购价格、资金筹集来源以及具体支付方式等问题。首先，收购公司需要确定支付给目标公司的货币数额；其次，需要确定资金筹集来源及具体交付方式，如使用股票、使用现金或者两者兼有；最后，需要选择交易的会计处理方式，因为这会影响到目标公司的税款缴纳以及收购公司的资产负债表和利润表。

（4）处理其他并购后续事项。这是企业并购的最后一步，或许也是在交易完成后使并购动机能够顺利实现的最具挑战性的一步。因为并非所有并购都会取得成功。一些并购在完成后并没有实现预期的高效率和协同效应，从而成为失败的并购案例；也有些企业在前一阶段的效益考核中被认为是失败的并购，但在后期的发展中又成功实现了企业增值，转而被视为是成功的并购案例；甚至有个别恶意的收购行为最终也被认为是成功案例。

Text* 正文

When analysing investment decisions, we neglect the largest investment decisions that most firms make in details, i.e., their acquisitions of other firms. Boeing's largest investment of the last decade was not a new commercial aircraft but its acquisition of McDonnell Douglas in 1996. At the time of the acquisition, Boeing's managers were optimistic about the merger, claiming substantial value for the stockholders of both firms. What are the principles that govern acquisitions? Should they be judged differently from other investments?

Firms are acquired for a number of reasons. In the 1960s and 1970s, firms such as Gulf and Western and ITT built themselves into conglomerates by acquiring firms in other lines of business. In the 1980s, corporate giants such as Time, Beatrice and RJR Nabisco were acquired by other firms, their own management or wealthy <u>raiders</u> who saw potential value in restructuring or breaking up these firms. In the 1990s, we saw a wave of <u>consolidation</u> in the media business as telecommunications firms acquired

---

* Partly from: Damodaran A. Acquisitions and Takeover, Handbook of Finance. John Wiley & Sons, Inc., 2008:1-11.

entertainment firms, and entertainment firms acquired cable businesses. Through time, firms have also acquired or merged with other firms to gain the benefits of <u>synergy</u>, in the form of either higher growth, as in the Disney acquisition of <u>Capital Cities</u>, or lower costs.

Acquisitions seem to offer firms a short cut to their strategic objectives, but the process incurs costs. We examine the four basic steps in an acquisition: establishing an acquisition motive, the identification and valuation of a target firm, structuring and paying for the deal, and the most difficult, making the acquisition work after the deal is consummated.

1. The Process of an Acquisition

Acquisitions can be friendly or hostile events. In a friendly acquisition, the managers of the target firm welcome the acquisition and, in some cases, seek it out. In a hostile acquisition, the target firm's management resists to be acquired. The <u>acquiring firm</u> offers a price higher than the target firm's market price prior to the acquisition and invites stockholders in the target firm to tender their shares for the price.

In either friendly or hostile acquisitions, the difference between the acquisition price and the market price prior to the acquisition is called the <u>acquisition premium</u>. The acquisition price, in the context of mergers and consolidations, is the price that will be paid by the acquiring firm for each of the target firm's shares. The acquisition price is usually based upon negotiations between the acquiring firm and the target firm's managers. In a <u>tender offer</u>, it is the price at which the acquiring firm receives enough shares to gain control of the target firm. The price may be higher than the initial one offered by the acquirer, if other firms bid for the same target firm or if an insufficient number of stockholders tender at that initial price. For instance, in 1991, AT&T initially offered to buy NCR for $80 per share, a premium of $25 over the stock price at the time of the offer. AT&T ultimately paid $110 per share to complete the acquisition.

There is one final comparison that can be made, which is between the price paid on the acquisition and the accounting book value of the equity in the firm being acquired. Depending upon how the acquisition is accounted for, the difference can be recorded as goodwill on the acquiring firm's books or not be recorded at all.

2. Steps in an Acquisition

There are four basics, not necessarily sequential, steps in acquiring a target firm. The first is the development of a rationale and a strategy for acquisitions, and to investigate the resources requirement. The second is the choice of a target for the acquisition and the valuation of the target firm, with premiums for the value of control and any synergy. The third is the determination of how much to pay on the acquisition, how to raise funds, and whether to use stock or cash. The above decision has significant implications for the choice of accounting treatment for the acquisition. The final step in the acquisition, and perhaps the most challenging one, is to make the acquisition work after the deal is complete.

2.1 Developing an Acquisition Strategy

Not all firms that make acquisitions have acquisition strategies, and not all firms that have acquisition strategies stick with them. In this part, we consider a number of different motives for acquisitions and suggest that a coherent acquisition strategy has to be based on one or another of these motives.

2.1.1 Acquire undervalued firms

Firms that are undervalued by financial markets can be targeted for acquisition by those who recognize the mispricing. The acquirer can then gain the difference between the value and the purchase price as surplus.

2.1.2 Diversify to reduce risk

Diversification reduces an investor's exposure to firm-specific risk. In fact, the risk and return models have been built on the presumption that the firm-specific risk can be diversified away and hence not be rewarded. By buying firms in other businesses and diversifying, acquiring firms' managers believe that they can reduce earnings volatility and risk, and increase potential value.

2.1.3 Create operating or financial synergy

Create operating or financial synergy is the third reason to explain the significant premiums paid in most acquisitions is synergy. Synergy is the potential additional value from combining two firms. It is probably the most widely used and misused rationale for mergers and acquisitions.

2.1.4 Take over poorly managed firms and change management

Some firms are not managed optimally and others often believe they can run them better than the current managers. Acquiring poorly managed firms and removing incumbent management, or at least changing existing management policy or practices, should make these firms more valuable, allowing the acquirer to claim the increase in value. This value increase is often termed the value of control.

2.1.5 Cater to managerial self interest

In most acquisitions, it is the managers of the acquiring firm who decide whether to carry out the acquisition and how much to pay for it, rather than the stockholders of the same firm. Given these circumstances, the motive for some acquisitions may not be stockholder wealth maximization, but managerial self-interest.

2.2 Choosing a Target firm and valuing control/synergy

Once a firm has an acquisition motive, there are two key questions that need to be answered. The first relates to how to best identify a potential target firm for an acquisition. The other more concrete one is how to value a target firm.

2.3 Structuring the Acquisition

Once the target firm has been identified and valued, the acquisition moves forward into the structuring phase. There are three interrelated steps in this phase. The first is to decide the amount payable to the target firm, given that we have valued it, with synergy and control built into the valuation. The second is to decide the payment method, i.e., using stock, cash or some combination of the two, and borrowing any of the funds needed. The final step is the choice of the accounting treatment of the deal because it can affect both taxes paid by stockholders in the target firm and how the purchase is accounted for in the acquiring firm's income statement and balance sheets.

2.4 Following up on the Acquisition

We have described how firms value, pay for's and structure an acquisition. However, the real work in an acquisition occurs after the transaction. We examine the evidence on the success or failure of mergers at enhancing value and the reasons why mergers are easy to fail.

Many studies examine the extent to which mergers and acquisitions succeed or fail after the firms combine. Most studies conclude that many mergers fail, and even those that do deliver the promised efficiency seldom create value for the acquirers' stockholders.

There are clearly exceptions to this pattern of failure. Some firms, such as GE, Cisco and Browning Ferris, have successfully increased value over time using acquisitions. Even those firms classified as failures in the studies quoted in the previous section can claim that it takes time for acquisitions to work and create value. Some studies also find improvements in operating efficiency after mergers, especially hostile ones.

3. Operating and Financial Synergy

3.1 Sources of Operating Synergy

Operating synergies are those synergies that increase firm operating income, growth or both. We categorize operating synergies into five types:

(a) Economies of scale that may arise from the merger, allowing the combined firm more cost-efficient and profitable.

(b) Greater pricing power from reduced competition and higher market share, which results in higher margins and operating income.

(c) Combination of different functional strengths, as would be the case when a firm with strong marketing skills acquires a firm with a good product line.

(d) Higher growth in new or existing markets, arising from the combination of the two firms, would be the case when a US consumer products firm acquires an emerging market firm, with an established distribution network and brand name recognition, and uses these strengths to increase sales of its products.

(e) Operating synergies can affect margins and growth, through which the value of the firms involve in the merger or acquisition.

3.2 Sources of Financial Synergy

With financial synergies, the payoff can take the form of either higher cash flows or a lower cost of capital (discount rate), as shown by the following:

(a) A combination of a firm with excess cash, or cash slack, (and limited project opportunities) and a firm with high-return projects (and limited cash) can yield a payoff in terms of higher value for the combined firm. The increase in value comes from the projects taken with the excess cash that otherwise would not have been taken. The synergy is likely to show up most often for large firms acquiring smaller firms, or for publicly traded firms acquiring private businesses.

(b) Debt capacity can increase, because firms' earnings and cash flows may become more stable and predictable when two firms combine, allowing them to borrow more than they could have as individual entities, which creates a tax benefit for the combined firm. The tax benefit can either be shown as higher cash flows, or take the form of a lower cost of capital for the combined firm.

(c) Tax benefits can arise either from the acquisition taking advantage of tax laws or from the use of net operating losses to shelter income. Thus, a profitable firm that acquires a money-losing firm may be able to use the net operating losses of the latter to reduce its tax burden. Alternatively, a firm capable of increasing its depreciation charges after an acquisition can save in taxes, and increase its value.

Clearly, there is potential for synergy in many mergers. The important issues are whether or not the synergy can be valued and, if so, how to value it.

Finally, on the issue of synergy, the KPMG study of the 700 largest deals from 1996 to 1998 concludes the following:

(a) Firms that valuate synergy carefully before an acquisition are 28% more likely to succeed than firms that do not.

(b) Cost saving synergies associated with reducing the number of employees is more likely to be accomplished than new product development or R&D synergies. For instance, only a quarter to a third of firms succeeded on the latter, whereas 66% of firms were able to reduce headcount after mergers.

Core Words and Expressions 核心术语

raider	入侵者
consolidation	合并
synergy	协同效应
Capital Cities	大都会通讯公司
acquiring firm	收购方
acquisition premium	收购溢价
tender offer	要约收购
value of control	控制权价值
stockholder wealth maximization	股东财富最大化

Questions and Discussion 问题与讨论

1. Please summarize the article briefly.
2. Please explain the significant premiums paid in most acquisitions.
3. Please analyse how the synergy in M&A should be valued.

Information Extension

思政微课堂

2021年,《中华人民共和国国民经济和社会发展第十四个五年规划和2035年远景目标纲要》提出,要"实施高标准市场体系建设行动,健全市场体系基础制度,坚持平等准入、公正监管、开放有序、诚信守法,形成高效规范、公平竞争的国内统一市场""健全协同高效的监督机制,严格责任追究,切实防止国有资产流失"。2022年,党的二十大报告强调,要"构建高水平社会主义市场经济体制""完善产权保护、市场准入、公平竞争、社会信用等市场经济基础制度,优化营商环境""深化国资国企改革,加快国有经济布局优化和结构调整,推动国有资本和国有企业做强做优做大,提升企业核心竞争力"。资产评估行业作为现代高端服务业,是经济社会发展中的重要专业力量,在提升市场信息披露质量、促进国有资产保值增值、保障资本市场良性运行和国有资产安全等方面发挥着不可或缺的作用。资产评估介入市场主体的产权交易,既抑制了交易主体的非理性行为,也为政府有效监管提供了"数据库"。正是资产评估职能的发挥,才将"看不见的手"和"看得见的手"融合,使"公开、公平、公正"的经济秩序得以维护和优化。

中国是世界第一工业大国、世界第一人口大国、世界第二经济强国。国有企业是中国特色社会主义的重要物质基础和政治基础,是中国共产党执政兴国的重要支柱和依靠力量。2022年,全国国有企业营业收入达到82.6万亿元,利润总额为4.3万亿元;国有上市公司也通过并购重组继续深化践行国企改革行动方案,依旧是上市公司重大资产重组的主力,反映了国资产业布局、战略性重组和专业化整合持续向纵深推进的趋势。在服务于国有企业的评估业务类型中,资产评估以维护国家利益为最高准则,以防止国有资产的流失为目标,为国有资产的确认、登记、并购、增资、股权转让等经济行为提供专业化的评估服务,力求更好促进国有资本和国有企业高质量发展。30多年来,我国出台了多项法律法规和行业准则以规范资产评估行为,促进国有资产有序流转。例如,为了正确体现国有资产的价值量,保护国有资产所有者和经营者、使用者的合法权益,国务院于1991年发布《国有资产评估管理办法》(国务院令第91号),标志着我国资产评估行业走上法制化的道路;国务院国有资产监督管理委员会于2005年颁布《企业国有资产评估管理办法》(国务院国资委第12号令);财政部于2007年颁布《金融企业国有资产评估监督管理暂行办法》(财政部第47号令)。2009年,国务院国有资产监督管理委员会印发《关于企业国有资产评估报告审核工作有关事项的通知》,要求各级国有资产监督管理机构应依照中国资产评估协会发布的《企业国有资产评估报告指南》(中评协〔2008〕218号)进行审核。2012年,财政部颁布《中央文化企业国有资产评估管理暂行办法》(财文资〔2012〕15号),进一步加强中央文化企业国有资产评估管理。根据2016年出台的《中华人民共和国资产评估法》,中国资产评估协会新修订的《资产评估执业准则——企业价值》(中评协〔2018〕38号)自2019年1月1日起施行,《企业国有资产评估报告指南》(中评协〔2017〕42号)和《金融企业国有资产评估报告指南》(中评协〔2017〕43号）自2017年10月1日起施行。纵观我国经济所有制改革的发展历程，资产评估基于防止国有资产流失、维护国有资产权益的需求而产生，在改革开放和建立社会主义市场经济体制过程中逐渐兴起，在历次经济体制改革中发挥了不可或缺的重要作用。现阶段，国有企业发展进入崭新阶段，资产评估将继续在"十四五"以及未来新发展格局下，为维护国有资产出资人合法权益、促进企业国有产权有序流转、国有资产公平定价和人民财富保值增值等目标的实现提供服务支撑。

Chapter 7
Valuations for Financial Reporting
以财务报告为目的的评估

Wisdom
名人名言

岁终,则会计其政。

——周公旦

零星算之为计,总合算之为会。

——焦循

Financial statements are like fine perfume; to be sniffed but not swallowed.

—Abraham Briloff

The future is not what it used to be.

—Paul Valery

Chapter 7 Valuations for Financial Reporting 以财务报告为目的的评估

Rudimentary Knowledge
基本知识

Abstract 中文摘要

以财务报告为目的的评估主要服务于在财务报告准备过程中不同的财务目的，包括对需要计入报表的资产和负债价值的衡量、企业合并对价分摊、减值测试、租赁分类以及资产折旧费用的计算等具体类型，并需要参照国际财务报告准则（IFRS）、国际会计准则（IAS）和当地会计准则的相关要求进行。中国资产评估会于2017年修订发布了《以财务报告为目的的评估指南》（中评协〔2017〕45号），对以财务报告为目的的评估行为予以规范。

公允价值计量是以财务报告为目的的评估中必不可少的环节。以财务报告为目的的评估中所指公允价值与资产评估价值类型中市场价值、公平价值的概念比较接近。与此同时，公允价值（公允市场价值）在不同会计准则框架下的定义又略有差异。例如，国际财务报告准则（IFRS）和中国《企业会计准则第39号——公允价值计量》都将公允价值定义为：市场参与者在计量日发生的有序交易中，出售一项资产所能收到或者转移一项负债所需支付的价格；经济合作与发展组织（OECD）将公允市场价值定义为：在公开市场上，自愿买方和自愿卖方的交易价格。国际评估准则理事会（IVSC）在制定国际评估准则（IVS）时，对出自不同会计准则框架下的公允价值的定义分别进行了引用，并给予了实质性调整。此外，资产评估中的贬值与财务报告中的折旧存在一定差异。

Text* 正文

Valuations are required for different accounting purposes in the preparation of the financial reports or statements of companies and other entities. Examples of different accounting purposes include measurement of the value of an asset or liability for

---

* Partly from: The International Valuation Standards Council (IVSC), International Valuation Standards, 2011 Edition, 2011; The International Valuation Standards Council (IVSC), International Valuation Standards, 2022 Edition, 2021.

inclusion on the statement of financial position, allocation of the purchase price of an acquired business, impairment testing, lease classification and valuation inputs to the calculation of depreciation charges in the profit and loss account. And it requires to reference the International Financial Reporting Standards (IFRS), International Accounting Standards (IAS) and local accounting standards.

1. Purchase Price Allocation

Goodwill is the difference between the acquisition price paid in the transfer of the business and the fair value of the vendor's net identifiable assets acquired. Following a business combination, i.e., the acquisition of a controlling interest in one or more other businesses, it requires the acquirer to account for the transaction by recognizing the vendor's separately identifiable assets acquired and liabilities assumed at fair value.

Actually, a business's tangible assets are generally readily identifiable and can be separately valued. However, the identification and valuation of the separately identifiable intangible assets can be more challenging. Moreover, in addition to the general situation, there are some exceptions to the recognition and/or measurement of identifiable assets and liabilities including contingent liabilities, income taxes, employee benefits, indemnification assets, reacquired rights, share-based payment awards and assets held for sale, which need special requirements.

2. Impairment Testing

Impairment arises if the carrying amount of an asset exceeds the amount that can be recovered from either its continued use and/or the sale of the asset. An entity is required to review certain categories of asset at the date of each statement of financial position to determine whether an asset may be impaired. Impairment might be indicated by a reduction in the value of the asset because of market or technological changes, obsolescence of the asset, asset underperformance in comparison to the expected return, or an intention to discontinue or restructure operations. Certain assets, such as goodwill and intangibles with an indefinite life or not yet available for use, would be tested for impairment on an annual basis.

If impairment has arisen, the carrying amount of the asset, whether derived from either historic cost or a previous valuation, should be written down to the "recoverable amount", which is the higher of the value in use and fair value less costs to sell. It is not necessary to determine both values, if either exceeds the asset's carrying amount, the asset is not impaired and it is not necessary to estimate the other one.

2.1 Value in Use

Value in use is the present value of the future cash flows expected to be derived from the asset or cash-generating unit, which is the smallest identifiable group of assets that generates cash inflows. Value in use is specific to the entity as it reflects the cash flows that the entity expects to obtain from continuing use of an asset over its anticipated useful life, including any proceeds from its ultimate disposal.

The following shall be considered in the calculation of value in use:

(a) an estimate of the future cash flows the entity expects to derive from the asset,

(b) expectations about possible variations in the amount or timing of those future cash flows,

(c) the time value of money, represented by the current market risk free rate of interest,

(d) the price for bearing the uncertainty inherent in the asset,

(e) other factors, such as illiquidity, that market participants would reflect in pricing the future cash flows the entity expects to derive from the asset.

The expected cash flows need be tested for reasonableness by ensuring that the assumptions on which the entity's projections are based are consistent with past actual outcomes, provided the effects of subsequent events or circumstances that do not exist if those actual cash flows are generated appropriately. Cash flows of the asset are estimated based on asset's current condition and therefore the expected cash flows should not reflect any increase due to any restructuring or reconditioning of the asset to which the entity is not currently committed.

The appropriate discount rate reflects the return that market participants would require for an investment that would generate cash flows of amounts, timing and risk profile equivalent to those that the entity expects to derive from the asset.

2.2 Fair Value Less Costs to Sell

The fair value less costs to sell of an asset or cash-generating unit is the amount obtainable from its sale in an arm's length transaction between knowledgeable, willing parties, less the costs of disposal. They attributable to the transaction directly, e.g., legal fees, marketing costs, removal costs, unrecoverable transaction taxes and any costs directly incurred in preparing the asset or cash-generating unit for sale, but exclude consequential costs such as those involved in reorganising the business following the disposal.

3. Investment Property Measurement

Investment property is defined as property held by the owner to earn rentals or for capital appreciation, or both including land or a building, or part of a building, or both. Furthermore, investment property includes property constructed or developed for future use as investment property. While property intended for sale in the ordinary course of business or in the process of construction or development for such sale is not regarded as investment property.

Investment property is initially recognized in financial statements at its cost of purchase plus any directly attributable costs. For subsequent recognition, the entity may adopt either the fair value model or the cost model for all its investment property.

The fair value model presumes that the fair value can be reliably determined on a continuing basis. In some exceptional circumstances, an entity may adopt the cost model for that property, e.g., when the market for comparable properties is inactive while methods such as discounted cash flow cannot be used to provide a reliable measurement. The fact that this is only permissible in exceptional circumstances is reinforced by the general requirement in the standard that if an entity has previously measured an investment property at fair value, it shall continue to measure the property at fair value even if comparable market transactions become less frequent or market prices become less readily available. If the fair value of an investment property under construction cannot be reliably measured, it can be measured at cost, until either its fair value becomes reliably measurable or construction is completed, whichever is earlier.

4. Leases

Leases are classified for inclusion in financial statements as either operating leases or <u>finance leases</u>. A finance lease is a lease that transfers substantially all the risks and rewards incidental to ownership of an asset. Title may or may not be eventually transferred. An operating lease is a lease other than a finance lease. For leases of property (real estate), special rules apply. Other than for investment property, the land and buildings elements of a property interest have to be considered separately for classification as either a finance lease or an operating lease.

4.1 Lease Classification

The classification test depends on the substance rather than the form of the contract.

The following examples could be indicative of a finance lease, either individually or in combination. These are illustrations rather than absolute tests:

(a) The lease transfers ownership of the asset to the lessee by the end of the <u>lease term</u>,

(b) The lessee has the option to purchase the asset at a price expected to be sufficiently lower than the fair value at the date the option becomes exercisable for it to be reasonably certain, at the inception of the lease, that the option will be exercised,

(c) The lease term is for the major part of the economic life of the asset even if title is not transferred,

(d) At the inception of the lease, the present value of the minimum lease payments amounts to at least substantially all of the fair value of the leased asset,

(e) The leased assets are of such a specialized nature that only the lessee can use without major modifications,

(f) If the lessee can cancel the lease, the lessor's losses associated with the cancellation are borne by the lessee,

(g) Gains or losses from the fluctuation in the fair value of the residual accrue to the lessee,

(h) The lessee has the ability to continue the lease for a secondary period at a rent that is substantially lower than market rent.

It is emphasized that the criteria listed are examples and indicators and may not be conclusive. If it is clear from other features that the lease does not transfer substantially all risks and rewards incidental to ownership, the lease is classified as an operating lease. For example, if ownership of the asset transfers at the end of the lease for a variable payment equal to its then value, or if regular reviews of the rent exist, to the market level or by reference to inflation index. Lease classification is made at the inception of the lease. Classification involves an assessment of the degree to which economic benefits are transferred. In many cases a qualitative assessment of the lease terms indicates the correct classification without the need for a valuation of the different lease interests. However, valuations may be required to help establish benefits accruing to the lessor and lessee respectively, e.g., in estimating the residual value at the end of the lease to establish if the lease is for a major part of the asset's economic life.

4.2 Classification of Property Leases

A lease of land and a building or buildings together requires that the two elements be considered separately for the purposes of classification. If it appears that the element of the lease attributable to the building could be a finance lease, it is necessary to make an allocation of the initial rent based on the relative fair values of the interest in each element at the inception of the lease.

For most property leases the interest in the leased land and buildings reverts to the lessor at the end of the lease. There are provisions for the rent to be reviewed periodically to reflect changes in the value of the property, and frequently an obligation on the lessee to return the buildings back to the lessor in good condition. Above indicate that the lessor did not transfer substantially all the risks and rewards of ownership of either the buildings or the land to the lessee when the lease was granted. Consequently, many leases of land and buildings are readily identifiable as operating leases.

Finance leases of land and buildings generally arise if the lease is clearly created as a way of funding the eventual purchase of the property by the lessee, e.g., by means of an option to acquire the lessor's interest for a nominal sum after the specified rental payments have been made. Occasionally, leases not clearly structured as finance agreements may meet some of the criteria of a finance lease, e.g., where the rental payments do not reflect the underlying value of the property. In such cases, a more detailed analysis of the value of the risks and benefits transferred from lessor to lessee may be required in order to determine the correct classification.

Wherever a lease is of a plot of land and a building is constructed upon it, allocating the rent to each element is a task that can be undertaken reliably where there is an active market for land for similar development in the locality. If the lease is of part of a multi-let building with no identifiable land attributable to any particular lease, reliable allocation may be impossible. The whole lease should be treated as a finance lease, unless it is clear that both elements are operating leases. If both elements are operating leases from the outset, the allocation exercise would not be necessary.

In practice, leases of part of a multi-let building are normally operating leases and the whole property is classified as investment property by the lessor. In such cases, allocation is unnecessary. If the building element is clearly a finance lease, the land element is likely to be identifiable. It is comparatively rare for the building element to meet the criteria for classification as a finance lease and for the land element not to be clearly identifiable. However, if such a case is identified, an allocation between the land and the building element should not be attempted based on unreliable criteria. In such circumstances, the whole of the leased property should be accounted for as a finance lease.

4.3 Leased Investment Property

It is not necessary to make an allocation between the land and buildings elements of an investment property held under a lease and accounted for using the fair value model.

Investment property is frequently held by an investor under a lease, e.g., a long lease of land on which it has developed buildings, which are then leased as an investment. Because land does not normally depreciate, a lease of land would appear to be correctly classified as an operating lease and therefore excluded from the statement of financial position. However, since many substantial investment properties are held on this basis, the initial recognition an investment property held under a lease shall be accounted for as though it were a finance lease.

Although the foregoing provisions mean that questions of classification and allocation do not generally arise in relation to investment property, a potential anomaly remains. The value of the investor's interest in an investment property held under a lease reflects the difference between the payments under the superior lease and the receipts or potential receipts under the sub lease or leases. However, it is inappropriate for the liabilities for leased assets to be presented in the financial statements as a deduction from the leased assets.

In order to comply with this requirement, wherever a valuation of an investment property held under a lease is net of all payments expected to be made, it is necessary to add back any recognized lease liability to arrive at the carrying amount. It should be noted that this is an accounting adjustment only and should neither be reflected nor anticipated in the valuation of the investor's (lessor's) interest.

4.4 Valuing the Lease Asset or Liability

Wherever a lease is identified as a finance lease, lessees are required to account for the asset and liability based on either the fair value of the leased asset or the present value of the minimum lease payments, whichever is lower, each determined as at the inception of the lease.

The value of the asset is considered separately from any liability created by the lease. When accounting for a lessee's interest in a finance lease it is therefore necessary to measure the asset by assessing the value of the benefit that a market participant would accrue from the right to use the asset for the duration of the lease. In terms of leases of property, other than investment property, it is important to note that this is not the same as the value of the lessee's interest created by the lease, as the latter reflects the lease liability as well as the value of the asset.

In summary, they are the payments over the lease term that the lessee is required to make, excluding any contingent rent, taxes and amounts paid to the lessor for services. The minimum lease payments include any residual value guaranteed by the lessee to the lessor. Since contingent rents are excluded from the calculation of the minimum lease payments and the payments should be clear from the face of the lease, valuations are not normally required.

The present value of the minimum lease payments should be calculated using a discount rate equivalent to the interest rate implicit in the lease or, if this is not practicably determinable, the lessee's incremental borrowing rate. The calculation of the interest rate implicit in the lease requires the fair value of the unencumbered leased asset at the date of the lease inception and its residual value at the end of the lease.

5. Depreciation

International Accounting Standards include a requirement for an entity to account for the depreciation of property, plant and equipment. Depreciation in the context of financial reporting is a charge made against income in the financial statements to reflect the consumption of an asset over its useful life to the entity. To depreciate separately components of an asset that have a cost that is significant in relation to the whole is required. Components that have a similar useful life and that are depreciated in a similar manner may be grouped. Land is not normally depreciated. Valuations are often required to support the calculation of the depreciable amount.

The term depreciation is used differently in valuation and in financial reporting. In the context of valuation, depreciation often refers to the adjustments made when using the cost approach to the cost of reproducing or replacing the asset to reflect obsolescence in order to indicate the value of the asset when no direct sales evidence available. In the context of financial reporting, depreciation refers to the charge made against income to reflect the systematic allocation of the depreciable amount of an asset over its useful life to the entity.

In order to assess the depreciation charge to be made, the depreciable amount has to be determined, which is the cost of an asset or other amount substituted for cost in the financial statements, less its residual value. It means the difference between the carrying amount of the asset and its residual value. Carrying amount is the amount at which an asset is recognized after deducting any accumulated depreciation or amortization and accumulated impairment losses thereon. And residual value is the estimated amount that an entity would currently obtain from disposal of an asset, after deducting the estimated costs of disposal, if the asset is of the age and in the condition expected at the end of its useful life. In order to determine the residual value, the useful life of the asset, the period over which an asset is expected to be available for use by an entity, or the number of production or similar units expected to be obtained from the asset by an entity, has also to be determined.

Furthermore, it should be noted that the carrying amount may be based on either historic cost or fair value, less accumulated depreciation (amortization) and accumulated impairment losses. The residual value and the useful life have to be reviewed at least at every financial year end.

5.1 Depreciation: Land and Buildings

Land normally has an unlimited useful life. Therefore, it should be accounted for separately and not depreciated. The first step in establishing the depreciable amount attributable to a property, or a part of a property, is therefore to establish the value of the land component, which is normally done by establishing the value of the land at the date of the relevant financial statement and then deducting from the carrying amount for the property interest, i.e., the land and buildings combined, in order to establish the element that can be attributed to the buildings. This is a notional value as it would not be realized as buildings usually cannot be sold without the land on which they sit.

Having established the notional value for the building component, the residual value of the building needs to be estimated. The useful life needs to be established. It is important to note that it may not be the same as the remaining economic life as would be recognized by a typical market participant. The useful life is specific to the entity. If the property would not be available to the entity for the whole life or if the entity determines that the building is surplus to its requirements in a shorter period, it is the useful life.

The residual value is a value as of the date of the financial statement and on the assumption that the asset is at the end of its useful life and in a condition commensurate with that assumption. Buildings may have an economic life that extends beyond the period for which they will be available to or required by the entity and therefore may have a significant residual value.

5.2 Depreciation: Plant and Equipment

The useful life of an item of plant or equipment is more likely to coincide with the economic life of the item because rates of obsolescence are generally higher than for buildings, with the result that economic lives are shorter. However, the distinction between the useful life to the entity and remaining economic life should be considered.

5.3 Depreciation: Componentization

While the carrying amount is based on historic cost, the cost of those components that both have a significant cost in relation to the total and that have a materially different useful life should be readily identifiable.

Wherever the carrying amount is based on the fair value of the item, an allocation need to be made of the fair value of the item between the components. It may be possible to determine the value attributable to a component of an item of plant or equipment if there is an active market for those components, otherwise the components may not be actively traded. The latter is normally the case with components of a building, e.g., buildings are rarely sold without the mechanical and electrical services needed for heating, lighting and ventilation, and the installed plant could not be sold without the building. If the value of the individual components cannot be reliably determined, the value attributable to the whole is apportioned to the components. The ratio of the cost of the item to the cost of the whole may be an appropriate basis for such an apportionment.

Core Words and Expressions 核心术语

allocation of the purchase price	对价分摊，购买价格分配
impairment testing	减值测试
lease classification	租赁分类
depreciation charge	折旧费
indemnification	赔偿，保护，赦免，补偿金

recoverable amount	可回收金额
finance lease	融资租赁
lease term	租赁期
proviso	附带条件，附文，限制性条款
residual value	剩余价值，残值
amortization	分期偿还，摊销
useful life	使用寿命，有效期

Questions and Discussion 问题与讨论

1. What are the types of valuations for Financial Reporting?

2. Please describe what impairing test is and how it is done?

3. Find a financial report from the internet and try to analyse its fair value to the best of your knowledge.

More Knowledge
知识扩展

Topic 1: Fair Value and Financial Reporting
公允价值与财务报告

Abstract 中文摘要

公允价值及其计量在会计与审计的处理中起到了越来越重要的作用。其中，最突出的变化就是处理方式从以基础规则为指导逐步过渡为以实际原则为指导。这要求专业人士在工作中要根据特定情况原则来做出合理判断。这也意味着财务报告已经进入了一个会计范式与经济信息相适应的新时代。

财务报告中的公允价值不简单等同于市价。它是在计量日市场参与者之间的有序交易中，出售一项资产所收到的或转让一项负债所支付的对价。公允价值的计量，根据市场的可观察性和报告主体进入活跃市场的程度可分为三个层级：

第一层级：输入值为可观察的输入值，即在计量日企业有能力进入的活跃市场中相同资产或负债的报价；

第二层级：输入值为可观察的输入值，但是除第一层级以外，对于资产或负债直接或间接可观察到的价格；

第三层级：此时输入值对于目标资产或负债是不可观察的。

第一层级和第二层级中的输入值有时被称为是"市场对市场"的输入，第三层级中的输入值有时被称为是由"市场到模型"的输入。

被用来计量公允价值的估值技术与市场法、收益法和成本法相一致，且其目标是最大限度地利用市场输入值。市场法以替代原则为基础，反映市场对投入或拥有的事物的预期回报态度；收益法用以量化资产预期产生的回报；成本法以重置成本为基础，反映资产的拥有和投入。

Text* 正文

1. Fair Value

The fair value measurement standard establishes a framework for making fair value measurements and requires additional disclosures about the measurements. The pronouncement does not establish any new areas in financial reporting where fair value accounting is required. Rather, it interacts with other accounting literature (in fact, it is woven throughout the Accounting standard codification, ASC) that requires or permits fair value measurements.

For financial reporting, the Accounting Standard Codification (ASC) provides a single authoritative definition of fair value: Fair value is the price that would be received to sell an asset or paid to transfer a liability in an orderly transaction between

---

* Partly from: Mard M J, Hitchner J R, Hyden S D. Valuation for Financial Reporting: Fair Value, Business Combinations, Intangible Assets, Goodwill, and Impairment Analysis, 3rd edition, John Wiltey & Sons, Inc. 2011: 6-12.

market participants at the measurement date. An important distinction to the FASB definition is that fair value may not consider synergies and attributes of a specific buyer and a specific seller, but may consider synergies available to market participants.

Fair value for financial reporting is not quite the same as fair market value as used with the IRS and other purposes. Characteristics of fair value in business combinations under GAAP include:

(a) Valuation methodologies specified in accounting literature and/or acceptable to the auditors;

(b) Generally established on an asset-by-asset and a situation-by-situation basis;

(c) Typically a control value, but more specifically, driven by the unit of account;

(d) The fair values of individual assets do not include a specific buyer's unique synergies unless such synergies are also those of "market participants";

(e) The additional purchase price paid in a business combination because a synergistic component is recorded as goodwill and subsequently is subject to impairment testing;

(f) In the absence of quoted market prices, the technique used to estimate fair value is the method producing a fair value best approximating quoted market prices;

(g) Typically includes tax amortization benefits for individual assets in a business combination;

(h) Transaction costs are not an attribute of the assets or liability and thus purchase price is not adjusted;

(i) Considers the highest and best use of market participants in the principal market to establish the valuation premise (in-use or in-exchange);

(j) Considers a reporting entity's credit standing, or the credit standing of the creditor in the case of liabilities;

(k) Requires the use of market participant assumptions in assessing management's prospective financial information (projections).

Chapter 7 Valuations for Financial Reporting 以财务报告为目的的评估

2. Fair Value Hierarchy

The FASB has specified a <u>hierarchical</u> approach to determining fair value. The ASC defines a hierarchy in the development of fair value measurements as follows:

2.1 Level 1

Inputs are observable market inputs that reflect <u>quoted prices</u> for identical assets or liabilities in active markets the reporting entity has the ability to access at the measurement date.

2.2 Level 2

Inputs are observable market inputs other than quoted prices for identical assets or liabilities in active markets the reporting entity has the ability to access at the measurement date. Level 2 inputs include:

(a) Quoted prices for similar assets or liabilities in active markets;

(b) Quoted prices for identical or similar assets or liabilities in markets that are not active; the prices are not active; that is, a market is one with few transactions for assets or liability, the prices are not current, or price quotations vary substantially either over time or among market makers or in which little information is released publicly;

(c) Market inputs other than quoted prices directly observable for the asset or liability. For example, interest rates, <u>yield curves</u>, volatilities, and <u>default rates</u> observable at the commonly quoted <u>intervals</u>;

(d) Market inputs not directly observable for the asset or liability but that are derived principally from or <u>corroborated</u> by other observable market data through correlation or by other means. For example, inputs derived through extrapolation or interpolation that are corroborated by other observable market data.

2.3 Level 3

Inputs are unobservable markets inputs. For example, inputs derived through extrapolation or interpolation unable to be corroborated by observable market data. Unobservable market inputs shall be used to measure fair value if observable market inputs are unavailable, thereby allowing for little, if any, market activity for the asset or liability. However, the fair value measurement objective remains the same; that is, an exit price from the perspective of a market participant seller. Therefore, a fair value measurement using unobservable market inputs within level 3 shall consider the assumptions that market participants would use in pricing the asset or liability, including assumptions about the amount a market participant buyer would demand to assume the risk related to the unobservable market inputs used to measure fair value. The reporting entity's own data used to develop the inputs shall be adjusted to exclude factors specific to the available reporting entity information that market participants would use different assumptions.

Level 1 and Level 2 inputs are sometimes called market-to-market inputs, while Level 3 inputs are sometimes called market-to-model inputs.

3. Valuation Approaches: Market, Income, and Cost

Fair value measurement also calls for valuation techniques used to measure fair value consistent with the market approach, income approach, and cost approach. The measurement objective is to use a valuation technique (or a combination of techniques) appropriate for the circumstances, and to maximize the use of market inputs.

Fundamentally, value is a function of economics and is based on the return on assets. The cost approach represents the things owned or borrowed. The income approach quantifies the return these assets can be expected to produce. The market approach merely reflects the market's perceptions of the things owned and borrowed or their expected returns.

For the determination of fair value measurement, the cost approach is based on the current replacement cost—the amount at the measurement date would be required to replace the service capacity of the asset. It is based on the cost to a market participant to acquire or construction asset of comparable utility, adjusted for obsolescence whether physical, functional, or economic.

The income approach uses valuation techniques to convert future amounts to a single present amount and is based on the value indicated by current market expectations about those future amounts. The approach includes present value techniques such as <u>option-pricing models</u>, <u>binomial models</u>, and the <u>multi-period</u>

excess earnings method.

The market approach uses prices of market transactions (involving identical assets or liabilities, or similar ones). The fair value hierarchy is: Level 1, the identical assets or liabilities; Level 2, similar assets or liabilities. Therefore, the market approach maybe either a Level 1 or Level 2 determination. Further, matrix pricing is considered consistent with the market approach, which applies to debt securities that do not rely on the securities' relationship to other benchmark quoted securities. Because people often confuse the term "market approach" with "market value", the forthcoming exposure draft of the revised IVS uses the term "Direct Market Comparison Approach", rather than "Market Approach".

Core Words and Expressions 核心术语

Accounting standard codification (ASC)	会计准则汇编
quoted market price	市场报价
tax amortization benefit	税收摊销收益
credit standing	信用地位，商业信誉
hierarchical	分层的，分等级的
quoted price	报价
yield curve	收益曲线
default rate	违约率
interval	时间间隔
corroborate	证实
option-pricing model	期权定价模型
binomial models	二项式模型
multi-period	多周期

Questions and Discussion 问题与讨论

1. What is the difference in fair value definition between ASC and FASB?

2. Please summarize the Fair Value Hierarchy.

3. Please introduce the three valuation approaches for fair value measurement briefly.

Topic 2: Goodwill and Impairment 商誉和减值

Abstract 中文摘要

资产减值是指资产的可收回金额低于其账面价值。可收回金额则应当根据资产的公允价值减去处置费用后的净额和资产预计未来现金流量的现值二者之间的较高者确定。根据中国《企业会计准则第 8 号——资产减值》，企业应当在资产负债表日判断资产是否存在可能发生减值的迹象。对于存在减值迹象的资产应当进行减值测试，计算资产的可回收金额。可回收金额低于账面价值的，应当按照可回收金额低于账面价值的金额，计提减值准备。

表明资产可能发生了减值的迹象主要有：（1）资产的市价当期大幅度下跌，其跌幅明显高于因时间推移或者正常使用而预计的下跌；（2）企业经营所处的经济、技术或者法律环境发生重大变化，从而对企业产生不利影响；（3）市场利率或其他市场投资报酬率在当期已经提高，从而影响企业资产预计未来现金流的现值；（4）有证据表明资产已经陈旧过时或者实体已经损坏；（5）资产已经或者将被闲置、终止使用等；（6）企业内部报告的证据表明资产的经济绩效已经低于或者将低于预期；（7）其他表明资产可能发生减值的迹象。

因企业合并所形成的商誉和使用寿命不确定的无形资产，无论是否存在减值迹象，每年都应当进行减值测试。其中，商誉减值测试具体可分为两个步骤：第一步是报告单位公允价值的确定以及与账面价值之间的比较。当账面价值高于报告单位的公允价值时，就存在着商誉减值；第二步是在减值测试日分配一个新的购买价格，正如在减值日进行一项企业合并一样。新的估值工作应该包括确定公允价值，其中包括已经识别的资产以及在评估基准日没有被识别但是在基准日和测试日之间出现的新资产。

当存在减值损失时，需要进行财务报告的披露，包括对引起该减值的事实和环境等因素、减值金额以及用于确定公允价值的方法等的披露。如果减值的具体金额尚不能够被确定，则需对其影响原因和现状进行披露，也包括在后续的一定时间内可能影响减值的重要调整因素的披露。在以减值测试为目的的评估中，资产评估专业人员应当结合评估对象的特点、价值类型、资料收集情况和数据来源来分析市场法、收益法和成本法的适用性。

Text* 正文

1. Impairment

1.1 Reporting Units

An entity must establish its reporting units based on its current reporting structure and the reporting unit guidance from the Codification. Recognized net assets, excluding goodwill, should be assigned to those reporting units. Recognized assets and liabilities irrelevant to a reporting unit, such as an environmental liability for an operation previously disposed of, do not need to be assigned to a reporting unit. All goodwill recognized in an entity's statement of financial position should be assigned to one or more reporting units based on a reasonable and supportable analysis. Goodwill in each reporting unit should be tested for impairment annually and between annual tests when a possible event reduces the fair value of a reporting unit below its carrying amount.

All goodwill reported in the financial statements of a reporting unit should be tested for impairment as if the reporting unit was a stand-alone entity. A reporting unit is an operating segment or a component. A component of an operating segment is a reporting unit if the component constitutes a business for which discrete financial information is available and segment management regularly reviews the operating results of that component. Goodwill must be defined and allocated at this component level. Entities that are not required to report segment information are nevertheless required to test goodwill for impairment at the reporting unit level.

---

* *Partly from: Mard M J, Hitchner J R, Hyden S D. Valuation for Financial Reporting: Fair Value, Business Combinations, Intangible Assets, Goodwill, and Impairment Analysis, 3rd edition, John Wiltey & Sons, Inc. 2011: 135-141.*

The nature of fair value of a reporting unit is that the synergies of operating in a combined entity, especially for shared overhead costs, are a fundamental part of the fair value of a reporting unit.

Additionally, if you could not take into account the synergies of part of a combined entity, there would be an immediate impairment, being such economy of scale synergies are a typical part of a <u>control transaction</u>. Thus, when employing a quoted market price in determining the fair value of a reporting unit, one must consider a control premium.

All acquired goodwill must be assigned to reporting units, which depends on the assignment of other acquired assets and assumed liabilities. These assets and liabilities may be assigned to reporting units based on the following criteria:

(a) The asset will be employed in or the liability relates to the operations of a reporting unit;

(b) The asset or liability will be considered in determining the fair value of the reporting unit.

Goodwill is the excess cost over the assets acquired and liabilities assumed, but the definition is deceptively simple. The goodwill allocated to a reporting unit is contingent on the <u>expected benefits</u> of the combination to the reporting unit. The goodwill allocation is required even though other assets or liabilities of the acquired entity may not be assigned to that reporting unit. A relative fair value allocation approach, similar to that used when a portion of a reporting unit is disposed of, should be used to determine how goodwill should be allocated when an entity reorganises its reporting structure, in a manner that changes the composition of one or more of its reporting units. However, goodwill is ultimately tested for impairment.

1.2 Annual Testing

The measurement of the fair value of intangibles and goodwill can be performed at any time during the <u>fiscal year</u> as long as the timing is consistent from year to year. Although different measurement dates can differ from reporting units, this date selected for a reporting unit must be consistent from year to year. A detailed determination of the fair value of a reporting unit may be carried forward from one year to the next (i.e., no further impairment analysis is required) if all of the following criteria are met:

(a) The assets and liabilities that comprise the reporting unit have not changed significantly since the most recent fair value determination;

(b) The most recent fair value determination results in an amount that exceeds the carrying amount of the reporting unit by a substantial margin.

Based on an analysis of events, it is determined that the possibility is remote that a fair value determination is less than the current carrying amount of the reporting unit.

However, the annual impairment test is to be accelerated, and goodwill of a reporting unit should be tested for impairment on an interim basis if there is an event that would probably reduce the fair value of a reporting unit below its carrying value. Examples of such events are:

(a) A significant adverse change in legal factors or in the business climate;

(b) An adverse action or assessment by a regulator;

(c) Unanticipated competition;

(d) A loss of key personnel;

(e) A probable expectation that a reporting unit or a significant portion of a reporting unit will be sold or otherwise disposed of;

(f) The testing for recoverability of a significant, asset group within a reporting unit;

(g) Recognition of a goodwill impairment loss in the financial statements of a subsidiary that is a component of a reporting unit.

1.3 The Impairment Test

The impairment test of goodwill is a two-step process.

STEP 1 The fair value of the reporting unit is determined and compared with the carrying amount of the reporting unit, including goodwill.

The fair value of a reporting unit refers to the amount at which the unit as a whole could be bought or sold in a current transaction between willing parties. Quoted market prices in active markets are considered the best evidence of fair value and should be used as the basis for the measurement, if available. However, the market price of an individual share of stock may not be representative of the fair value of the reporting unit as a whole. Due to fluctuation, the low stock price at a certain date may not indicate impairment which has a connotation of permanence. Further, a quoted price gleaned from an inactive market may be considered a distressed transaction. If so, the asset is to be valued using other techniques, therefore, the quoted market price of an individual share of stock need not be the sole measurement basis of the fair value of a reporting unit. If a quoted market price of the shares of a reporting unit is unavailable, the estimate of fair value should be based on the best information available, including prices for similar assets and liabilities and the results of other valuation techniques.

A valuation technique based on multiples of earnings, revenue, or a similar performance measure may be used to estimate the fair value of a reporting unit, given the technique is consistent with the objective of measuring fair value. Such measures may be appropriate, for example, if the fair value of an entity, having comparable operations and economic characteristics, is observable, and the relevant multiples of a comparable entity are known. Conversely, use of multiples would be inappropriate when the operations or activities of an entity for which the multiples are known are not of a comparable nature, scope, or size as the reporting unit for which fair value is estimated.

Goodwill impairment exists if the carrying amount of the reporting unit, including goodwill, exceeds the fair value of the reporting unit. In such a case, the second step of the goodwill impairment test is triggered.

STEP 2 The second step of the goodwill impairment test requires performing what amounts to a new purchase price allocation as of the date of the impairment test is if a business combination is consummated on the date of the impairment test, with the fair value of the reporting unit serving as a <u>proxy</u> for the purchase price. The new valuation work should determine the new fair values of both the originally recognized assets and any new assets that may have been unrecognized at the valuation date but are developed between the acquisition date and the test date. The fair values of the assets at the test date are <u>deducted from</u> the fair value of the reporting unit to determine the implied fair value of goodwill at the test date. If the implied fair value of goodwill

Chapter 7 Valuations for Financial Reporting 以财务报告为目的的评估

at the test date is lower than its carrying amount, goodwill impairment is indicated, and the carrying amount of goodwill is written down to its implied fair value.

The assets (or asset groups) other than goodwill should be tested for impairment. Consequently, if the asset (or asset group) is impaired, the impairment loss would be recognized prior to the goodwill being tested for impairment, which means that, in addition to impairment of goodwill, impairment of other assets must also be recognized. Thus, the asset values recognized on the balance sheet as of the date of the impairment test is the lower of the carrying amount or fair value for each previously recognized tangible asset. For example, assume a company has a reporting unit whose assets have a fair value of $80 million, including goodwill of $35 million. For illustrative purposes, it is further assumed that the relative fair values of the assets have been valued and recorded on the books of the acquirer as follows:

Recognized Tangible Assets	$15,000,000
Recognized Identifiable Tangible Assets	$30,000,000
Goodwill	$35,000,000
Fair Value of Reporting Unit	$80,000,000

After one year, assume the carrying amounts of certain assets after amortization are:

Recognized Tangible Assets	$12,000,000
Recognized Identifiable Tangible Assets	25,000,000
Goodwill	35,000,000
Fair Value of Reporting Unit	$72,000,000

Now assume that an impairment test is performed at this time one year later, and the aggregate fair value of the assets of the reporting unit is $70 million. The decline in value indicates impairment (step one fails), but not necessarily, with a goodwill impairment charge of $10 million. A new asset allocation (step two) must be performed to determine the new goodwill amount. The assumptions of the fair value as of the date of the impairment test are:

Recognized Tangible Assets	$13,000,000
Unrecognized Tangible Assets*	$1,000,000
Recognized Identifiable Tangible Assets	$20,000,000
Unrecognized Identifiable Tangible Assets*	$7,000,000
Goodwill	$29,000,000
Fair Value of Reporting Unit	$70,000,000

* Assets acquired or developed after the acquisition date

the results of step two are:

	Net Carrying Amount	Fair Value	Impairment Amount
Recognized tangible assets	$12,000,000	$13,000,000	
Unrecognized tangible assets	0	$1,000,000	
Recognized identifiable intangible assets (with a defined life)	$25,000,000	$20,000,000	$5,000,000**
Unrecognized identifiable intangible assets	0	$7,000,000	
Goodwill	$35,000,000	$29,000,000	$6,000,000
Total	$72,000,000	$70,000,000	$11,000,000

**Assumes the asset or asset group failed the recoverability test and impairment must be measured. If the asset or asset group does not fail the recoverability test the asset is deemed to be not impaired even though the carrying amount exceeds fair value.

In this example, step one would fail by $2 million (the amount by which the total carrying amount of $72 million exceeds fair value of $70 million), but the step two analysis shows a required impairment expense of $11 million.

If the impairment test finds that the fair value of the reporting unit has not declined materially, no further analysis is required. The increase in goodwill value is never recognized.

2. Financial Reporting Disclosures

Disclosure is more involved when an impairment loss is recognized. In such a situation, the following disclosures are required:

(a) A description of the facts and circumstances leading to the impairment.

(b) The amount of the impairment loss and the method of determining the fair value of the associated reporting unit (based on quoted market prices, prices of comparable businesses, or a present value or other valuation technique).

If a recognized impairment loss is an estimate that has not yet been finalized, the fact and the reasons for it should be disclosed. In subsequent periods, the nature and amounts of any significant adjustments made to the initial estimate of the impairment loss must be disclosed.

The valuation analysts must make sure that the report and work papers provide the client and auditor the information necessary for these disclosures.

Core Words and Expressions 核心术语

control transaction	控制权交易
expected benefit	预期收益
fiscal year	会计年度
proxy	代理人，委托书
deduct from	扣除

Questions and Discussion 问题与讨论

1. What are the kinds of events that would probably reduce the fair value of a reporting unit below its carrying value?

2. What are the two steps of impairment test of goodwill?

Information Extension

思政微课堂

企业的财务报告不仅能够帮助经营管理人员、投资者、债权人和其他有关各方全面系统地了解企业一定时期的财务状况、经营成果和现金流量，也是财政、税务、工商、审计等部门监督企业经营管理的重要依据，以财务报告为目的评估业务也应需而生。为促进中国会计准则与国际财务报告准则接轨，2006年2月，财政部颁发了新《企业会计准则》，引入了公允价值的概念和计量模式。2014年7月，财政部发布《企业会计准则第39号——公允价值计量》，对公允价值计量进行了更加专业和细致的规范。公允价值计量模式的运用使会计信息责任体系发生了改变，由以往的会计责任和审计责任的二维责任体系，逐渐发展成为会计责任、评估责任和审计责任构成的三维责任体系。

为规范以财务报告为目的的评估行为，保护资产评估当事人合法权益和公共利益，中国资产评估协会于2017年9月修订发布了《以财务报告为目的的评估指南》（中评协〔2017〕45号）。根据该准则，以财务报告为目的的评估，是指资产评估机构及其资产评估专业人员遵守法律、行政法规、资产评估准则和企业会计准则及会计核算、披露的有关要求，根据委托对评估基准日以财务报告为目的所涉及的各类资产和负债公允价值或者特定价值进行评定和估算，并出具资产评估报告的专业服务行为；执行以财务报告为目的的评估业务，应当理解相关会计准则的概念、原则及其与资产评估准则相关概念、原则之间的联系与区别，具备相应的专业知识和实践经验，胜任所执行的评估业务；资产评估专业人员应当与企业和执行审计业务的注册会计师进行必要的沟通，明确评估业务基本事项并充分理解会计准则或者相关会计核算、披露的具体要求，并且需要根据会计准则或者相关会计核算与披露的具体要求、评估对象等相关条件明确价值类型；在评估方法的选择方面，资产评估专业人员应当根据评估对象、价值类型、资料收集情况和数据来源等相关条件，参照会计准则关于评估对象和计量方法的有关规定，恰当选择评估方法，关注所采用的评估数据，并知晓公允价值获取层级受评估方法选择及评估数据来源的影响。

Chapter 8
Tax Base Assessment
税基评估

Wisdom
名人名言

将欲茂枝叶，必先救根株。云何救根株，劝农均赋租。

——白居易

井税有常期，日晏犹得眠。

——元结

Like mothers, taxes are often misunderstood, but seldom forgotten.

— Lloyd Branwell

It is not the taxation itself that causes great harm to the country, but the way of taxation.

— Quesnay

Rudimentary Knowledge
基本知识

Abstract 中文摘要

税基即税收课税基础，是税收课征的经济基础和客观依据。税基评估是指具有胜任能力的资产评估专业人员以税收为特定评估目的，依据税法及相关法律、法规和评估准则，对税基的价值进行分析、估算并发表专业意见的行为和过程。

税基评估主要涉及三种现实需求：一是税收征收；二是税收缴纳；三是解决税务争议。按照税收对象的不同，税基评估可以划分为财产税基评估、流转税税基评估、所得税税基评估、资源税税基评估、行为税税基评估等；按照行为主体的不同，税基评估可以划分为政府税基评估、准政府税基评估和中介税基评估。

伴随世界各国税制的改革和完善，税基评估为包括财产税、关税、所得税、资源税等不同税种在内的税收征管工作提供了专业支持。资产评估专业人员在搜集信息资料的过程中，需要重点查阅与所评税基相关的税收法律、法规、规章制度和税收政策，以此作为评定估算的主要依据。随着税收制度的优化、税收管理的精细化和征管措施的逐步完善，运用现代评估技术来提高税收征管效率成为必然趋势。

Text* 正文

1. Definition and Related Concepts of Tax Base Assessment

Tax base refers to the economic basis and objective basis of tax collection, including the dual meanings of qualitative and quantitative stipulations. Qualitative stipulation refers to the specific object of taxation; quantitative stipulation refers to how many objects of taxation can be used as the base for calculating the amount of tax payable.

Tax base assessment refers to the professional activities of assessment pricing,

---

* Partly from: Standard on Property Tax Policy, Edition: IAAO, 2010.

which independently, objectively, and fairly carried out by assessment institutions and assessors with competent in tax base assessment, following certain procedure and appropriate assessment standards and methods, in accordance with corresponding tax laws and the purpose of tax. The object of assessment is the tax base without specific ad valorem tax value.

It is necessary for professionals of assessment institutions to provide assessment services related to tax. Tax base assessment provides professional support for the improvement of tax collection and management. With the reform and improvement of tax system in various countries, especially the reform and improvement of specific taxes such as property tax, tariff, income tax and resource tax, tax base assessment has attracted the attention of all countries and has been paid attention by the assessment community.

1.1 Subject of Tax Base Assessment

The subject of tax base assessment refers to behaviour subject engaged in tax base assessment, which is, the assessment organisation and personnel who undertake the business of tax base assessment. For the same subject of tax base assessment, there are both tax base assessment subjects serving for the tax collector and the tax payer at the same time.

1.2 Object of Tax Base Assessment

The object of tax base assessment is not the same as the general assets assessment object for it emphasizes the subject matter of taxation or tax object. At the same time, not all the assets related to tax collection are tax, base assessment objects. Therefore, the tax base assessment object must be the subject matter of the assessment object which is related to the collection and payment of tax and mainly cannot directly define the ad valorem tax value. According to the classification standard of the current tax system, the tax base assessment object can be divided into property tax base, income tax base, turnover tax base, resource tax base and conduct tax base.

2. The Main Characteristics of Tax Base Assessment

The tax base assessment is an important branch in the field of asset assessment. Its activities involve two fields: tax and asset assessment. Its business content is a special assessment business which combines tax activities and asset assessment activities. Therefore, it not only has the characteristics of general assets valuation, but also has its own main characteristics:

(a) Tax base assessment is an assessment with tax as a specific purpose;

(b) There are two or more different assessment subjects in the same assessment object at the same time;

(c) The appraisal value standard is mainly ad valorem tax value;

(d) The valuation targets are diversified and complicated.

3. Classification of Tax Base Assessment

3.1 Classification According to Specific Needs of Tax Activities

According to the specific needs of tax activities, tax base assessment can be divided into tax base assessment for tax collection, tax base assessment for paying tax, and tax base assessment for solving tax disputes. The specific purposes and interests of the three tax base assessments are not the same.

(a) Tax base assessment for tax collection

The tax base assessment for tax collection is mainly to provide ad valorem tax base value for tax collection declaration and facilitate tax payment. It is the tax base assessment value to inform the taxpayer on behalf of the tax collector.

(b)Tax base assessment for paying tax

The purpose of the tax base assessment is not only to calculate the ad valorem tax amount for tax declaration, but also to provide the tax base assessment value to serve tax payers' tax avoidance purpose.

(c)Tax base assessment for solving tax disputes

Tax base assessment for solving tax disputes is mainly to solve the tax disputes between tax collectors and payers in the process of tax collection. The tax assessment can be promoted by tax collectors and payers respectively and be put forward to the adjudicators for the tax bases in dispute.

3.2 Classification According to the Object of Tax Base Assessment

According to the object classification of tax base assessment, tax base assessment can be divided into tax base assessment of property tax, tax base assessment of turnover tax, tax base assessment of income tax, tax base assessment of resource tax, tax base assessment of conduct tax.

(a) Property tax base assessment

Property tax base assessment is aimed at assessing the tax base of property tax, specifically including the tax base assessment of real estate tax, inheritance tax, property tax and other property taxes. The property tax base assessment is an important part of the tax base assessment in the countries and regions where the tax base assessment is established.

(b) Turnover tax base assessment

Turnover tax base assessment is aimed at assessing the tax base of turnover tax, including the valuation of tariff, business tax, value-added tax, consumption tax, and other tax bases. Turnover tax base assessment also includes tariff-based assessment and other turnover-tax-based assessment.

(c) Income tax base assessment

Income tax base assessment is aimed at assessing the specific tax bases of income tax, such as enterprise (company) income tax and individual income tax. At present, there are many assessments of such tax base in other counties or regions, mainly for the purpose of solving tax disputes, and the targets involved are relatively large. If the personal income, level of social accounting, the improvement of tax collection and management ability will rise, and equity transfer of joint-stock companies will increase in the future, the business involved in this kind of tax base assessment will grow rapidly.

(d) Resource tax base assessment

Resource tax base assessment is aimed at assessing the tax base of the resource tax category involving various natural resources, such as mineral resources, forest resources, water resources, cultivated land protection and ecological protection, etc. Resource tax base assessment may become an important part of tax base assessment.

(e) Behavioural purpose tax base assessment

Behavioural purpose tax base assessment is aimed at assessing the tax base of the behavioural purpose tax category. In the tax system, there are many kinds of specific taxes of purpose tax crossing or overlapping with property tax or resource tax or turnover tax. In many countries or regions, behavioural purpose tax mainly includes land value-added tax, consumption tax, and other taxes.

3.3 Classification According to the Behaviour Subject by Tax Base Assessment

(a) <u>Government tax base assessment</u>

The main characteristics of this kind of tax base assessment are as follows: the behavioural subject of the valuation is the government's valuation agency; the tax base assessment is the government's management activity; the tax base assessment is a free public service activity, and the funds needed for the tax base assessment are all listed in the government's financial budget.

(b) <u>Quasi-government tax base assessment</u>

The main characteristic of this kind of tax base assessment is that the behavioural subject of the valuation is the quasi-government valuation organisation, and the tax base assessment is also a free public service activity. The cost of the tax base assessment is mainly provided by the public financial budget of the government. Some differences between quasi-government tax base assessment and government tax base assessment lie in that the assessors are not civil servants, but business establishment. On the premise of completing the duty of tax base assessment, the assessment institution also provides some paid services related to assessment to the society.

(c) <u>Intermediary tax base assessment</u>

The main characteristic of this kind of tax base assessment is that the behavioural subject of the valuation is the social intermediary valuation organisation, the tax base assessment is the paid social intermediary service activity, and the expenses needed to carry out the tax base assessment are paid by the entrusting party. In some cases, the intermediary tax base assessment is also entrusted by the tax collector to carry out paid tax base assessment services.

4. Tax Base Assessment of Some Overseas Countries and Regions

4.1 Tax Base Assessment in the United States

In the United States, the property tax is the main source of income for local finance, and its tax object is mainly the <u>stock real estate</u>. The property tax rate is not fixed in the form of law, but calculated according to the actual amount of fiscal year expenditure budget and the total value of taxable real estate. Every year, local governments in the United States valuate real estate in their jurisdictions to determine the property tax that taxpayers are required to pay. The appraiser confirms the location of the real estate and the owner of the property, and the tax and other administrative departments establish the database, valuate the property value, determine the scope of collection, and calculate the value. After the compilation of the roster, the government shall notify the property owners to confirm the appraisal value, and the property owners who have objections to the declaration and payment of the property tax may reconsider or even appeal the appraisal, which shall be finally decided by the government or the court.

4.2 Tax Base Assessment in Canada

The property tax in Canada is not a single tax, but a composite tax consisting of multiple elements. It mainly includes real estate property tax, special property tax, business property tax, <u>alternative taxes</u> paid by NGOs and other fees. And there is no national property tax rate in Canada. Some of the property tax bases are assessed by government agencies while some are assessed by quasi-government agencies.

4.3 Tax Base Assessment in Japan

Japan has established a property tax base assessment system dominated by the government, and has made it clear that the tax subjects of fixed assets tax are city, town, and village level governments, and their incomes are all controlled by city, town, and village. For public welfare undertakings and residential land (disaster area), a certain proportion of the amount of property appraisal shall be deducted. Japan's fixed assets tax is based on the valuation result of the real estate market.

4.4 Tax Base Assessment in Hong Kong

Hong Kong's tax related assessment is mainly based on the assessment of the rating tax base in Hong Kong. The tax base assessment method of rating tax in Hong Kong is mainly mass appraisal. The assessment shall be fair and just, and the uniform assessment period (October 1 of each year) shall be stipulated. Rates need to be reassessed every year, which can reflect the economic changes of the market every year, as well as the mechanism of objection and appeal against the unfair assessment.

4.5 Tax Base Assessment in Taiwan

Taiwan's tax base assessment includes land price tax, housing tax base assessment and tax related assessment to resolve income tax disputes. Taiwan's land and real estate are taxed separately, and their tax base assessments are all government assessments.

Core Words and Expressions 核心术语

tax base assessment	税基评估
ad valorem tax	从价税
property tax	财产税
tariff	关税
income tax	所得税
subject of tax base assessment	税基评估主体
tax collector	征税人
tax payer	纳税人
object of tax base assessment	税基评估客体
turnover tax	流转税
resource tax	资源税
conduct tax	行为税
real estate tax	不动产税
inheritance tax	遗产税
stock real estate	存量房地产

government tax base assessment	政府税基评估
quasi-government tax base assessment	准政府税基评估
intermediary tax base assessment	中介税基评估
alternative taxes	替代税
rates tax	差饷税（中国香港）

Questions and Discussion 问题与讨论

1. What is tax base assessment?

2. Why do we have a tax base assessment?

3. What are the types of tax base assessment?

More Knowledge
知识扩展

Topic 1: Mass Appraisal of Real Property 房地产批量评估

Abstract 中文摘要

在税基评估的理论与实践中，所采用的评估方式主要分为批量评估方式和单宗评估方式，其中单宗评估方式更多应用于非涉税评估领域，而批量评估由于其自身特点，主要应用于房地产的财产税和房地产交易的税基评估中。批量评估是指在评估基准日运用统一的数据、标准化的方法和统计检验技术对一组房地产进行价值评估的过程。资产评估专业人员需要根据评估对象和特定的评估环境选择相适应的评估方法（如成本法、市场法和收益法）作为评估模型设定的理论依据，再根据所设定的模型和所能获得的信息数据，应用具体的数理计量方法来校准技术，进而获得所需要的目标房地产价值估计。

全世界范围内有关房地产批量评估技术的研究可追溯至19世纪70年代。

Carbone 和 Longini(1977)借助数理统计理论构建基于房地产信息的 MRA(Multiple Regression Analysis，多元回归分析）方程，将 AVMs（Automated Valuation Models，自动评估模型）用于房地产批量评估。由于 AVMs 的可信度取决于数据质量和建模者技术能力，部分学者尝试对传统 AVMs 进行理论修正；也有部分学者借助人工神经网络、粗糙集理论、遗传模糊规则、空间分析、地理统计学加权回归等理论或方法，推动批量评估理论的不断发展和完善。在此过程中，尤为重要的是计算机辅助技术和 GIS（Geographic Information System，地理信息系统）软件的引入。Mccluskey et al.（1997）研究提出 CAMA（Computer Aided Mass Appraisal，计算机辅助批量评估）方案，极大地减轻了评估师的工作量；Borst et al.（1997）对批量评估技术和 GIS 展开关联研究，开创了 GIS 应用于房地产批量评估的先河。经过长期的理论探索与评估实践，国际估税官协会（IAAO）、欧洲评估师协会联合会（TEGOVA）、美国评估促进会（TAF）、英国皇家特许测量师学会（RICS）等国际评估组织基本形成了将数理统计、计算机辅助技术、GIS 等与传统评估方法有机结合的房地产批量评估技术体系。特征价格法（Hedonic Price Method, HPM）和基准修正法（Benchmark Correction Method, BCM）是其中的典型代表。在中国香港，批量评估已广泛应用于税收领域，计算机辅助批量评估技术也已经应用到工厂、住宅等房地产评估实务中。2006 年，浙江杭州开始研究并计划建立统一的自动评估模型，对房屋交易税价进行公平评估和管理；随后，广东深圳也开始建立对于存量房屋的房产税批量评估制度。*

Text** 正文

1. The Introduction of Mass Appraisal

<u>Mass appraisal</u> refers to the method of standardized data and statistical inspection technology used by valuation institutions and personnel to valuate the value of the whole batch of valuation objects on a specific date. An important feature of mass

---

* *Chen Lei, Zhou Yanqiu, He Qing, Public Service Quality and Real Estate Tax Base Assessment under the Situation of Real Estate Tax Reform Pilot - Simulation Calculation from Empirical Data of 35 Large and Medium Sized Cities in China, Journal of Macro-quality Research, 2021. Chen Lei, Zhou Yanqiu, Qin Qizhi, Benchmark Correction Path for Mass Appraisal of Real Estate Tax Base: Innovation and Practice, Appraisal Journal of China, 2021.*
** *Partly from: Standard on Mass Appraisal of Real Property, Edition: IAAO,2017; Guidance on International Mass Appraisal and Related Tax Policy, Edition: IAAO,2014.*

appraisal is that it brings a large number of mathematical tools such as measurement, statistical testing into the valuation process. In the application of measurement tools (especially multiple regression), the mass appraisal method considers that the value of the real estate to be valuated is affected by many factors, such as the area, orientation, building structure and so on. Through the analysis of the existing housing feature data and value data, we can calculate the contribution of each feature to the housing value. After obtaining the coefficients of each variable in the econometric model, the characteristics of the real estate to be valuated can be input into the model, so that the value of multiple real estate can be valuated in one appraisal.

Mass appraisal models apply to all three approaches to value: the cost approach, the market approach, and the income approach.

2. The Difference Between Mass Appraisal and Single Case Appraisal

<u>Single case appraisal</u> refers to the appraisal of the tax base value of a taxable property in one valuation. It means that in one valuation, the appraisal object is a single one. On this point, it is the same as the general asset appraisal practice, and its appraisal method is mainly based on the market approach, cost approach, and income approach. The most fundamental difference between mass appraisal and single case appraisal is that the object of one appraisal is a batch of real estate, or a single object. It is such a fundamental difference that leads to significant differences between mass appraisal and single case appraisal in guiding ideology, specific methods, means, steps, and procedures. At present, judging from the practice of real estate tax base assessment in various countries, mass appraisal has become the mainstream. Only when the mass appraisal is not effective due to various factors (such as the large difference of property types in the assessment area, etc.), can single case appraisal be adopted.

3. The Approaches of Mass Appraisal Models

3.1 The Cost Approach

The cost approach is applicable to virtually all improved parcels and, if used properly, can produce accurate valuations. The cost approach is more reliable for newer structures of standard materials, design, and workmanship. It produces an estimate of the value of the fee simple interest in a property.

Reliable cost data are imperative in any successful application of the cost approach. The data must be complete, typical, and current. Current construction costs should be based on the cost of replacing a structure with one of equal utility, using current materials, design, and building standards. In addition to specific property types, cost models should include the cost of individual construction components and building items in order to adjust for features that differ from base specifications. These costs should be incorporated into a construction cost manual and related computer software. The software can perform the valuation function, and the manual, in addition to providing documentation, can be used when non-automated calculations are required.

The most difficult aspects of the cost approach are estimates of <u>land value</u> and accrued depreciation. These estimates must be based on non-cost data (primarily sales) and can involve considerable subjectivity. Land values used in the cost approach must be current and consistent.

3.2 The Market Approach

The market approach, also called sales comparison approach, estimates the value of a subject property by statistically analysing the sale prices of similar properties. This approach is usually preferred when estimating the values of residential and other property types with adequate sales.

Applications of the market approach include direct market models and comparable sales algorithms. Comparable sales algorithms are most akin to single-property appraisal applications of the market approach. They have the advantages of being easily explained and can compensate for less well specified or calibrated models, because the models are used only to make adjustments to the selected <u>comparables</u>. They can be problematic if the selected comparables are not well validated or representative of market value. Direct market models depend more heavily on careful model specification and calibration, because they predict market value directly. Their advantages include efficiency and consistency, since the same model is directly applied against all properties in the model area.

3.3 The Income Approach

In general, for income-producing properties, the income approach is the preferred valuation approach when reliable income and expense data are available, along with well-supported income multipliers, overall rates, and required rates of return on investment. Successful application of the income approach requires the collection, maintenance, and careful analysis of income and expense data.

Mass appraisal applications of the income approach begin with collecting and processing income and expense data. Appraisers should then compute normal or typical gross incomes, vacancy rates, net incomes, and <u>expense ratios</u> for various homogeneous strata of properties. These figures can be used to judge the reasonableness of reported data for individual parcels and to estimate income and expense figures for parcels with unreported data.

Alternatively, models for estimating gross or net income and expense ratios can be developed by using actual income and expense data from a sample of properties and calibrated by using <u>multiple regression analysis</u>. The developed income figures can be capitalized into estimates of value in a number of ways. The most direct method involves the application of gross income multipliers, which expresses the ratio of market value to gross income. At a more refined level, net income multipliers or their reciprocals, overall capitalization rates, can be developed and applied. Provided there are adequate sales data, these multipliers and rates should be extracted from a comparison of actual or estimated incomes with sale prices (older income and sales data should be adjusted to the valuation date as appropriate). Income multipliers and overall rates developed in this manner tend to provide reliable, consistent, and readily supported valuations when good sales and income data are available. When adequate sales are not available, relevant publications and local market participants can be consulted.

4. Approach Applicability Analysis

The appropriateness of each valuation approach varies with the type of property under consideration. Table 1 ranks the relative usefulness of the three approaches in the mass appraisal of major types of properties. The table assumes that there are no major statutory barriers to using all three approaches or to obtaining cost, sales, and income data. Although relying only on the single best approach for a given type of property can have advantages in terms of efficiency and consistency, the use of two or more approaches provides helpful cross-checks and flexibility and can thus produce greater accuracy, particularly for less typical properties.

The table below shows the rank of typical usefulness of the three approaches to valuation in the mass appraisal of major types of property.

Type of Property	Cost Approach	Market Approach	Income Approach
Single-family residential	2nd	1st	3rd
Multifamily residential	3rd	1st or 2nd	1st or 2nd
Commercial	3rd	2nd	1st
Industrial	1st or 2nd	3rd	1st or 2nd
Non-agricultural land	-	1st	2nd
Agricultural*	-	2nd	1st
Special-purpose**	1st	2nd or 3rd	2nd or 3rd

5. Application Status of Mass Appraisal at Home and Abroad

In Canada, Columbia Province began to design the computer-aided asset appraisal system in the 1980s. It applies the emerging information technology, database and computer technology to the real estate tax base assessment. The integrated geographic information system can automatically connect with the relevant management departments, display data maps and carry out graphic analysis according to the needs, establish mathematical models, and calibrate them repeatedly according to the collected data.

The United States, the United Kingdom, Australia, Singapore, Thailand, South Africa and other countries or regions have begun to apply mass appraisal technology in tax collection and management, and the use of this technology has become a global trend.

---

* Includes farm, ranch, and forest properties.
** Includes institutional, governmental, and recreation properties.

In Hong Kong, mass appraisal technology is widely used in rates collection. At present, the computer-aided mass appraisal system is widely used in residential, office and factory buildings in Hong Kong.

Hangzhou city began to study and plan to establish a unified automatic assessment model in October 2006 to fairly valuate and manage the house transaction tax price. In April 2008, the system was officially put into operation. Without increasing the number of tax department staff, the mode completed the investigation of residential buildings, villas, and commercial shops in Hangzhou in a short time, and finally established the Hangzhou tax mass appraisal system based on market comparison method and cost method.

As early as 2007, Shenzhen began to build a mass appraisal system for the tax price of existing housing. On the basis of the "hedonic price method", they made corresponding amendments to avoid some unreasonable interference. They adopted the "urban overall assessment method". Through the decomposition and analysis of various factors, they obtained the coefficient table of 1.54 million housing stock in Shenzhen. The system also uses GIS technology and 3D GIS technology to show the real estate related factors directly and improve the accuracy of valuation.

Core Words and Expressions 核心术语

mass appraisal	批量评估
single case appraisal	单宗评估
comparables	可比案例
land value	土地价值
expense ratios	费用率
multiple regression analysis	多元回归分析
computer-aided mass appraisal system	计算机辅助批量评估系统
hedonic price method	特征价格法
urban overall assessment method	城市整体评估法

Questions and Discussion 问题与讨论

1. What is the mass appraisal?
2. What are the common methods to valuate the tax base of real estate tax?
3. What are the differences between mass appraisal and single case appraisal?
4. How to valuate the tax base of real estate tax for single family residence?

Topic 2: Automated Valuation Models (AVMs) 自动评估模型

Abstract 中文摘要

计算机应用在税基批量评估中的演进可以划分为三个阶段：第一阶段是资产评估专业人员将收集到的数据填入计算机电子表格中进行处理；第二阶段是收集数据环节的计算机化，即按满足一定的数据记录和数据输入格式的方式收集有关的财产数据；第三阶段是评估程序的自动化，即将数据输入预先设定的计算公式而获得应该结果，自动评估模型（AVMs）就是应用于此阶段，是批量评估方法体系的关键技术。

AVMs技术的应用需要满足一系列前提条件，即：具有较高的透明度和可信度，具有广泛的适用性，具有足够的统计信息和质量保证。其通过数据验证、数据分析、市场分析和持续质量控制等方式，为各方使用者提供客观的评估结果。目前，AVMs不仅应用于财产税税基批量评估，还被广泛应用于抵押财产的批量评估业务中。

在税基评估中应用AVMs技术时，资产评估专业人员首先根据地图、不动产所有权凭证、所在位置，对不动产的所有者、特征以及权利进行确认；其次，确定AVMs应用中所有的假设，包括特别的限制条件和逆向假设条件；再次，确定不动产样本的经济域，即具有相似特征财产所构成的群体；最后，在保证所收集数据质量的基础上，资产评估专业人员可以决定AVMs的类型以及模型中应用的变量，进而根据所选择的模型具体形式，寻找能够校准的统计学技术与计算机技术。

Text* 正文

1. Definition of AVMs

Automated Valuation Models (AVMs) is a mathematically-based computer software program that market analysts use to produce an estimate of market value based on market analysis of location, market conditions, and real estate characteristics from information that was previously and separately collected. The distinguishing feature of an AVM is that it is a market appraisal produced through mathematical modelling. The credibility of an AVM is dependent on the data used and the skills of the modeler producing the AVM. AVMs should be developed by appropriately qualified market analysts, e.g., appraisers/valuers, who use statistically-based applications to analyse data and select the best simulation of market activity for the analysis of location, market conditions, and property characteristics from previously collected data. AVMs are designed to generate value estimates for properties at specified points in time (retrospective or prospective dates as required by client).

2. Principle of AVMs

• Transparency

• Public trust – providing confidence for the stakeholders

• Broad applicability

• Based on statistically sufficient information

• Certification and quality assurance

This standard provides guidance for public and private sector property valuation that depends on Automated Valuation Models (AVMs) systems. AVMs can be used when sufficient economic data exists to permit development of representative and valid statistical samples. Models that adhere to the best practices for data verification, data analysis, market analysis, and ongoing quality control would present the most reliable value estimates. The general format of development and use of an AVM described in this standard is shown in Figure 8-1.

---

* *Partly from: Standard on Automated Valuation Models (AVMs), Edition: IAAO, 2018.*

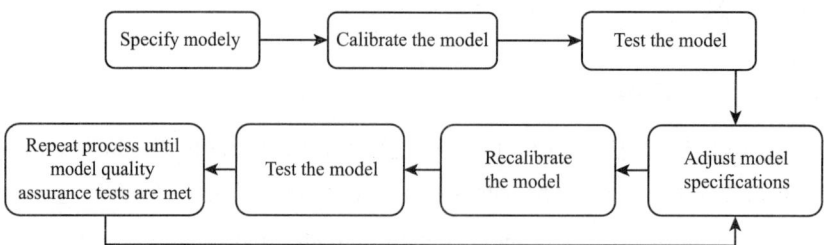

Figure 8-1 General Format of AVMs System

3. Purpose of AVMs

The purpose of an AVM is to efficiently provide an accurate, uniform, equitable estimate of fair market value. Fair market value defined; <u>allowable variance</u>; factors to be considered in determining fair market value; generally accepted appraisal procedures to be utilized. "Fair market value" means the amount in terms of money that a well-informed buyer is justified in paying and a well-informed seller is justified in accepting for property in an <u>open and competitive market</u>, assuming that the parties are acting without undue compulsion. All AVMs value should be reviewed for reliability. AVMs value generated in compliance with regulations of the governing bodies are considered as appraisals. Models that adhere to the best practices for data verification, data analysis, market analysis, and ongoing quality assurance present the most reliable value estimates.

4. Development and application of AVMs

AVMs are developed using appraisal principles and techniques. Data are acquired and analysed to develop a market valuation model that can be applied to equivalent properties (sold or unsold) in the same market area. Two major components of valuation modelling are specification and calibration. The <u>model specification</u> process identifies property characteristics (variables) that impact, demand, and develops the proposed model structure. <u>Model calibration</u> is the process of deriving coefficients for the variables previously specified in addition variables are created through transformations to avoid <u>collinearity</u> problems. Specification and calibration techniques vary with the purpose of the AVMs, type of property, available data, and the experience and knowledge of the market analyst.

The basic steps in the development of an AVM are:

• Creation of a scope of work

• Identification and acquisition of property data

• Exploratory data analysis

• <u>Stratification</u>

• Determination of <u>data representativeness</u>

• Model specification

• Model calibration

• Quality assurance

• Model application and value review

Model specification, calibration, and quality assurance are iterative processes that are repeated until statistical diagnostics are satisfactory.

Core Words and Expressions 核心术语

Automated Valuation Models (AVMs)	自动评估模型
market value	市场价值
market analysis	市场分析
mathematical modelling	数学建模
allowable variance	许可偏差
open and competitive market	公开竞争市场
model specification	模型选择
model calibration	模型校准
collinearity	共线性
stratification	分层
data representativeness	数据代表性

Questions and Discussion 问题与讨论

1. What is the Automated Valuation Model ?
2. What is the principle of AVMs?
3. Why AVMs are used in real estate mass appraisal?
4. What is the process of AVMs?

Information Extension
思政微课堂

　　税基评估在推进依法治税、加大税收对于收入分配的调节力度、加强对税源的科学化和精细化管理等方面具有重要作用。2005年3月，国家税务总局制定了《纳税评估管理办法（试行）》（国税发〔2005〕43号），对纳税评估通用分析指标及其使用方法，纳税评估分税种特定分析指标及其使用方法作了要求和说明。2010年7月，《国家税务总局关于发布〈企业重组业务企业所得税管理办法〉的公告》（国家税务总局公告2010年第4号）和《财政部 国家税务总局关于企业重组业务企业所得税处理若干问题的通知》（财税〔2009〕59号）对企业重组业务的企业所得税管理进行了规范和加强。其中规定，企业重组是指企业在日常经营活动以外发生的法律结构或经济结构重大改变的交易，包括企业法律形式改变、债务重组、股权收购、资产收购、合并、分立等各类重组。而企业重组的税务处理，区分不同条件分别适用一般性税务处理规定和特殊性税务处理规定。除了债务重组以及适用一般性税务处理规定的股权收购和资产收购等情形外，企业重组相关当事方企业在向税务机关报送资料时，均必须提供评估机构对计税基础和所涉及资产或股权的公允价值出具的资产评估报告。

　　作为"深化税收制度改革，健全地方税体系"的重要税种，房地产税税基价值评估的规范性和合理性对房地产税征收的公平而言也是至关重要。为深入推进房地产税收一体化管理，规范房地产交易计税价格核定办法，财政部、国家税务总局于2009年7月发布《关于开展应用房地产评税技术核定交易环节计税价格工作的通知》（财税〔2009〕100号），决定在全国范围内开展应用房地产评税技术核定交易环节计税价格工作；为加快推进房地产评估技术应用，加强存量房交易税收征管工作，财政部、国家税务总局于2010年10月进一步发布《国家税务总局关于推进应用房地产评估技术加强存量房交易税收征管工作的通知》（财税〔2010〕105号）。随后，自沪、渝两地于2011年实施房产税试点改革以来，我国房地产税改革方案一直处于探索实践阶段。从"研究推进房地产税改革"到"加快房地产税立法并适时推进改革"，从"做好房地产税立法相关工作"到"完善地方税体系，稳妥、稳步推进房地产税立法"，不难看出，有序推进并择时出台房地产税，是当前中央与地方政府共同努力的方向。2021年3月，《中华人民共和国国民经济和社会发展第十四个五年规划和2035年远景目标纲要》中提出，要"优化税制结构，健全直接税体系，适当提高直接税比重"；"推进房地产税立法，健全地方税体系，逐步扩大地方税政管理权"。2021年10月，全国人大常务委员会第三十一次会议作出决定：为积极稳妥推进房地产税的立法与改革，授权国务院在部分地区开展房地产税改革试点工作。2022年10月，党的二十大报告提出，要"完善分配制度"；"加大税收、社会保障、转移支付等的调节力度"；"健全现代预算制度，优化税制结构"。从"立法先行、充分授权、分步推进"到"稳步""稳妥"推进立法，房地产税改革已进入关键酝酿期。应当看到，推进房地产税"良法善治"的基本前提之一，是对房地产税税基进行科学评估。房地产税税基评估覆盖面广、复杂性强，这也为评估行业在实践基础上不断推进技术创新提供了新的机遇和挑战。

Chapter 9
Other Assets Valuation
其他资产评估

Wisdom
名人名言

河海不择细流,故能就其深。

——李斯

取之有度,用之有节。

——司马光

Invest for maximum total real return. This means the return after inflation. This is the only rational objective for most long-term investors.

—John Templeton

The line separating investment and speculation is never bright and clear.

—Warren Buffett

Part Ⅰ: Financial Instruments Valuation
　　　金融工具评估

Abstract 中文摘要

　　金融工具是一种以合约形式存在的资产，是证明债权债务关系并据以进行货币资金交易的合法凭证，是货币资金或者金融资产借以转让的工具。金融工具可以进一步划分现金类金融工具和衍生类金融工具。前者主要是证券和其他现金（存款或贷款）；后者主要包括交易所交易的金融衍生品和柜台金融衍生品。伴随金融工具在现实生活中的日益普及，金融工具评估逐渐发展成为经济社会活动中新兴的资产评估业务类型。

　　在金融工具评估中，资产评估专业人员需要综合考虑金融工具的市场交易情况、市场流动性和变现性、自身信用风险以及信息来源等多个方面的因素。例如，金融工具的市场交易情况可以采用某一指定期间内的相对交易量指标来衡量；市场流动性和变现性具体体现为将其转让以换取现金或现金等价物的便捷程度；自身信用风险包括交易对手方违约风险以及次级贷款、杠杆、抵押资产的风险等，一般可以通过建立组网协议、第三方违约保护等手段来降低风险。市场法、成本法和收益法均可以不同程度地适用于金融工具评估。

Text* 正文

1. Definition and Market for Financial Instruments

　　A financial instrument is a contract that creates rights or obligations between specified parties to receive or pay cash or other financial consideration, or an equity instrument that authorize a contract to create a residual interest in the assets of an entity after deducting all of its liabilities. The financial instrument may require the receipt or payment to be made on or before a specific date or be triggered by a specified event. It can be broadly divided into either "cash instruments", which include loans, deposits, securities and bonds, or "<u>derivative instruments</u>", which derive a return from one or

---

* Partly from: The International Valuation Standards Council (IVSC), International Valuation Standards, 2011 Edition: IVS 250, 2011.

more underlying assets.

Valuations of financial instruments are required for many different purposes, including but not limited to:

(a) acquisitions, mergers and sales of businesses or parts of businesses;

(b) financial reporting;

(c) regulatory requirements, in particular banking solvency requirements;

(d) internal risk and compliance procedures;

(e) establishing the net asset value of insurance company funds;

(f) pricing and performance measurement of investment funds.

A thorough understanding of the instrument being valued is required to identify and valuate the relevant market information available for identical or similar instruments. Such information includes prices from recent transactions in the same or a similar instrument, quotes from dealer brokers or pricing services, indices or any other inputs to the valuation process, such as the appropriate interest rate curve, or pricing volatility.

Liquid instruments, such as stock in a major company, a government bond or a futures contract for a recognized commodity, are traded on major exchanges and real time prices are readily available, to active market participants and through various media outlets. Some liquid derivative instruments, e.g., forward stock options and commodity futures, are also traded on exchanges.

However, many types of instruments, including many types of derivatives or non-liquid cash instruments, are not traded on public exchanges and vary in degrees of illiquidity. Trades of these instruments are negotiated in the over the counter (OTC) market. Although the overall size of the market for OTC traded instruments is many times greater than that for instruments traded on public exchanges, the volume of trades varies significantly. Some common or "vanilla" swaps are traded daily in large volumes, whereas for some bespoke swaps, there is often no trade at all after the initial deal is struck, because either the terms of the contract prohibit assignment or no market for that class of instrument exists.

2. Liquidity and Market Activity

The consideration of the liquidity of an instrument or the current level of market activity is important in determining the most appropriate valuation approach. The liquidity of an asset is a measure of how easily and quickly it can be transferred in return for cash or a cash equivalent. Market activity is a measure of the volume of trading at any given time, and is a relative rather than an absolute measure.

Although a separate concept, illiquidity or low levels of market activity poses valuation challenges through a lack of relevant market data, i.e., data that is either current at the valuation date or that relates to a sufficiently similar reliable asset. The lower the liquidity or market activity, the greater the reliance that will be needed on valuation approaches that use techniques to adjust or weight the inputs based on the evidence of other transactions to reflect either market changes or differing characteristics of the asset.

3. The Risk of Valuation

3.1 Credit Risk

Understanding the credit risk is an important aspect of valuing any debt instrument. Common factors that need to be considered in establishing and measuring credit risk include the following:

3.1.1 Counterparty risk

The financial strength of the issuer or any credit support providers involve consideration of not only the trading history and profitability of the relevant entity but also performance and prospects for the industry sector generally.

3.1.2 Subordination

Establishing the priority of an instrument is critical in assessing the default risk. Other instruments may have priority over an issuer's assets or the cash flows that support the instrument.

3.1.3 Leverage

The amount of debt used to fund the assets from which an instrument's return is derived affects the volatility of returns to the issuer and can affect credit risk.

3.1.4 *Collateral asset quality*

The assets to which the holder of an instrument has recourse in the event of default must be considered. In particular, it needs to be understood whether recourse is to all the assets of the issuer or only to specified assets. The greater the value and quality of the assets to which an entity has recourse in the event of default, the lower the credit risk of the instrument.

3.1.5 *Netting agreements*

While derivative instruments are held between counterparties, credit risk may be reduced by a netting or offset agreement that limits the obligations to the net value of the transactions, i.e., if one party becomes insolvent, the other party has the right to offset sums owed to the insolvent party against sums due under other instruments.

3.1.6 *Default protection*

Many instruments contain some form of protection to reduce the risk of non-payment to the holder. Protection might take the form of a guarantee by a third party, an insurance contract, a credit default swap or more assets to support the instrument than are needed to make the payments. The default risk is also reduced if subordinated instruments take the first losses on the underlying assets and therefore reduce the risk to more senior instruments. When protection is in the form of a guarantee, an insurance contract or a credit default swap, it is necessary to identify the party providing the protection and assess that party's credit worthiness. Considering the credit worthiness of a third party involves not only the current position but also the possible effect of other guarantees or insurance contracts that it might have written. If the provider of a guarantee also guarantees many correlated debt securities, the risk of its non-performance might increase significantly.

For parties with limited information, it might be necessary to use information available for entities with similar risk characteristics. Published credit indices may assist in the process. If secondary trading in structured debt exists, there might be sufficient market data to provide evidence of the appropriate risk adjustment. The varying sensitivities of different liabilities to credit risk should be taken into account in valuating which source of credit data provides the most relevant information. The risk adjustment or credit spread applied is based on the amount a market participant would require for the particular instrument.

3.2 Own Credit Risk

Because the credit risk associated with a liability is important to its value, when valuing the interest of the issuer of a liability, the credit risk of the issuer is relevant to its value in any transfer of that liability. Wherever it is necessary to assume a transfer of the liability regardless of any actual constraints on the ability of the counterparties to do so, e.g., in order to comply with financial reporting requirements, various potential sources for reflecting own credit risk exist in the valuation of liabilities. These include the yield curve for the entity's own bonds or other debt issued and credit default swap spreads or by reference to the value of the corresponding asset. However, in many cases the issuer of a liability lacks the ability to transfer it but can only settle the liability with the counterparty.

When adjusting for own credit risk, it is also important to consider the nature of the collateral available for the liabilities valued. Collateral legally separated from the issuer normally reduces the credit risk. If liabilities are subject to a daily collateralization process, a material own credit risk adjustment is unnecessary because the counterparty is protected from loss in the event of default. However, collateral provided to one counterparty is not available to other counterparties. Thus, although some collateralized liabilities might not be subject to significant credit risk, the existence of that collateral might affect the credit risk of other liabilities.

3.3 Control Environment Risk

Compared with other asset classes, the volume of financial instruments in circulation is vast but the number of active market participants relatively few. The nature and volume of instruments and their frequency of valuation means that valuation is often undertaken using computer-based models linked to trading platforms. As a consequence of these factors, many instruments are routinely valued by the holding entity, even if the valuation is to be relied upon by external parties such as investors or regulatory authorities. The incidence of valuation by independent third-party experts is less common than that of other asset classes.

Valuation by the holding entity creates a significant risk to the perceived objectivity of valuations. If valuations are for external consumption, steps should be taken to ensure that an adequate control environment exists to minimize threats to the independence of the valuation.

As a general principle, valuations produced by an entity's "front office" brokerage and market making activities that are to be included in financial statements or otherwise relied on by third parties are subject to "back office" scrutiny and approval. Ultimate authority for such valuations should be separate from, and fully independent of, the risk-taking functions. The practical means of achieving a separation of the function may vary according to the nature of the entity, the type of instrument valued and the materiality of the value of the particular class of instrument to the overall objective. The appropriate protocols and controls should be determined by careful consideration of the threats to objectivity that would be perceived by a third party relying on the valuation.

Examples of typical components of the control environment include:

(a) establishing a governance group responsible for valuation policies and procedures and for oversight of the entity's valuation process, including some members external to the entity;

(b) a protocol for the frequency and methods for calibration and testing of valuation models;

(c) criteria for verification of certain valuations by different internal or external experts;

(d) identifying thresholds or events that trigger more thorough investigation or secondary approval requirements;

(e) identifying procedures for establishing significant inputs not directly observable in the market, e.g., by establishing pricing or audit committees.

4. Valuation Inputs

Except for liquid instruments traded on public exchanges whose current prices are both observable and accessible to all market participants, valuation inputs or sources of data may come from different sources. Commonly used input sources are broker dealer quotations and consensus pricing services.

Although not as reliable as the evidence of a contemporary and relevant trade, wherever such information is unavailable, broker dealer quotations can provide the next best evidence of how market participants would price the asset. However, problems associated with broker dealer quotations that can affect their reliability as a valuation input include the following:

(a) Broker dealers are normally only willing to make markets and provide bids in respect of more popular instruments and may not extend coverage to fewer liquid issues. Because liquidity often reduces with time, quotations may be harder to find for older instruments. A dealer's prime interest is in dealing, not supporting valuation, and he/she has little incentive to research a quotation provided for a valuation as thoroughly as he/she would for an actual buy or sell enquiry, which can impact the quality of the information.

(b) There is an inherent conflict of interest for the broker dealers to be counterparties to an instrument.

(c) Broker dealers have an incentive to weight advice to buyer clients in a way that favourably reflects the holding.

Consensus pricing services operate by collecting price information about an instrument from several participating subscribers. They reflect a pool of quotations from different sources, with or without statistical adjustment to reflect standard deviations or the distribution of the quotations.

Consensus pricing services overcome the conflict-of-interest problems associated with single broker dealers. However, the coverage of such services is at least as limited as that for single broker dealer quotations. As with any data set used as a valuation input, understanding the sources and how the sources are statistically adjusted by the provider is essential to understand the reliance that should be given to it in the valuation process.

5. Valuation Approaches

Many types of instruments, particularly those traded on exchanges, are routinely valued using computer-based automated valuation models that use <u>algorithms</u> to analyse market transactions and produce valuations on the required asset. These models are often linked to proprietary trading platforms.

No matter automated or manual, the various valuation methods used in financial markets are mostly based on variations of the market approach, the income approach or the cost approach. It is important to use a particular valuation method or model to ensure that it is calibrated with observable market information on a regular basis. The above process ensures the model to reflect current market conditions and identify any potential deficiencies. As market conditions change, it might become necessary either to change the models used or to make additional adjustments to the valuations. Those adjustments should be made to ensure that the outcome most closely results in the required valuation objective.

5.1 Market Approach

A price obtained from trading on a recognized exchange platform on or very close to the time or date of valuation best indicates the market value of a holding of the identical instrument. If recent relevant trades are rare, the evidence of quoted or offered prices may also be relevant.

Although no need for adjustment of the price information if the instrument is identical, the information recently relevant and the holding similar, some adjustments may be necessary. Examples for adjustment or weighting of the evidence of traded prices may be required are:

(a) if the instrument being valued has different characteristics to the ones for which prices are available;

(b) if there are differences in the size or volume of the reported trade to the holding being valued;

(c) if the trade was not between willing parties acting independently;

(d) the timing of the trade, which may be accentuated by the closure of exchanges.

Chapter 9 Other Assets Valuation 其他资产评估

A further factor that can create a difference between an exchange traded price and the instruments to be valued can arise if the transfer of the holding results in either the creation of a controlling interest or prospect of a change of control.

5.2 Income Approach

The value of a financial instrument may be determined using a discounted cash flow method.

The cash flows may be fixed for the life of the instrument or variable. If future cash flows are not based on fixed contracted amounts, estimates of the probable income needs to be made in order to provide the necessary inputs. The terms of an instrument determine, or allow estimation of, the undiscounted cash flows. The terms of a financial instrument typically set out:

(a) the timing of the cash flows, i.e., when the entity expects to realize the cash flows related to the instrument;

(b) the calculation of the cash flows, e.g., for a debt instrument, the interest rate that applies, i.e., the coupon, or for a derivative instrument, how the cash flows are calculated in relation to the underlying instrument or index (or indices);

(d) the timing and conditions for any options in the contract, e.g., put or call, prepayment, extension or <u>conversion options</u>;

(e) protection of the rights of the parties of the instrument, e.g., terms relating to credit risk in debt instruments or the priority over or subordination to other instruments held.

In establishing the appropriate discount rate, it is necessary to assess the return that would be required on the instrument to compensate for the time cost of money and risks related to the terms and conditions of the instrument, the liquidity and marketability, the tax status and environment, etc. The determination of the discount rate also requires assumptions about the risks such as the credit risk, the risk of changes to the regulatory or legal environment. Besides, it needs to be consistent with the cash flows, e.g., if the tax flows are gross of tax, then the discount rate should be derived from other gross of tax instruments.

Depending on the purpose of the valuation, the inputs and assumptions made into the cash flow model need to reflect the assumptions that are either to be made by market participants, or based on the holder's current expectations or targets. For example, if the purpose of the valuation is to determine market value or fair value, the assumptions should reflect the ones of market participants. If the purpose is to measure performance of an asset against management determined benchmarks, e.g., a target's <u>internal rate of return</u>, then using alternative assumptions may be appropriate.

5.3 Cost Approach

The substitution principle inherent in the cost approach is applied to the valuation of financial instruments through the use of the replication method. The method provides an indication of the current value of an instrument or portfolio by reproducing or "replicating" its risks and cash flows in a hypothetical, or synthetic, alternative. An alternative is based on a combination of securities and/or simple derivatives in order to estimate the cost of offsetting, or hedging, the position at the valuation date. Portfolio replication is often used to simplify the procedures applied to value a portfolio of complex financial instruments, e.g., expected insurance claims or structured products, by substituting a replicating portfolio of assets easier to value and therefore more efficiently risk managed on a daily basis.

Core Words and Expressions 核心术语

derivative instrument	衍生金融工具
underlying asset	标的资产
solvency	偿付能力
internal risk	内部风险
dealer brokers	证券交易商之间的经纪人
pricing volatility	价格波动
forward stock option	远期股票期权
commodity future	期货

over the counter (OTC) market	场外交易
bespoke swap	定制掉期交易
counterparty risk	交易对手风险
collateral asset quality	抵押资产质量
netting agreement	组网协议
default protection	违约保护
collateralization	以…作抵押
protocol	协议
threshold	门槛，开端
algorithms	算法式
conversion options	可转换期权
internal rate of return	内部收益率

Questions and Discussion 问题与讨论

1. After studying this part, what is your understanding of financial instrument being valued?

2. When referring to markets for financial instruments, what are the main points?

3. What are the differences between liquidity and market activity?

4. What are the various valuation methods used in financial markets?

Part II : Non-Cash Flow Producing Assets Valuation 无法产生现金流量的资产的评估

Abstract 中文摘要

对于无法产生现金流量的资产，其价值主要源自供给稀缺、消费效用、个人认知等一系列因素。资产评估专业人员无法采用现金流折现模型即收益法的思路对其进行评估；而市场法虽然在此时具有更强的适用性，但也不可避免地受到这类资产价值的易变、市场流通性的缺乏以及评估的主观性等因素的影响。因此，如何对无法产生现金流量的资产价值进行最佳估计，仍然是资产评估领域的难题。

Text* 正文

Assets that produce no cash flows cannot be valued using discounted cash flow models. The assets derive their value from a combination of factors: a scarcity of supply relative to demand, consumption utility and individual perceptions. While they can be valued relative to comparables, their values are much more <u>volatile</u> since the values are based entirely upon perceptions.

1. Special Issues in Non-Cash Flow Producing Assets Valuation

The biggest difference between these assets and cash flow generating assets is that no <u>intrinsic</u> value backs up the price. Consequently, the only way to value these assets is by relative valuation, i.e., how similar assets are priced in the market. The process of using comparables in valuing an asset is fairly straightforward in theory.

The first step of the process is to collect a group of comparable assets. The second is to estimate a measure of standardized value for this group. The third is to control for differences between assets in this group and the asset being valued to arrive at a measure of reasonable value for the asset.

There will be several problems when one applies this approach. First of all, finding comparable assets may be difficult for some non-cash flow producing assets. While there are indices compiled on various unconventional assets, there are substantial differences between the assets within each index. And the markets for many of these assets are neither liquid nor public. Many transactions are private and the reported prices are therefore unreliable, therefore it is hard to get the comparable transactions. It is also unclear how one controls for differences across comparable assets, since these

---

* Partly from: Damodaran A. Investment valuation: Tools and Techniques for Determining the Value of Any Asset.3rd Edition,John Wiley & Sons, Inc., 2012: 775-777.

Chapter 9 Other Assets Valuation 其他资产评估

are qualitative differences relate to perception.

In addition, the prices of many of these assets are directly related to how scarce the supply of the asset is. For instance, the Honus Wagner T-206 baseball card is the most highly valued card in the market because only 58 cards known to exist in mint condition. One card sold for $640,000 in 1996 to Michael Gidwitz, an investor from Chicago. The card had been earlier owned by Wayne Gretzky, who bought it for $451,000 in 1991. Hence, any event that alters the balance may affect the price. A surprise finding of another mint condition Honus Wagner card in someone's attic can cause the price to change dramatically.

2. Take Art and Collectibles as Examples

Many investors view investments in art and collectibles as part of their overall portfolio. To account for these investments, valuers need to first think about several issues in exerting investments.

The first issue relates to the type of returns that these investments generate for investors over long periods. A number of studies have investigated this question. Among comprehensive analysis of art as an investment, the most famous index is Mei & Moses All Art Index. By studying the relationship between artwork and stock market from 1810 to 2000, Jianping Mei, an assistant professor of New York University, and his colleague Michael Moses found that art, as a stand-alone investment, earned low returns historically. However, the low correlation between the returns of art and stocks may give art a place in a well-diversified portfolio of financial assets, but only at the margin.

The second issue relates to how to optimally value investments in art and collectibles. In practice, they are almost always valued on a relative basis. Thus, a Picasso is usually valued based on what other Picassos have sold for recently.

Generally speaking, there are at least three problems when one values these assets. The first one is that market is illiquid and relatively few transactions exist. The most recent sale of a Picasso was three years ago and a great extent might have changed in the art market since then. The second problem is that no two Picassos are alike and there are substantial differences both in style and value across different paintings. The third problem is that there is the very real possibility of <u>forgery and fraud</u> and much of these can be detected only by an expert. Consequently, the relative valuation of art and collectibles remains the province of expert appraisers who try to overcome these problems and estimate a fair value. All analysts are susceptible to market moods and bubbles and busts are just as common in this market as they are in other ones.

Hence, what are the lessons for individual investors? The first one is that while art and collectibles, as a class, may balance a portfolio, you have to spend substantially more time acquiring specialized knowledge to be successful with these investments than that you would with financial investments. The second lesson is that you should expect to have much higher transaction costs with investments in art and collectibles, especially at the high end of the market. The third lesson is that you should collect baseball cards or Old Master paintings because you enjoy them instead of as mere investments. The psychological returns may compensate for the sub-standard financial returns.

Core Words and Expressions 核心术语

volatile	不稳定的
intrinsic	本质的，固有的
art and collectibles	艺术品，收藏品
portfolio	证券投资组合
Mei & Moses All Art Index	梅摩艺术指数
forgery and fraud	伪造和欺诈

Questions and Discussion 问题与讨论

1. Which method would you prefer to value the non-cash flow producing assets? What are their advantages and disadvantages?

2. Describe other types of non-cash flow producing asset to your classmates.

Part III: Mineral Rights Valuation 矿业权评估

Abstract 中文摘要

一般而言，一个国家或地区绝大部分的矿产和土地资源是由国家或政府所有的，其矿业权和土地的价值评估与所属国家或地区的矿产和土地资源法律制度也是密切相关的。这类法律制度是对矿产资源进行权属确定、评估定价、市场交易等事项的法律依据，也是构建矿业权评估理论和技术体系的重要基础。

数据显示，对国有矿产资源进行价值评估的现实需求巨大。由于受到政府运营、宏观政策等因素的影响，矿业权的价值会随着时间的推移不断发生变化，甚至出现很大波动。当矿业权的价值上升时，国家、政府等持有主体会因此获得高额收益，这些收益可能被用于公共部门的运转所需，也可能被用于税收减免和民生改善，进而促进整体经济的有效运行。

本节首先对资源性资产进行分析，在此基础上，以美国相关的历史数据为例，进一步对矿业权、原油天然气开采权、国有土地等资源性资产的价值变动及其评估途径进行介绍。

Text* 正文

Generally speaking, the state or government owns a substantial fraction of the mineral rights and land in a country or region. The value of these resources varies substantially over time, with both the acquisitions and sales of these assets and changes in the prices of the minerals and land involved. Whether or not one is interested in measures of national wealth, land management policy as part of efficient government operations, or long-run macroeconomic fiscal policy issues, time series estimates of the value of mineral rights and land are potentially valuable information. At one extreme, consider a country or state which owns substantial mineral rights if the price of those minerals skyrockets. The additional revenues, potentially available either for use in the public sector, or to allow tax cuts to provide greater private income, may alter

---

* Partly from: Boskin M J, Kumar P. New Estimates of the Value of Federal Mineral Rights and Land. Ucla Economics Working Papers, 1986, 16(5):1314-1317.

the course of the economy. There are historical precedents. Saudi Arabia was able to virtually abolish taxation due to revenues from the sale of mineral rights, and Alaska actually used oil-based revenues to provide cash grants on a per capita basis to its citizens, thereby increasing their private wealth and consumption opportunities.

The microeconomics of sensible resource allocation, within the public sector and between the public and private sector, relies on careful cost-benefit valuations of the value of public services and the opportunity costs of providing them. These in turn are only possible with accurate information on actual and potential revenue sources, including the opportunity costs of purchases and sales of assets, as well as traditional flows of income into and out of the public sector. Therefore, the value of mineral rights and land is potentially an important piece of information for a host of public policy questions.

This section provides new time series estimates of the value of government mineral rights and land using relevant data from the post-war period United States as an example. It brings together various data sources in a way as consistent as possible, uses reasonable economic theory to infer the value of mineral rights, and compares the results with previous estimates. The results suggest that the value of government mineral rights and land is quite substantial, and can fluctuate by tens of billions of dollars annually. These sorts of changes, if aggregated over any substantial period, may suggest a reappraisal of traditional land management policy as part of a comprehensive overall fiscal policy.

1. Methodologies for Valuing Mineral Rights

The base year value of government mineral rights is the sum of three components: future royalties on proven reserves, future royalties on estimated undiscovered reserves and future bonuses on unleased land.

To obtain the value for any future year, the value for the previous year can be taken by adding capital gains or losses, and subtracting bonus and royalty payments received. Capital gains and losses are calculated by assuming that the price in that year is the base from which future prices grow at the interest rate. Since all three components of the base year value are proportional to the current price, the capital gain is just the change in price times the previous year's value. Using this method, the base year value can be projected backwards as well.

When the government leases the mineral rights in a particular area, it reduced its wealth by transferring the mineral rights to the private sector. In return, the government receives some payment immediately in the form of a bonus, with the rest of the payments deferred as royalties or rental payments. By the time reserves are proven, their only value to the government is the present value of the royalties they represent.

Ignoring undiscovered reserves can cause several problems in the wealth and income accounts of the government. For example, the sale of leases would be treated as an increase in government receipts and wealth rather than an asset sale, and future royalty rights would not appear in the accounts until drilling is successful. Alternative, but economically identical, forms of payment would appear to have changed the wealth of the government. Further, capital gains and losses associated with price changes would only be counted on proven reserves. Government real capital formation would be overstated, since the sale of assets in the form of possible reserves would be ignored.

For all of these reasons, it is likely to believe accurate resource accounting for the government sector requires estimating a value for the undiscovered reserves on government land. This only needs to be done for a base year; changes can enter using the perpetual inventory method. For the base year calculation, Department of the Interior can be used to estimate for the expected undiscovered reserves for onshore government land and offshore. To value the royalties on these undiscovered reserves, an assumption regarding future prices needs to be made. The strong and convenient assumption that future prices are expected to increase at the rate of interest can be chosen. The assumption means that the history of production is irrelevant, and all production patterns yield the same present value of royalties. Such time independence is especially useful for undiscovered reserves since there is a substantial and uncertain time until the resource can be extracted.

2. The Value of Oil and Gas Mineral Rights

The estimates for the value of federal <u>oil and gas mineral rights</u> in 1981 have two striking facts. Firstly, the present value of bonuses from <u>offshore mineral</u> leases far exceeds the corresponding figure for <u>onshore</u> leases. The reason is that offshore bonuses were much greater than onshore bonuses in the period 1954-1979. For example, since 1971, offshore bonuses have annually exceeded one billion dollars whereas onshore bonuses did not reach twenty million dollars. The difference is reflected in the estimate of the present value of bonuses through equation. Secondly, the present value of future royalties from economically recoverable undiscovered reserves similarly dominates the corresponding figure for proven reserves. The explanation is straightforward: estimates of undiscovered resources are much larger than currently proven reserves.

The current value of over $800 billion is the single largest asset in the complete balance sheet of the federal government. It is substantially larger than the value of federal land. In fact, it is approximately the combined value of all federal tangible assets or all federal financial assets. Prior to 1974, the total series was quite stable in nominal dollars, and therefore it exhibited a slight downward decline in real terms. While the dollar value has increased sharply recently, prior to the increases in energy prices, the values for oil and gas were substantial.

3. The Value of Land

It may be tempting to simply add the value of land to mineral rights. However, there are theoretical reasons to suspect that at least some of the value of mineral rights is capitalized into the value of the land bearing the minerals. In that case, it would be necessary to discount the value of the land before aggregating the land and the mineral rights. Since the extent of capitalization is uncertain, the disaggregated components rather than their sum should be focused on. Clearly, to obtain the total value of land and mineral rights, it is necessary to add some, if not all, of the value of land to the estimate of the value of mineral rights.

4. Summery and Conclusion

The value of federal oil and gas mineral rights to be very substantial is

Chapter 9 Other Assets Valuation 其他资产评估

estimated, particularly following the sharp rises in energy prices in 1974 and 1979. In 1981, the <u>magnitude</u> exceeds the privately held national debt. The contributions of this study include attention to the composition of the holdings of land. It is unique in its effort to determine the value of the federal government's mineral rights. The information about undiscovered reserves and royalty and bonus payments to the government is exploited. This methodology can be extended to both other minerals and the private sector.

Therefore, there remains room for considerable research on both the value of government land and its mineral rights. A new benchmark estimate for the value of land in a particular year is especially important. A more detailed disaggregation of the types of land holdings and improved and updated corresponding price information would also be helpful. Improved estimates of the size of other mineral resources on land and estimates of the relationship between the quantity of economically recoverable unproven reserves of oil and gas and their prices would enable us to produce more comprehensive measures of wealth.

Finally, such estimates are important for sensible government <u>budgetary decisions</u>. These decisions include land management policy, general cost-benefit analysis incorporating proper measures of the opportunity cost of resources, and perhaps even, in some contexts, fiscal policy.

Core Words and Expressions 核心术语

mineral right	矿业权
minerals and land	矿产和土地
skyrocket	飞涨，猛涨
per capita basis	人均基础
unleased land	未出租的土地
bonus	红利，收益
undiscovered reserves	未发现的储备

are proportional to	与……成比例的
oil and gas mineral right	石油和天然气矿产开采权
offshore mineral	近海矿产
onshore	陆上的，岸上的
magnitude	规模
budgetary decisions	预算决策

Questions and Discussion 问题与讨论

1. What are the factors that influence the valuation of mineral rights?

2. What can we learn from the two striking facts of value of oil and gas mineral rights?

Information Extension

思政微课堂

资产评估是现代高端服务业，是经济社会发展中的重要专业力量。现阶段，我国经济发展正处于转变发展方式、优化经济结构、转换增长动力的关键时期，在数字经济、社会治理、民生保障、绿色生态、科技创新等领域都提出了一系列新的发展战略。这对资产评估行业的服务领域、服务类型、服务质量提出了更高要求。

为推动资产评估行业健康有序发展，拓展资产评估市场领域，推进资产评估机构转型升级，中国资产评估协会于2019年7月修订印发了《资产评估行业市场开拓路线指引（2019年）》（中评协办〔2019〕64号）。该指引根据现有法律法规及相关政策文件，收集、分析、整理并归集出涉及深化国有企业改革、加强金融监管、加强行政事业单位国有资产管理以及新经济发展等方面的业务类型，不仅涵盖了传统评估业务，也囊括了许多值得评估机构积极拓展的新业务。当前，新经济、新业态触发的新业务包括但不限于数字经济时代的数据资产价值评估、

"双碳"目标下的生态产品价值评估、ESG视角下的企业价值重估等，资产评估业务日益呈现多元化发展态势。

以新发展理念为统领，以高质量发展为主题，紧密衔接"十四五"时期国家和重大发展战略，中国资产评估协会于2021年9月发布了《"十四五"时期资产评估行业发展规划》（中评协〔2021〕21号），分析资产评估行业发展的现状和面临的形势，明确了"十四五"时期资产评估行业发展的指导思想、基本原则、基本目标和主要任务。该规划提出，资产评估行业要积极服务国家重大发展战略，包括：服务知识产权有序流转，健全知识产权评估体系；服务生态文明建设，拓展生态系统资产评估业务；服务资本市场，助力提高上市公司信息披露质量；服务新经济、新业态，强化对新评估业务的纵深研究；紧跟现代财税体制改革，全面服务财政中心工作；加快推进行业数字化转型，全面提升信息化水平及服务能力等。

例如，生态系统资产评估是资源资产化管理的重要环节。高度重视生态系统资产价值，显化自然资源的资产和资本属性，是真实反映自然资源稀缺性的必然选择，也是建设生态文明、有效保护和持续利用自然资源、推动高质量发展的必然要求。党的二十大报告提出，"中国式现代化是人与自然和谐共生的现代化""必须牢固树立和践行绿水青山就是金山银山的理念，站在人与自然和谐共生的高度谋划发展"。鉴于此，资产评估行业应顺应国家发展理念，在生态资源开发和绿色产业发展中有效发挥价值尺度专业优势，开展山水林田湖草沙冰等自然资源资产评估研究，加强生态工程绩效、生态环境损害价值、生态补偿价值评价评估和绿色金融等领域的专业实践，积极探索"绿水青山就是金山银山"的有效转化途径，助力人与自然和谐发展的现代化建设新格局的形成。

Chapter 10
Valuation Reporting
资产评估报告

Wisdom
名人名言

道虽迩，不行不至；事虽小，不为不成。

——荀子

悟已往之不谏，知来者之可追。

——陶渊明

I know only that what is moral is what you feel good after and what is immoral is what you feel bad after.

—Ernest Hemingway

It takes 20 years to build a reputation and five minutes to ruin it. If you think about that, you'll do things differently.

—Warren Buffett

Rudimentary Knowledge
基本知识

Abstract 中文摘要

资产评估报告是指资产评估机构及其资产评估专业人员遵守法律、行政法规和资产评估准则，根据委托履行必要的评估程序后，由资产评估机构对评估对象在评估基准日特定目的下的价值出具的专业报告。资产评估专业人员应当根据评估业务的具体情况，为委托方和其他评估报告使用者提供简明、清晰的价值说明和必要信息，使评估报告使用者能够正确理解和使用评估结论；资产评估报告不应存在歧义或者误导性信息。资产评估专业人员可以根据评估目的、评估对象的复杂程度、委托方的合理要求等综合确定资产评估报告的详略程度。

从具体内容来看，资产评估报告应当载明工作范围，并应当按照一定格式和要求进行编制，反映评估主体、委托方及其他评估报告使用者、评估目的、评估对象、价值类型、评估基准日、调查范围、信息来源、评估假设、使用限制说明、准则依据、评估方法、评估结果、评估报告日等基本信息。例如，根据中国资产评估协会修订发布的《资产评估执业准则——资产评估报告》（中评协〔2018〕35号），资产评估报告的内容包括标题及文号、目录、声明、摘要、正文、附件，其标题格式一般为"企业名称+经济行为关键词+评估对象+资产评估报告"，其文号格式一般包括资产评估机构特征字、种类特征字、年份、报告序号；资产评估报告载明的评估目的应当唯一，明确评估结论的具体用途，并应当载明评估对象和评估范围，描述评估对象的基本情况；资产评估报告应当说明选择的价值类型名称、定义及选择理由，应当说明所选用的评估方法名称、定义及选择理由，应当说明采用的法律法规依据、准则依据、权属依据及取价依据等，应当说明资产评估程序实施过程中现场调查、收集整理评估资料、评定估算等主要内容，应当披露所使用的资产评估假设；资产评估报告应当以文字和数字形式表述评估结论，并明确评估结论的使用有效期，其评估结论可以是确定的数值、区间值或者其他形式的专业意见；资产评估报告应当至少由两名承办该业务的资产评估专业人员签名，最后加盖资产评估机构的印章，法定业务资产评估报告的正文应当由至少两名承办该业务的资产评估师签名。此外，资产评估报告应当使用中文撰写；

对于同时出具中外文资产评估报告的，若中外文资产评估报告存在不一致，应当以中文资产评估报告为准；资产评估报告一般以人民币为计量币种，使用其他币种计量的，应当注明该币种在评估基准日与人民币的汇率。

资产评估报告是资产评估机构及其资产评估专业人员针对评估对象发表专家意见的载体和履行评估合同的劳动成果；工作底稿是资产评估专业人员在执行评估业务过程中形成的反映评估程序实施情况、支持评估结论的工作记录和相关资料。资产评估业务完成后，资产评估专业人员应将资产评估报告与工作底稿等归集形成资产评估档案，并按照有关法律、法规及资产评估准则的规定，以适当的期限妥善保管。

Text* 正文

1. General Principles

The final step in the valuation process is communicating the value to commissioning party and any other intended users. It is essential that the valuation report communicates the information necessary for proper understanding of the valuation. A valuation report shall be unambiguous, providing the intended reader with a clear understanding of the valuation.

To provide comparability, relevance and credibility, the valuation report shall set out a clear and accurate description of the scope of the assignment, its purpose and intended use, confirmation of the basis of value used and disclosure of any assumptions, special assumptions, material uncertainty or limiting conditions that directly affect the valuation.

2. Scope of Work

The purpose of the valuation, the complexity of the asset valued and the users' requirements determine the level of detail appropriate to the valuation report. The format of the report and any exclusion from the content requirements should be

---

* Partly from: The International Valuation Standards Council (IVSC), International Valuation Standards, 2022 Edition, 2021.

agreed and recorded in the scope of work. The scope of work also sets out the agreed purpose of the valuation, the <u>extent of investigation</u>, procedures that will be adopted, assumptions that will be made and the limitations that will apply. The scope of work may be prepared at the outset or during the progress of the valuation assignment but before the valuation and report are finalized. It is recommended that the scope of work be referred to in the report.

3. Specific Report Contents

All valuation reports shall include reference to the matters listed below, some of which are also recorded in the scope of work.

3.1 Identification and Status of the Valuer

The statement needs to confirm the identity of the valuer who can be an individual or a firm. Moreover, the valuer is in a position to provide an objective and unbiased valuation and is competent to undertake the valuation. If the valuer has obtained material assistance from others in relation to any aspect of the assignment, the nature of such assistance and the extent of reliance shall be referenced in the report.

The report shall also include the signature of the individual or firm responsible for the valuation. And check whether the valuer has any material connection or involvement with the subject of the valuation or the party commissioning the valuation.

3.2 Identification of the Client and Intended Users

The party commissioning the valuation shall be identified together with any other parties whose decisions may rely on the valuation. Confirmation of those for whom the valuation assignment is being produced is important when determining the form and content of the report to ensure that it contains information relevant to their needs. It is also important to understand whether there are any other intended users of the valuation report, their identity and their needs, to ensure that the report content and format meets those users' needs.

3.3 Purpose of the Valuation

The purpose of the valuation determines the basis of value, which is very important and shall be clearly stated, such as for loan security, to support a share transfer, etc. The purpose for which the valuation assignment is being prepared must be clearly identified as it is important that valuation advice is not used out of context or for purposes for which it is not intended. The purpose of the valuation will also typically influence or determine the basis/bases of value to be used.

3.4 Identification of the Asset or Liability

Clarification may be needed to distinguish between an asset and an interest in or right of use of that asset. If the valuation is of an asset utilized in conjunction with other assets, it is necessary to clarify whether the <u>group or portfolio of assets</u> is to be valued or each of the assets individually. If it is the latter, it is also important to clarify whether each asset is assumed to be valued as an individual item and to assume that the other assets are available to a buyer or assuming that the other assets are not available.

3.5 Basis of Value

It is a statement of the fundamental measurement assumptions of a valuation and shall be appropriate for the purpose. The source of the definition of any basis of value used shall be cited or the basis explained. As we have mentioned in Chapter 1, the basis of valuation can fall into three principal categories. The first is to indicate the most probable price that would be achieved in a hypothetical exchange in a free and open market, such as market value. The second is to indicate the benefits that a person or an entity enjoys from ownership of an asset, such as investment value and special value. The third is to indicate the price that would be reasonably agreed between two specific parties for the exchange of an asset, such as fair value.

3.6 Valuation Date

The valuation date is defined as the date on which the opinion of value applies. The valuation date may be different from the date on which the valuation report is issued or the date on which investigations are to be undertaken or completed. Wherever relevant, these dates shall be clearly distinguished in the report.

3.7 Extent of Investigation

The extent of the investigations undertaken shall be <u>disclosed</u> in the report including the limitations on those investigations that set out in the scope of work such as the limitations or restrictions on the inspection, inquiry, and analysis for the purpose of the valuation.

3.8 Nature and Source of the Information Relied upon

The nature and source of any relevant information relied upon in the valuation process without specific verification by the valuer shall be disclosed. The nature and source of any relevant information that is to be relied upon and the extent of any verification to be undertaken during the valuation process must be identified. Besides, the nature and source of the valuation inputs must be consistent with the basis of value, which in turn must have regard to the valuation purpose. For example, various approaches and methods may be used to arrive at an opinion of value providing they use market-derived data. The market approach will, by definition, use market-derived inputs. To indicate market value, the income approach should be applied, using inputs and assumptions that would be adopted by participants. To indicate market value with the cost approach, the cost of an asset of equal utility and the appropriate depreciation should be determined by analysis of market-based costs and depreciation.

3.9 Assumptions and Special Assumptions

All assumptions made shall be clearly stated. Assumptions are matters that are reasonable to accept as facts in the context of the valuation assignment without specific investigation or verification. They are matters that, once stated, are to be accepted in understanding the valuation.

A special assumption is the assumption that either assumes facts that differ from the actual facts existing at the valuation date or that would not be made by a typical market participant in a transaction on the valuation date. Special assumptions are often used to illustrate the effect of changed circumstances on value.

3.10 Restrictions on Use, Distribution or Publication

Wherever it is necessary or desirable to restrict the use of the valuation or those relying upon it, this shall be stated.

3.11 Valuation Has Been Undertaken in Accordance with Valuation Standards

While confirmation of conformity with valuation standards is required, the purpose of the valuation requires a departure from the standards. Any such departure shall be identified, together with justification for that departure. A departure would not be justified if it results in a misleading valuation.

3.12 Valuation Approach and Reasoning

More than one valuation approach or method may be used to arrive at an indication of value, when insufficient factual or observable inputs prevent a single method to produce a reliable conclusion. If more than one approach and method is used, the resulting indications of value should be analysed and reconciled to reach a valuation conclusion.

To understand the valuation figure in context, the report shall make reference to the approach or approaches adopted, the key inputs used and the principal reasons for the conclusions reached. The process requirement does not apply, if it has been specifically agreed and recorded in the scope of work that a valuation report shall be provided without reasons or other supporting information.

3.13 Amount of the Valuation

This shall be expressed in the applicable currency. It is stated that the currency for the valuation and the final valuation report or conclusion must be established. For example, a valuation might be prepared in RMB euros or US dollars. This requirement is particularly important for valuation assignments involving assets in multiple countries and/or cash flows in multiple currencies.

3.14 Date of the Valuation Report

The date on which the report is issued shall be included, which may be different from the valuation date. Valuers must disclose or report the date of value that is the basis of their analyses, opinions or conclusions. Valuers must also state the date they disclose or report their valuation.

4. Valuation Record

A record shall be kept of the work done during the valuation process for a reasonable period in regard to any relevant legal or regulatory requirements. The record subject to any such requirements shall include the key inputs, all calculations, investigations and analyses relevant to the final conclusion, and a <u>copy</u> of any <u>draft or final report</u> provided to the client.

Core Words and Expressions 核心术语

commissioning party	委托方
intended user	期望使用者
comparability	可比性
relevance	相关性
credibility	可信性
extent of investigation	调查程度
group or portfolio of assets	资产组或投资组合
factual or observable inputs	事实的或可观察输入
copy	备份
draft or final report	报告草稿或终稿

Questions and Discussion 问题与讨论

1. Is there any relation between valuation report contents and scope of work?

2. Please summarize the basic contents of a valuation report.

3. Why are valuation approaches and reasoning required in a valuation report?

4. What is the difference between the date of the valuation report and valuation date?

More Knowledge

知识扩展

Topic: Reporting under Valuation Standards

Abstract 中文摘要

编制资产评估报告作为资产评估程序的最后一步,其重要性在于为委托方和其他评估报告使用者提供资产评估结论。本节主要以由国际评估准则理事会(IVSC)制定的国际评估准则(IVS)和美国评估促进会(TAF)制定的专业评估执业统一准则(USPAP)为例,对资产评估准则中关于评估报告的内容进行介绍。

根据国际评估准则(IVS),资产评估专业人员应当在资产评估报告中清楚、明确地阐述评估结论,说明工作范围、评估目的和评估对象的预期用途,并披露可能影响评估结论的评估假设和限制条件。根据专业评估执业统一准则(USPAP),不动产和动产评估报告可以划分为三类,即完整评估报告、概述型评估报告和限制用途评估报告;企业价值评估报告可以划分为一般评估报告和限制用途评估报告两种类型。

此外,"Valuation Certificate"在不同资产评估准则语境下的含义略有不同。在国际评估准则(IVS)中,其主要代表一种扼要的评估报告,简明地提供评估结论及相关信息;而在专业评估执业统一准则(USPAP)中,其主要作为评估师在评估报告结尾部分进行的声明,以表明评估师工作的独立性、与评估准则的一致性等相关内容。

Text* 正文

1. Valuation Report under Standards

A valuation report is a document that indicates the value conclusion recording

---

* Partly from: The International Valuation Standards Council (IVSC), International Valuation Standards, 2022 Edition, 2021; The Appraisal Foundation (TAF), 2020-2021 Uniform Standards of Professional Appraisal Practice, 2021; Wang Chengjun, Professional English, Appraisal Journal of China, 2007.

the instructions for the assignment, the basis and purpose of the valuation, and the results of the analysis, etc. A valuation report may explain the analytical processes of valuation, and present meaningful information used in the analysis. It also needs to identify the property and property rights subject to the valuation and disclose all underlying assumptions and limiting conditions and specifies the dates of valuation and reporting. In addition, it describes the extent of the inspection, refers to the applicability of valuation standards and any required disclosures, and includes the valuer's signature. The analytical processes and empirical data used to arrive at the value conclusion may also be included in the valuation report to guide the reader the procedures and evidence that a valuer used to develop the valuation.

Each analysis, opinion, or conclusion that results from a valuation must be communicated in a manner meaningful to the intended user and should be accurate. The type, content and length of a report vary according to the intended user, legal requirements, the property type, and the nature and complexity of the assignment. However, even if a client asks for a report that excludes detailed documentation, the valuer must undertake the analysis required by the assignment as set by the scope of work. In this case, all material, data, and working papers used to prepare the valuation are kept in the valuer's file. The extent of file documentation depends on the type of report prepared. A less detailed report requires more file documentation, while a more detailed report may require little external documentation. Usually, a report is presented in the format requested by the intended user. In some countries, a valuation report may be oral or written, and the written reports may be form or narrative reports.

In this section, two widely-used valuation standards which contains valuation report requirement are introduced.

1.1 Valuation Report Under IVS

International Valuation Standards (IVS) has made requirement of valuation reporting, which are voluntarily used by valuers. It applies to all valuation reports or reports on the outcome of a valuation review which may range from comprehensive narrative reports to abbreviated summary reports. Taking IVS 2022 edition as an example, the terms of IVS 103 states the standard in introduction of reporting, the general requirement of reports, valuation reports and valuation review reports.

It is essential that the valuation report communicates the information necessary for proper understanding of the valuation or valuation review. A report must provide the intended users with a clear understanding of the valuation. To provide useful information, the report must set out a clear and accurate description of the scope of the assignment, its purpose and intended use (including any limitations on that use) and disclosure of any assumptions, special assumptions, significant uncertainty or limiting conditions that directly affect the valuation.

The purpose of the valuation, the complexity of the asset being valued and the users' requirements will altogether determine the level of detail appropriate to the valuation report. The format of the report should be agreed with all parties as part of establishing a scope of work. Compliance with this standard does not require a particular form or format of report; however, the report must be sufficient to communicate to the intended users the scope of the valuation assignment, the work performed and the conclusions reached. The report should also be sufficient for an appropriately experienced valuation professional with no prior involvement with the valuation engagement to review the report and understand the items which must be conveyed in the report or review report.

Where the report is the result of an assignment involving the valuation of an asset or assets, the report must convey: the scope of the work performed, intended use, intended users, the purpose, the approach or approaches adopted, the method or methods applied, the key inputs used, the assumptions made, the conclusion(s) of value and principal reasons for any conclusions reached, and the date of the report (which may differ from the valuation date).

Where the report is the result of a valuation review, the report must convey: the scope of the review performed, the valuation report being reviewed and the inputs and assumptions upon which that valuation was based, the valuation report being reviewed and the inputs and assumptions upon which that valuation was based, and the date of the report (which may differ from the valuation date).

1.2 Valuation Report Under USPAP

In the United States, professional valuers are required to conduct their valuation activities in compliance with the requirement of Uniform Standards of Professional Appraisal Practice (USPAP). According to USPAP, valuation reports for real property and personal property are divided into three types: self-contained appraisal report, summary appraisal report, and restricted use appraisal report; while valuation reports for business valuation are divided into appraisal report and restricted use appraisal report.

The essential difference between these reporting options is the level of detail required in certain areas of presentation and the accompanying work file. The restricted use appraisal report is different from self-contained report and summary report in that only the client is the intended user of the restricted use report, while in self-contained report and summary report, the intended users of the report could either be client or other intended users defined by clients.

2. Concept Analysis: Certificate in Valuation Report

There are different contents of valuation certificate in different areas. In some countries such as the UK, the term valuation certificate is similar to the term valuation report and could be used interchangeably. Valuation certificate designates a document in which the valuer certifies the amount of the valuation of a property. Although it may also take the form of a detailed report, it is usually a short letter including the valuation date, purpose of the assignment, date of the certificate, assumptions upon which the valuation is based, and the name, address, and qualification of the valuer. While in other countries such as the United States, a valuation certificate usually means a statement in which the valuer affirms that the facts presented are correct and the valuer has performed the valuation in compliance with ethical and professional standards, etc.

2.1 Certificate Under IVS

According to International Valuation Standards (IVS), each valuation report shall clearly and accurately set forth the conclusions of the valuation in an accurate manner. A valuer should identify the client, the intended use of the valuation, basis of value and relevant dates such as valuation date, the date of report and the date of inspection.

Moreover, the valuer should identify the property rights or interests and physical and legal characteristics of the property, and also describe the scope of the work used to develop the valuation. In addition, he/she should specify all assumptions and limiting conditions upon which the value conclusion is contingent, identify special, unusual, or extraordinary assumptions, and address the probability that such conditions may occur. The valuers should also give a description of the information and data <u>examined</u>, the market analysis performed, the valuation approaches and procedures followed, and the reasoning that supports the analyses, opinions, and conclusions in the report.

To protect the valuer's interests, he/she should contain a clause in the report prohibiting the publication of the report in whole or in part, or any reference thereto, or to the <u>valuation figures</u> contained therein, or to the names and <u>professional affiliation</u> of the valuers, without the written approval of the valuer.

2.2 Certificate Under USPAP

Valuation Certificate is used in appraisal report in the United States and some other countries to attest to the fact that the appraiser follows the ethical and professional requirements in performing the assignment. <u>A signed certification</u> is an integral part of the appraisal report. The appraiser, who signs any part of the appraisal report, including <u>a letter of transmittal</u>, must also sign this certification. According to USPAP, each written appraisal report must contain a signed certification similar in content to the following form:

"I certify that, to the best of my knowledge and belief:

(a) The statements of fact contained in this report are true and correct.

(b) The reported analyses, opinions, and conclusions are limited only by the reported assumptions and limiting conditions and are based on my personal, impartial, and unbiased professional analyses, opinions, and conclusions.

(c) I have no (or the specified) present or prospective interest in the property that is the subject of this report and no (or the specified) personal interest with respect to the parties involved.

(d) My engagement in this assignment is not contingent upon developing or reporting predetermined results.

(e) My compensation for completing this assignment is not contingent upon the development or reporting of a predetermined value or direction in value that favours the cause of the client, the amount of the value opinion, the attainment of a stipulated result, or the occurrence of a subsequent event directly related to the intended use of this appraisal.

(f) My analyses, opinions, and conclusions are developed, and this report is prepared, in conformity with the Uniform Standards of Professional Appraisal Practice.

(g) I have (or have not) made a personal inspection of the property that is the subject of this report. (If more than one person signs this certification, the certification must clearly specify which individuals did and which individuals did not make a personal inspection of the appraised property.)

(h) No one provided significant appraisal assistance to the person signing this certification. (If there are exceptions, the name of those providing significant appraisal assistance must be stated.)."

Core Words and Expressions 核心术语

analytical process	分析程序
underlying assumptions and limiting conditions	基本假设和限制条件
the extent of the inspection	勘查的情况（范围／程度）
the valuer's signature	评估专业人员（评估师）的签名
legal requirements	法律要求
detailed documentation	详细的文件
working papers	工作文件
the valuer's file	评估专业人员（评估师）的底稿文件
file documentation	工作底稿

external documentation	外部文件
written report	书面报告
form or narrative report	表格型的报告或叙述型的报告
professional valuer	职业评估师
self-contained appraisal report	完整评估报告
summary appraisal report	概述型评估报告
restricted use appraisal report	限制用途评估报告
appraisal report	（一般）评估报告
reporting options	报告选择权，报告类型
the level of detail	详细程度
accompanying work file	作为附件的工作文件
valuation certificate	评估声明
ethical and professional standards	职业道德和行业准则
examined	经检验的
valuation figures	评估数据
professional affiliation	职业从属关系
a signed certification	经评估师签署的评估声明
a letter of transmittal	提交函

Questions and Discussion 问题与讨论

1. What is appraisal report? And what is restricted use appraisal report?

2. What is the different meaning of valuation certificate under IVS and USPAP?

Information Extension
思政微课堂

我国的资产评估行政管理部门一直非常重视对资产评估报告的规范。20 世纪 90 年代，资产评估主要服务于国有企业的改革和对外开放，对资产评估报告的规范最初也由国有资产管理部门制定。1992 年，国家国有资产管理局出台《国有资产评估管理办法施行细则》（国资办发〔1992〕36 号），对国务院《国有资产评估管理办法》（国务院令第 91 号）要求资产评估机构出具的资产评估结果报告书应当包含的内容提出了要求。1993 年，国家国有资产管理局制定和发布《关于资产评估报告书的规范意见》，进一步规范了资产评估报告书的出具和内容。1996 年，国家国有资产管理局转发了中国资产评估协会制定的《资产评估操作规范意见（试行）》，规定了资产评估报告书及送审专用材料、资产评估工作底稿和项目档案管理的具体要求。1999 年，财政部印发《资产评估报告基本内容与格式的暂行规定》（财评字〔1999〕91 号），对原有的资产评估报告制度进一步修改完善。2021 年，为健全国有资产报告制度、规范国有资产报告编报工作，财政部印发了《国有资产报告编报工作暂行办法》（财资〔2021〕123 号），要求国有资产报告编制要实现全口径、全覆盖，采取价值量与实物量相结合的方式，全面、科学反映各级各类国有资产管理情况；国有资产报告应采取综合报告和专项报告相结合的方式。

与此同时，在资产评估行业自律管理层面，为规范资产评估执业行为、保证资产评估执业质量，中国资产评估协会修订发布的《资产评估执业准则——资产评估报告》（中评协〔2018〕35 号）明确了资产评估报告的基本遵循、基本内容和出具要求；为规范企业国有资产评估报告编制和出具行为、保护资产评估当事人合法权益和公共利益，中国资产评估协会修订发布的《企业国有资产评估报告指南》（中评协〔2017〕42 号）和《金融企业国有资产评估报告指南》（中评协〔2017〕43 号），具体从国有资产评估报告的基本内容与格式方面，对评估报告的编制、出具与装订等作出了规定。国有资产评估报告主要包括企业国有资产评估报告、金融企业国有资产评估报告、文化企业国有资产评估报告、行政事业单位国有资产评估报告等。与非国有资产评估报告的编制相比，国有资产评估报告在具体内容和要求上还涉及一系列特殊要求。例如，国有资产评估业务要求在资产评估报告的"评估依据"部分披露本次评估业务所对应的经济行为依据；国有资产评估报告的附件应当包括与评估目的相对应的经济行为文件、被评估单位的专项审计报告、资产评估委托合同等。需要强调的是，国有企业改革作为国有资本保值增值、提高国有经济竞争力、放大国有资本功能的重大战略举措，已成为我国整个经济体制改革的中心环节，对于社会主义市场经济体制的建立和完善具有重大意义。其中，资产评估是国有企业改革得以顺利实现的重要环节，为维护各类资产出资人合法权益、促进企业产权有序流转、保障资产公平定价、防止资产流失提供了价值标尺，为国有企业改革与发展提供了基本支撑。

Chapter 11
Valuation Standards
资产评估准则

Wisdom
名人名言

悬衡而知平,设规而知圆。

——韩非子

欲知平直,则必准绳;欲知方则圆,则必规矩。

——吕不韦

It is easier to fight for principles than to live up to them.

—Adlai Stevenson

All men are liable to error; and most men are, in many points, by passion or interest, under temptation to it.

—John Locke

Rudimentary Knowledge
基本知识

Abstract 中文摘要

资产评估准则（Valuation Standards, VS）是资产评估机构及其资产评估专业人员执行资产评估业务的技术规范和职业道德规范的总称，是保证其执业质量的行业公认标准。资产评估准则的完善和成熟程度反映了一国资产评估行业发展的状况。

资产评估准则的功能主要体现在以下三个方面：一是规范和指导资产评估机构及其资产评估专业人员的执业行为，保证资产评估结果质量，防范资产评估执业风险；二是促使其他相关领域理解资产评估专业服务的作用，为资产评估报告使用人正确理解和使用评估结论提供重要依据；三是为国家监管部门和行业协会评价资产评估专业服务质量提供重要标尺，有效维护社会公共利益和资产评估各方当事人合法权益，促进资产评估行业健康发展，提升资产评估行业公信力。

资产评估准则的制定是一项复杂的系统性工程，不仅对专业性、技术性有很高要求，而且需要反映所对应的经济、社会、文化、法律等背景和环境条件。根据发布主体及应用范围，资产评估准则可以划分为国际组织评估准则、区域组织评估准则、中国评估准则和外国评估准则。其中，国际评估准则理事会（IVSC）制定的国际评估准则（IVS）、欧洲评估师联合会（TEGOVA）制定的欧洲评估准则（EVS）、美国评估促进会（TAF）制定的专业评估执业统一准则（USPAP）、英国皇家特许测量师学会（RICS）制定的红皮书（Red Book）、中国财政部及中国资产评估协会（CAS）制定的中国资产评估准则（CVS）等都是在全球具有较大影响力的资产评估准则。

伴随经济发展全球化、产权主体多元化以及资产评估行业专业化程度的不断提升，资产评估准则在世界范围内呈现一系列发展特征和趋势：一是资产评估准则的涵盖范围不断变化，包括由单纯不动产评估向综合化评估方向发展，由一般资产评估向新型社会资源评估方向发展，由原生品资产评估向衍生品资产评估方向发展；二是资产评估准则的原则性和规则性更替共存，例如，一些国际评估组织和区域评估组织更侧重于从原则性、通用性层面进行准则规范的制定，一些国家则基于本国法律框架和评估业务实际，侧重于在规则性、本土化准则规范的制定方面给予较多探索；三是国际准则、区域准则和国家准则基于各自差异化的制定宗旨与发展定位，相互促进、共同发展；四是资产评估理论和实践相互促进、共同完善，例如，在评估理论有效指导业务实践的同时，评估实践也会在一定程度上助推理论体系的完善。

Text 正文

1. Introduction of Valuation Standards

Valuation standards are the general term for technical specifications and professional ethics that regulate and guide valuation institutions and their valuers when they undertake valuation assignments. Valuation standards are recognised standards in the industry to ensure the quality of their practice. The maturity of valuation standards reflects the development of a country's valuation industry.

Valuation standards play a very important role in the guidance towards practical valuation. The formulation of valuation standards is a complex and systematic project. It requires not only high-level professionalism and technology, but also supports of corresponding economic, social, cultural, legal conditions. According to the issuing entity and the scope of application, valuation standards include international organisation valuation standards, regional organisation valuation standards, Chinese valuation standards and foreign valuation standards.

There are several critical standards with huge impacts, such as International Valuation Standards (IVS), European Valuation Standards (EVS), Uniform Standards of Professional Appraisal Practice (USPAP), RICS Red Book, and Chinese Valuation Standards (CVS).

2. Function of Valuation Standards

The functions of valuation standards are mainly reflected in the following three aspects:

(a) When valuation institutions and valuers undertaking assignments, valuation standards can guide their practice conduct and address their ethical and performance problem so that to guarantee the quality of assets valuation, and it can also prevent valuation risks through definitions, rules, standards, standards rules, and statements.

(b) Valuation standards helps valuers to develop and communicate their analyses, opinions, and conclusions with intended users of valuation report, providing important basis for they to understand and use the valuation conclusion correctly.

(c) Valuation standards provides an important benchmark for national regulatory authorities and industry associations to evaluate the quality of professional services for asset valuation, and it can also protect the legitimate rights of public interest and interests of all parties involved in assets valuation, promoting the healthy development and enhancing the credibility of the assets valuation industry.

3. Development Characteristics of Valuation Standards in the Worldwide

Nowadays, the valuation standards need to be developed in order to satisfy the increasing need of valuation in the worldwide. The development trend of valuation standards is mainly reflected in four aspects.

■ Firstly, valuation standards coverage has changed:

(a) from real property interests valuation to comprehensive valuation.

Assets valuation is originated from real property interests valuation, before experienced the expansion from real property interests valuation to other assets valuation by the market. Assets valuation developed from single assets valuation to comprehensive valuation, including intangible assets and business valuation. In this trend, valuation standards gradually move towards the integration, which reflects the characteristics of the valuation meeting the needs of economic development.

(b) from general assets valuation to new social resources valuation.

As environment, resources, health, and safety become more important in economic life, the concept of the environment impact assessment, strategic environment assessment, renewable energy and energy efficiency is also exceptionally bright and have gradually entered the view of the assessment and valuation.

(c) from primary assets valuation to derivative assets valuation.

As the development of the financial instruments, various financial derivatives had been developed. The valuation of this kind of assets have become increasingly important.

- Secondly, the development characteristics includes the co-existence of principled and regular international standards. For example, some international appraisal organisations and regional appraisal organisations focus more on the principle and universality of standards, while some countries focus more on the formulation of regular and localized the standards based on local legal frameworks and valuation practices.

- Thirdly, the international, regional standards and national guidelines promoted each other and developed together based on their differentiated formulation purposes and development position;

- Finally, the theory and practice of valuation standard promote and improved together. For example, while valuation theory effectively guides business practice, valuation practice will also cause the improvement of valuation theory.

Core Words and Expressions 核心术语

European Valuation Standards (EVS)	欧洲评估准则
Royal Institution of Chartered surveyors (RICS)	英国皇家特许测量师学会
RICS Red Book	英国评估准则 / 英国红皮书
Chinese Valuation Standards (CVS)	中国资产评估准则
social resources valuation	社会资源评估
primary assets valuation	原生品资产评估
derivative assets valuation	衍生品资产评估
financial derivatives	金融衍生品
quality of assets valuation	资产评估质量
legitimate rights	合法权益
public interest	公共利益

Questions and Discussion 问题与讨论

1. Please state the definition of valuation standards and give examples.

2. What are the development characteristics of valuation standards in the worldwide?

3. Please illustrate the function of valuation standards.

More Knowledge
知识扩展

Topic 1: Chinese Valuation Standards (CVS) 中国评估准则

Abstract 中文摘要

根据《中华人民共和国资产评估法》,"评估机构及其评估专业人员开展业务应当遵守法律、行政法规和评估准则,遵循独立、客观、公正的原则"。其中,中国评估准则(Chinese Valuation Standards, CVS),即中国资产评估准则,是指由中华人民共和国财政部(MOF of the PRC)制定的资产评估基本准则以及由中国资产评估协会(China Appraisal Society, CAS)根据资产评估基本准则制定的资产评估执业准则和资产评估职业道德准则。凡是作为中国资产评估协会会员的资产评估机构和资产评估专业人员执行资产评估业务时,都应当遵守和执行中国资产评估准则。

20世纪80年代末,为适应经济体制和国有企业改革需要,中国资产评估行业在政府颁布法令的形式下产生。为促进资产评估行业的健康规范发展,财政部和中国资产评估协会先后制定并发布了一系列资产评估准则规范。2001年,财政部发布资产评估行业第一项准则《资产评估准则——无形资产》(财会〔2001〕1051号),标志着我国资产评估准则建设迈出第一步。2004年,财政部发布两项基本准则《资产评估准则——基本准则》《资产评估职业道德准则——基本准则》(财企〔2004〕20号),确立了我国资产评估准则的基本理念和基本要求。2007年11月28日,财政部、中国资产评估协会在人民大会堂举行中国资产评估准则体系发布会，正式发布包括8项新准则在内的15项资产评估准则，涉及主要评估程序和主要执业领域的资产评估准则体系基本建成。此后，我国资产评估准则建设继续推进，于2016年合计达到28项。2016年7月2日，第十二届全国人大常委会第二十一次会议审议通过的《中华人民共和国资产评估法》规定了评估准则的制定和实施方式，进一步明确了评估准则在评估行业的履行、监管和使用中的基础地位，为评估准则体系建设奠定了坚实的法律保障。2017年，在《中华人民共和国资产评估法》和《资产评估行业财政监督管理办法》（财政部令第86号）出台并施行后，我国资产评估准则体系得到了系统、全面的修订和完善。其中，《资产评估基本准则》（财资〔2017〕43号）由财政部发布；截至2023年9月，我国资产评估准则共计33项，其体系框架*详见图11-1。

我国现已形成较为完善的资产评估准则体系，并主要呈现两大特征：一是综合性和系统性较强，涵盖了资产评估基本准则、资产评估执业准则、资产评估职业道德准则等多个层次，规定了评估执业行为和职业道德行为的要求，覆盖了各类评估对象和主要市场领域，实现了与国际评估准则在基本专业理念、主要技术方法、重要专业术语等方面的趋同；二是专业性准则与程序性准则并重，既包括针对各类资产和经济权益、主要资产评估业务制定的实体性技术规范，又包括针对主要专业流程及其履行制定的程序性执业规范，在提升行业公信力、规范执业行为、加强行业监管、促进评估结论使用、增进行业国际交流等方面发挥了重要作用。在中国资产评估准则体系中，资产评估基本准则是资产评估机构及其资产评估专业人员执行各种资产类型、各种评估目的资产评估业务应当共同遵循的基本规范，是资产评估执业准则和资产评估职业道德准则的制定依据。资产评估执业准则是资产评估机构及其资产评估专业人员在执行资产评估业务过程中应当遵循的程序规范和技术规范，包括具体准则、评估指南和指导意见：资产评估具体准则分为程序性准则和实体性准则两个部分；资产评估指南是针对特定评估目的的评估业务和某些重要事项制定的规范；资产评估指导意见是为资产的细分类别资产提供评估规范和为资产评估业务中某些具体问题提供指导性意见。资产评估道德准则从专业能力、独立性、与委托方和其他相关当事人的关系、与其他资产评估机构及资产评估专业人员的关系等方面对资产评估机构及其资产评估专业人员应当具备的道德品质和体现的道德行为进行了规范。

---

* China Appraisal Society (CAS), *Fundamentals of Assets Valuation*, China Financial & Economic Publishing House, 2023.

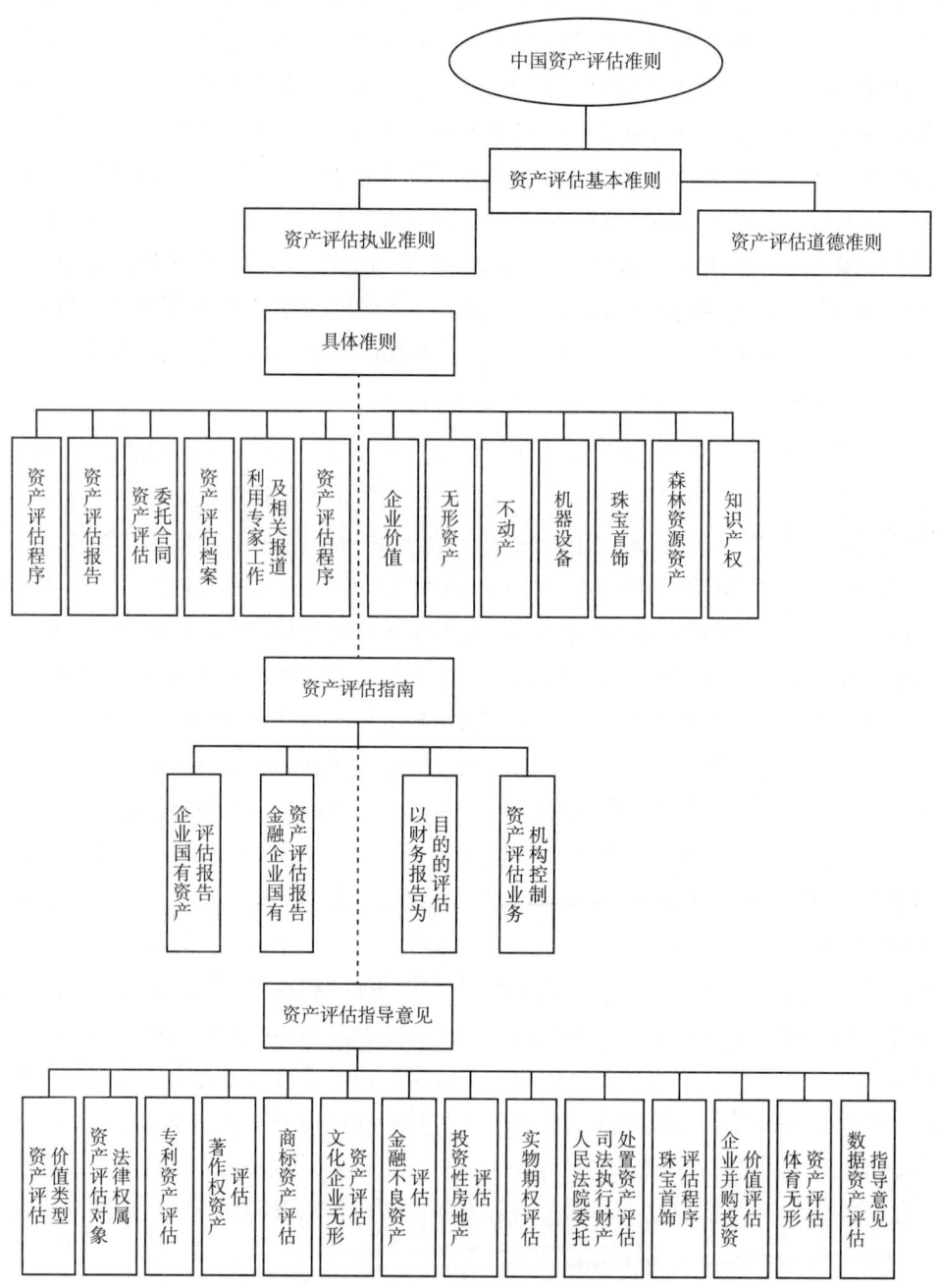

图 11-1 中国资产评估准则体系框架

现阶段，中国资产评估准则体系的动态更新机制已然建成，具体由中国资产评估协会在财政部指导下，结合监管需求、执业需求、理论和实践发展需要，以新增准则和修订准则相结合的方式对资产评估准则体系进行持续动态更新，并具体表现为三种方式：一是吸收资产评估行政管理部门、行业协会发布的规范性文件内容，新增制定和发布资产评估准则；二是对已经发布并执行一段时期的资产评估准则进行部分内容的修订；三是将已经发布并执行一段时期的资产评估指南和资产评估指导意见上升为资产评估具体准则。此外，除资产评估准则体系外，根据资产评估特定业务发展需要，中国资产评估协会不定期制定和更新发布资产评估专家指引，但其不作为评估机构执业的强制性标准，仅作为执业参考。

Text 正文

1. Background

China Valuation Standards (CVS) refer to the General Valuation Standard formulated by Ministry of Finance of the People's Republic of China (MOF of the PRC), with the Valuation Practicing Standard and Valuation Ethics Standard formulated by China Appraisal Society (CAS) in accordance with the General Valuation Standard.

At the end of the 1980s, in order to meet the needs of the economic system and state-owned assets reform, the industry of assets valuation in China was created. Over the past decades, MOF of the PRC and CAS have been focusing on enhancing the creditability of the industry and building up the core competitiveness of the profession with an aim of serving the overall economic and social development. Making full reference to the advanced international valuation philosophy and based on extensive practical experience of the valuation industry, MOF of the PRC and CAS studied the construction of CVS System. Basing on the organisational framework for standard formulation, MOF of the PRC established the Committee for the Valuation Standards while CAS established the Technical Committee for the Valuation Standards. During this process of standard formulation, MOF of the PRC and CAS have pulled efforts of all relevant parties of asset valuation.

In 2001, MOF of the PRC issued the first valuation standard, "Valuation Standards-Intangible Assets", marking the first step in the construction of valuation standards in China. In 2004, two basic standards, "Valuation Standards - Basic Standards" and "Valuation Standards - Operational Standards", were released by MOF of the PRC, which established basic concepts and requirements of CVS. In 2007, MOF of the PRC and CAS officially released CVS System including fifteen valuation standards in Great Hall of the People, which basically completed the valuation standards system involving major valuation procedures and practice areas. In 2016, the Asset Appraisal Law of the PRC enacted. The law specifies the formulation and implementation of valuation standards, stipulates the important terms, valuation procedures, valuation methods, and valuation reports of valuation standards. In 2017, in accordance with the Asset Appraisal Law of the PRC, MOF of the PRC and CAS systematically and comprehensively revised and improved CVS System and twenty-six standards were revised, standardising the behaviour of valuers and valuation practitioners. As of September 2023, there are a total of 33 valuation standards in China.

2. Applicable Scope

All appraisal institutions and appraisal professionals who are members of CAS must comply with CVS when performing a valuation assignment. All valuation standards are mandatory. At present, more than 5,500 assets valuation institutions and over 43,000 Public Valuers in China comply with CVS.

3. Update Mode

Now, the dynamic update mechanism of China valuation standard system has been established. Under this mechanism, CAS adds new guidelines and revises standards under the guidance of MOF of the PRC.

There are three forms of update: firstly, formulate and release the valuation standards again by absorbing the contents of the regulatory documents that issued by the administrative departments and the appraisal society, and combining the needs of the development of the appraisal theory and practice; secondly, update some contents of the valuation standards, which issued and implemented for a period of time; thirdly, upgrade the Valuation Practice Notes and Valuation Guidance Notes, which issued and implemented for a period of time, to specific standards.

4. Fundamental Contents

Presently, CVS System includes three major sectors: General Valuation Standard, Valuation Ethical Standard and Valuation Practicing Standards. These standards basically satisfy the need for practice and supervision of the valuation industry. Among these, the General Valuation Standard is promulgated by MOF of the PRC whereas other standards are issued by CAS.

- General Valuation Standard: It is the basic standard that appraisal institutions and their appraisal professionals should follow when performing valuation assignment. General Valuation Standard is also the basis for formulating the Valuation Ethical Standard and the Valuation Practicing Standards.

- Valuation Ethical Standard: It regulates the ethical behaviour, which appraisal institutions and their appraisal professionals should present, from aspects of professional competence, independence and relationship with relevant parties.

- Valuation Practicing Standards: They present the procedural standards and technical standards that asset appraisal institutions and their asset appraisal professionals should follow in the process of performing valuation assignment, including Specific Standards, Valuation Practice Notes, and Valuation Guidance Notes.

  ♦ Specific Standards: This part includes six Procedure Standards and seven Assets Standards. The specific standards comprise:

    • Valuation Practicing Standard-Valuation Procedures

    • Valuation Practicing Standard-Valuation Report

    • Valuation Practicing Standard-Engagement Letter

    • Valuation Practicing Standard-Valuation Case Files

    • Valuation Practicing Standard-Use of Expert's Work and Related Reports

    • Valuation Practicing Standard-Valuation Methods

    • Valuation Practicing Standard-Business Value

    • Valuation Practicing Standard-Intangible Asset

- Valuation Practicing Standard-Real Property
- Valuation Practicing Standard-Machinery and Equipment
- Valuation Practicing Standard-Forest Resources
- Valuation Practicing Standard-Jewellery
- Valuation Practicing Standard-Intellectual Property

◆ Valuation Practice Notes: This part is specifically developed for the valuation assignment with specific valuation purposes and certain important matters. The practice notes comprise:

- Practice Note-Valuation Reports for Enterprises' State-Owned Assets
- Practice Note-Valuation Report for State-Owned Assets of Financial Institutions
- Practice Note-Valuation for Financial Reporting Purpose
- Practice Note-Quality Control of Valuation Firm

◆ Valuation Guidance: This part provides specific valuation guidance for sub-categories assets and certain specific issues in valuation assignment. The guidance notes comprise:

- Guidance Note-Bases of Value
- Guidance Note-Legal Ownership of The Valuation Subject
- Guidance Note-Patent Valuation
- Guidance Note-Copyright Asset Valuation
- Guidance Note-Trademark Valuation
- Guidance Note-Non-Performing Financial Asset Valuation
- Guidance Note-Investment Property Valuation
- Guidance Note-Real Option Valuation
- Guidance Note-Valuation of Intangible Assets of Cultural Companies
- Guidance Note-Valuation of Property Disposition in Judicial Enforcement Entrusted by The People's Court

- Guidance Note-Jewellery Valuation Procedure
- Guidance Note-Investment Value in M&A Valuation
- Guidance Note-Valuation of Intangible Assets of Sports
- Guidance Note-Valuation of Data Assets

To sum up, the valuation professions in China have formed a complete system of valuation standards which cover key procedures and areas of asset valuation, conform to domestic conditions, and converge with international standards.

Core Words and Expressions 核心术语

General Valuation Standard	资产评估基本准则
Ministry of Finance of the People's Republic of China (MOF of the PRC)	中华人民共和国财政部
Valuation Practicing Standard	资产评估执业准则
Valuation Ethical Standard	资产评估职业道德准则
appraisal institution	评估机构
appraisal professional	评估专业人员
Valuation Practice Note	资产评估指南
Valuation Guidance Note	资产评估指导意见
promulgate	颁布
Specific Standard	具体准则
Procedure Standard	程序性准则
Assets Standard	实体性准则
engagement letter	委托合同
enterprises' state-owned assets	国有资产
copyright asset	著作权资产

non-performing financial asset	金融不良资产
real option	实物期权
M&A valuation	并购估值
data asset	数据资产

Questions and Discussion 问题与讨论

1. Please give a brief introduction of origin and development of the CVS.

2. Please list and explain the main parts of the CVS, giving some examples of the valuation standards.

Topic 2: International Valuation Standards (IVS) 国际评估准则

Abstract 中文摘要

　　国际评估准则（International Valuation Standards, IVS）是由国际评估准则理事会（International Valuation Standards Council, IVSC）制定和发布的推荐性、自愿性使用的评估准则，也是目前最具国际影响力的国际性评估准则。该准则旨在规范评估执业行为，提升评估执业质量，维护社会公共利益和评估各方当事人合法权益。第一版《国际评估准则》发布于 1985 年。目前，全球已有 137 个国家的 200 多个评估专业组织接受国际评估准则。

　　国际评估准则理事会作为一个独立的非营利性组织，是评估行业的全球标准制定者，目前在国际评估界发挥着主导作用。其前身为 1981 年成立的国际评估准则委员会（The International Assets Valuation Standards Committee, TIAVSC），总部设在英国伦敦，是 20 世纪 80 年代初在世界各国评估专业团体的推动下逐步发展起来的重要国际性评估专业组织。2008 年，国际评估准则委员会改组为国际评估准则理事会，下设包括国际评估准则委员会（International Valuation Standards Board, IVSB）在内的三个委员会。为满足财务报告、国际资本市场和国际经济领域的需要，国际评估准则理事会致力于为公共利益制定和发布评估准则和技术文件，并促使国际评估准则在世界范围内得到认可和遵守，实现国家或区域性评估准则与国际评估准则之间的协调和统一。

国际评估准则采用的是整版更新的方式。前六版《国际评估准则》分别发布于 1985 年、1994 年、1997 年、2000 年、2001 年和 2003 年。2005 年，为满足《国际会计准则》及相关实务的需要，国际评估准则委员会于 2005 年发布了第七版《国际评估准则》。2007 年，国际评估准则委员会发布的第八版《国际评估准则》全面修订了"市场价值以外的价值类型"准则和"以担保贷款为目的的评估"应用指南，新增了"以公共部门资产财务报告为目的的评估"和"历史性资产评估"两个应用指南。2011 年，国际评估准则理事会发布了第九版《国际评估准则》，该版准则与早期版本相比在语言和形式上发生了重大变化，准则的内容更突出原则性，准则的框架也更具有层次性。在此基础上，2013 年发布的第十版《国际评估准则》对"基本准则""资产准则""评估应用"部分进行了修订；2017 年发布的第十版《国际评估准则》删除了"评估应用"部分，同时在基本准则部分新增了"价值类型""评估的基本方法和具体方法"两项准则；2020 年生效的第十一版《国际评估准则》在资产准则部分新增了"非金融负债"；2022 年生效的第十二版《国际评估准则》在资产准则部分进一步新增了"存货"。现阶段，《国际评估准则 2022》（第十三版）已于 2022 年 1 月 31 日开始施行；《国际评估准则 2024》（第十四版）预计将于 2024 年 1 月发布，于 2024 年 7 月生效。

经过多次修订，国际评估准则现已形成相对稳定、比较完善的结构体系。《国际评估准则 2022》（第十三版）由国际评估准则简介、术语表、框架、基本准则和资产准则等部分构成。其中，"国际评估准则框架"是该准则的导言部分，包括遵循准则、资产和负债、评估师、客观性、专业胜任能力、背离情形等内容；"国际评估准则基本准则"阐明了执行所有评估业务的基本要求，包括工作范围、调查和遵循、评估报告、价值类型、评估途径和方法五项准则；"国际评估准则资产准则"包括对特定类型资产评估的相关要求，是对基本准则要求的细化或者扩充，包括企业及企业权益、无形资产、非金融负债、存货、机器设备（厂房和设备）、不动产权益、开发性不动产、金融工具八项准则。

Text 正文

1. Background

International Valuation Standards (IVS) are developed and published by the the International Valuation Standards Council (IVSC), which is headquartered in London, UK. The IVSC was founded in Melbourne, Australia, as <u>The International Assets Valuation Standards Committee (TIAVSC)</u> by 20 national valuation professional organisations in 1981. It is a <u>not-for-profit organisation</u> dedicated to establishing and promoting global valuation standards to serve the public interest.

The IVSC develops and maintains standards on how to undertake and report valuations, especially those that will be relied upon by investors and other third-party stakeholders. The IVSC also supports the need to develop a framework of guidance on best practice for valuations of the various classes of assets and liabilities and for the consistent delivery of the standards by properly trained professionals around the globe.

The first edition of IVS was published in 1985. The original purpose of IVSC was to develop a set of common international real estate valuation standards for purpose of financial reporting, in conjunction with the development of International Accounting Standards (IAS) by the International Accounting Standards Board (IASB). Since then, the IVSC have broadened their scope to encompass the harmonization of international real estate valuation practice in general. At present, all types of assets (such as real estate, business and non-tangible assets) have been introduced into the IVS.

The IVS have become globally agreed, high-level standards, establishing a consistent and transparent framework for valuation practice worldwide. As IVSC has been adopted by more countries and regions, IVS is playing an important role in supporting business and reducing financial markets risk for the public interest. The functions and features of IVS can be listed as follows:

(a) IVS establish a global framework for valuation providers, overcoming gaps in quality and consistency around the world;

(b) IVS set asset-specific guidelines on how a valuation should be done;

(c) IVS enable like-for-like comparisons of data, based on a consistent valuation methodology;

(d) IVS reflect the global nature of business, which operates across borders;

(e) IVS give a guarantee of quality and define international best practice;

(f) IVS are recognized and supported around the world by leading valuation organisation.

2. Applicable Scope

Nowadays, there are more than 200 member organisations of the IVSC, and more than 160 associations from 137 countries accept IVS. The adoption or use of any IVSC standards by any entity is entirely voluntary and at the user's risk. The IVSC does not control how or if any entity chooses to use the standards and does not and cannot ensure or require compliance with the standards. The IVSC does not audit, monitor, review, or control in any way the manner in which users apply the standards.

3. Update Mode

IVS is usually renewed in full page. Independent technical standards boards comprising specialist valuation experts from around the world lead the development of and consultation on IVS. The IVSC's technical standards boards undertake regular consultations to review and update the IVS, ensuring it reflects changing market needs and international best practice. The technical boards cover: Tangible Assets (including real estate, plant, and machinery), Intangible Assets (including business fair value and intellectual property), Financial Instruments (including derivatives and equity instruments).

So far, there are thirteen editions of IVS: IVS 1985, IVS 1994, IVS 1997, IVS 2000, IVS 2001, IVS 2003, IVS 2005, IVS 2007, IVS 2011, IVS 2013, IVS 2017, 2020, and the latest edition is IVS 2022, which has become effective from January 2022.

In the future, the IVSC Standards Board (IVSB) intends to continuously review the IVS and update or clarify the standards as needed to meet stakeholder and market needs. The IVSB has continuing projects that may result in additional standards being introduced or amendments being made to the standards in this publication at any time. Thus, the IVSC hosted a series of webinars in May 2023 to discuss the proposed changes. Following the consultation, the next edition of the IVS is expected to be published in January 2024, with an effective date of July 2024.

4. Fundamental Contents

The framework of IVS has changed over the reviewing and updating. For example, in IVS 2011 and IVS 2013, four parts are referred to, which are the IVS Framework, General Standards, Asset Standards, and Valuation Applications. However, in IVS 2017, IVS 2020 and IVS 2022, three parts are referred to, which are the IVS Framework, General Standards, and Asset Standards.

This section takes IVS 2022 as an example to illustrate the fundamental content of IVS. IVS 2022 comprises Introduction, Glossary, IVS Framework, five "General Standards" and eight "Asset-specific Standards". The IVS are arranged as follows:

- Introduction: This part introduces the basic information of IVS, and states the core principles that IVSC Standards Boards have taken into account when drafting the IVS.

- Glossary: This glossary defines certain terms used in the IVS, and it is only applicable to the IVS and does not attempt to define basic valuation, accounting or finance terms, as valuers are assumed to have an understanding of such terms.

- IVS Framework: This serves as a preamble to the IVS. The IVS Framework consists of general principles for valuers following the IVS regarding objectivity, judgement, competence and acceptable departures from the IVS. The specific content of IVS Framework includes:

    ◆ Compliance with Standards

    ◆ Assets and Liabilities

    ◆ Objectivity

    ◆ Competence

    ◆ Departures

- General Standards: These set forth requirements for the conduct of all valuation assignments including establishing the terms of a valuation engagement, bases of value, valuation approaches and methods, and reporting. They are designed to be applicable to valuations of all types of assets and for any valuation purpose. This part comprises:

- ◆ IVS 101 Scope of Work
- ◆ IVS 102 Investigation and Compliance
- ◆ IVS 103 Reporting,
- ◆ IVS 104 Basic Value
- ◆ IVS 105 Valuation Approaches and Methods

■ Assets Standards: The Asset Standards include requirements related to specific types of asset valuation, including background information on the characteristics of each asset type that influence value, and additional asset-specific requirements regarding common valuation approaches and methods used. This part comprises:

- ◆ IVS 200 Businesses and Business Interests
- ◆ IVS 210 Intangible Assets
- ◆ IVS 220 Non-Financial Liabilities
- ◆ IVS 230 Inventory
- ◆ IVS 300 Plant and Equipment
- ◆ IVS 400 Real Property Interests
- ◆ IVS 410 Development Property
- ◆ IVS 500 Financial Instruments

Core Words and Expressions 核心术语

The International Assets Valuation Standards Committee (TIAVSC)	国际评估准则委员会

not-for-profit organisation	非营利组织
general standards	通用准则
asset standards	资产准则
businesses and business interests	企业和企业权益
asset-specific requirements	资产相关的特定性要求
non-financial liabilities	非金融负债
development property	开发性房地产

Questions and Discussion 问题与讨论

1. Please give a brief introduction of origin and development of the IVS.

2. What role does the IVS play in the world, and how important is IVS?

3. Please list and explain the main parts of the IVS, giving some examples of the valuation standards.

Topic 3: European Valuation Standard (EVS) 欧洲评估准则

Abstract 中文摘要

　　欧洲评估准则（European Valuation Standards, EVS）是由欧洲评估师协会联合会（European Group of Valuers' Associations, TEGOVA）制定和发布的区域性评估准则。该准则的设计目标是为欧洲评估师、客户和政府部门提供易于理解的评估执业标准。第一版《欧洲评估准则》发布于 1978 年。目前，欧洲评估准则在欧盟范围内通行，分布在欧洲及全球 38 个国家的 71 个专业评估协会的超过 7 万名欧洲评估师自愿遵循和应用该准则。

　　欧洲评估师协会联合会的总部设在比利时布鲁塞尔，其前身是由比利时、法国、德国、爱尔兰和英国于 1977 年 4 月发起设立的欧洲固定资产评估师联合会

（The European Group of Valuers of Fixed Assets, TEGOVOFA）。欧洲评估师协会联合会是欧洲不动产评估领域的领先专业机构，致力于制定不动产评估准则、完善职业道德体系和提高执业质量。自1978年以来，为满足多元化评估执业的需要，欧洲评估准则的涵盖范围开始由单纯不动产评估向综合化评估方向发展，企业价值评估、无形资产评估、机器设备评估等内容逐渐被纳入欧洲评估准则的内容体系。在此基础上，欧洲评估师协会联合会进一步于2020年和2022年分别以独立版本的形式配套发布了第一版《欧洲企业价值评估准则》（EVS-BV）和第一版《欧洲机器设备评估准则》（EVS-PME）。

欧洲评估准则通常采用的是整版更新的方式。1978—2023年，《欧洲评估准则》共计经历了九个版本的更新，其中包括2000年的第四版、2003年的第五版、2009年的第六版、2012年的第七版、2016年的第八版。现阶段，最新发布的第九版《欧洲评估准则2020》已于2021年1月1日正式生效。此外，在不同版本的欧洲评估准则之间，欧洲评估师协会联合会也会根据现实需要对具体准则进行适时更新。例如，继第八版欧洲评估准则生效之后，欧洲评估师协会联合会曾于2017年新增发布欧洲评估准则6"自动化评估模型"（EVS 6 Automated Valuation Models <AVMs>）和欧洲评估指南11"评估师对统计工具的使用"（EVGN 11 The Valuer's Use of Statistical Tools）这两项具体准则，作为对第八版欧洲评估准则的有效补充。

欧洲评估准则现已形成多层次、较完善的综合化评估准则体系。其中，第九版《欧洲评估准则2020》由欧洲评估（基本）准则和评估指南，评估方法，评估与可持续性，欧洲评估信息文件，测量，教育与资格，欧洲评估师行为守则、欧盟立法与不动产评估七个部分构成；其欧洲评估（基本）准则进一步包括市场价值、市场价值以外的价值、评估师、评估程序、评估报告五项准则。第一版《欧洲企业价值评估准则》由欧洲企业价值评估准则、欧洲企业价值评估指南、企业价值评估与可持续性、企业价值评估师行为守则、欧盟立法与企业价值评估五个部分构成。第一版《欧洲机器设备评估准则》由欧洲机器设备评估准则和评估指南、欧洲机器设备评估信息文件、欧洲机器设备评估师行为守则、欧盟立法与机器设备评估四个部分构成。

Text 正文

1. Background

European Valuation Standards (EVS) are developed and published by The European Group of Valuers' Associations (TEGOVA). The TEGOVA was founded in Brussels, Belgian, as The European Group of Valuers of Fixed Assets (TEGOVOFA) by Belgium, France, Germany, Ireland and the United Kingdom in April 1977. It is a pan-European association of professional bodies working for standards, ethics and quality in the real estate valuation market. Its main objective is the creation and spreading of harmonised standards for valuation practice, for education and qualification as well as for corporate governance and ethics for valuers. It supports its member associations in the introduction and implementation of these standards.

TEGOVA is governed by the General Assembly and the Board of Directors, which are statutory bodies. The General Assembly consists of all Members. The Board of Directors of the association consists of at least five and maximum eight member associations. The Advisory Committees & Working Groups of TEGOVA include Recognition Committee, European Valuation Standards Board (EVSB), European Business Valuation Standards Board (EVSB-BV), and European Plant, Machinery & Equipment Valuation Standards Board (EVSB-PME).

The first edition of EVS named Guidance Notes for European Application was published in 1978. The nineth edition of EVS was launched on 2 November 2020 and effective from 1 January 2021. The EVSB drafts and promote EVS with particular attention to European Union law, and it also recommends a standard approach to valuation methodologies. The Standards were designed with the particular objective of providing standards that are relevant and easily comprehensible to valuers, clients, and the public authorities. They were also designed in the belief that the valuation profession must be conscious of the real added value that quality valuation brings to markets and society and must imbue clients and public authorities with an understanding of how the valuer reached the determination of value.

On the basis of EVS, TEGOVA developed the first edition of European Business Valuation Standards (EVS-BV) in 2020, providing harmonised European standards, guidance and technical information in business valuation. EVS-BV is effective from 24th March, 2020. After that, TEGOVA additionally published the first edition of European Plant, Machinery & Equipment Valuation Standards (EVS-PME) in 2022. EVS-PME was conceived and designed to foster convergence in PME valuation across Europe, providing common ground and best practice regarding methodology, reporting, and valuation approaches to a fast-mutating industrial landscape. EVS-PME 2022 is effective from 1st November, 2022.

2. Applicable Scope

EVS is widely and voluntarily used in European Union. TEGOVA unites 71 national valuers' associations from 37 countries representing 70,000 qualified valuers either self-employed or employed by specialist consultancies, private sector companies, government departments or financial institutions both local and international. EVS provides minimum standards that TEGOVA Member Associations (TMAs) must adopt in their own standards, supplementing such additional requirements as are deemed necessary by legislation, regulation or generally accepted practice within a specific state.

TEGOVA has developed the Recognised European Valuer (REV) and TEGOVA Residential Valuer (TRV) programmes for individual valuers, who have achieved this status are subject to additional requirements including continuing professional development. The REV and TRV statuses are the marks of excellence in real estate valuation. Additionally, Recognised European Plant, Machinery & Equipment Valuer (REV-PME) and Recognised European Business Valuer (REV-BV) refers to a valuer recognised by TEGOVA for her/his qualification, knowledge and professional experience in plant, machinery & equipment valuation, or business valuation.

3. Update Mode

The updating of EVS is a journey that started immediately after the latest edition was published. Each edition of EVS has been determined by extensive consultation and feedback. And when it comes to the new edition of EVS, the whole edition of the old one and practical and specific items may be renewed alternatively.

Since EVS 1978 (1st edition), TEGOVA has published nine editions for EVS, such as EVS 2000 (4th edition), EVS 2003 (5th edition), EVS 2009 (6th edition), EVS 2012 (7th edition), EVS 2016 (8th edition) and the latest edition, EVS 2020 (9th edition), which has been effective from 1 January 2021.

In addition, between different versions of EVS, TEGOVA updates the specific guidelines in the proper time, in order to satisfy practical needs of valuers. For example, after the effectiveness of EVS 2016 (8th edition), TEGOVA has additionally updated "EVS 6 Automated Valuation Models <AVMs>" and "EVGN 11 The Valuer's Use of Statistical Tools" as the supplement to this edition.

4. Fundamental Contents

In this section, the fundamental contents of EVS 2020, EVS-BV 2020, and EVS-PME 2022 are to be introduced.

4.1 European Valuation Standards (EVS)

The structure of EVS has changed with the publishing of its nine editions. In the fifth edition EVS 2003, there were nine standards and fourteen guidelines. In the sixth EVS 2009, the number of standards reduced to five and the number of guidelines reduced to five. In the seventh edition EVS 2012, the standards and guidelines combined as the first part, adding European Union Legislation and Property Valuation as the second part and Valuation Information Papers as the third part. In the eighth edition EVS 2016, it has been divided into four parts: European Valuation Standards and Guidance Notes, European Codes, European Union Legislation and Property Valuation, and Technical Documents. The latest edition EVS 2020 comprises mainly seven parts:

■ Part 1: European Valuation Standards and Guidance Notes

  ◆ Part 1 A: European Valuation Standards. This part formulates the standards first and then illustrates them in detail, including the definition and explanation of some important concepts, business terms and conditions. The standards and terms listed as follow:

  • EVS 1 Market Value

- EVS 2 Valuation Bases Other than Market Value

- EVS 3 The Qualified Valuer

- EVS 4 The Valuation Process

- EVS 5 Reporting the Valuation

- EVS 6 Valuation and Energy Efficiency

♦ Part 1 B: European valuation guidance notes. This part provides detailed analysis and explanation of key issues and approaches to be followed, including:

- EVGN 1 Portfolio Valuation

- EVGN 2 Fair Value for Financial Reporting

- EVGN 3 Valuation for Insurance Purposes,

- EVGN 4 Apportionment of Value between Land and Buildings.

■ Part 2: Valuation Methodology: This part elaborates the code of conduct and ethics of European valuers and the measurement of distance, area, and volume. EVS 2020 does not impose any specific valuation methodology, as (unless there is applicable regulation) they are a matter for the professional judgement of the valuer in each case, according to the nature of the property and the context and purpose of the valuation. It includes 11 sections:

- Introduction

- Scope

- Definitions

- Valuation approaches

- General observations

- The Comparative Method

- The Income Approach, methods and models

- The Cost Approach

- The Residual Method

- Using more than one valuation method
- The final check

■ Part 3: Valuation and Sustainability: This part mainly introduces the importance of concerning with environmental performance and sustainability to those concerned with property and buildings, where relevant to valuation. This part comprises:

♦ Introduction

♦ Sustainability

♦ Sustainability and property users

♦ Developing "green" standards for property

♦ Valuation and sustainability

■ Part 4: European Valuation Information Papers. This part includes:

♦ EVIP 1 The Impact of the Energy Performance of Buildings Directive on Property Valuation

♦ EVIP 2 Valuation and Other Issues for <u>Recurrent Property Taxation</u>

♦ EVIP 3 <u>Multiple Interests</u> in Residential Property

♦ EVIP 4 Listed Residential Property (property protected by law)

♦ EVIP 5 Residential Tenancies and Rent Control

♦ EVIP 6 Residential Valuations and Equity Release

♦ EVIP 7 <u>Advanced Statistical Models</u>

■ Part 5: Measurement, Education and Qualifications. This part includes:

♦ European Code of Measurement

♦ Summary of TEGOVA's Minimum Educational Requirements

♦ Recognition of Qualifications by TEGOVA.

■ Part 6: European Valuers' Code of Conduct. TEGOVA expects valuers in its member associations to adhere, as a matter of personal responsibility to this Code.

■ Part 7: European Union Legislation and Property Valuation. This part includes:

♦ General Introduction

♦ the EU Internal Market

♦ Energy

♦ Environment

♦ The Common Agricultural Policy

♦ Schedule of EU Legislation

4.2 European Business Valuation Standards (EVS-BV))

TEGOVA developed the first edition of EVS-BV in 2020. The aim of this standards is to impose the consistency of the most important issues of business valuation, which includes: the code of conduct, the <u>terms of engagement</u>, the definitions of bases of value, valuation approaches, and reporting the valuation. The EVS-BV mainly contains five parts:

■ European Business Valuation Standards, including:

♦ EBVS 1 Market Value and Bases of Value other than Market Value,

♦ EBVS 2 the Valuation Process Incorporates Detailed Terms of Engagement,

♦ EBVS 3 the Valuation Approaches and Methods,

♦ EBVS 4 Reporting the Valuation.

■ European Business Valuation Guidance Notes, including:

♦ EBVGN 1 Control Premiums and Discounts for Lack of Control and Discounts for Lack of Marketability

♦ EBVGN 2 Discount Rates in the Discounted Cash Flow Method

♦ EBVGN 3 Valuation of Intangible Assets.

■ Business Valuation and Sustainability

■ European Business Valuers' Code of Conduct

■ European Union Legislation and Business Valuation.

4.3 European Plant, Machinery & Equipment Valuation Standards (EVS-PME)

In 2022, the first edition of European Plant, Machinery & Equipment Valuation Standards (EVS-PME) has been developed by TEGOVA. In order to set a common language for valuation practice in the European Union, these standards define and standardise the concepts of "fixed assets" and "in situ"/"ex situ" and obsolescence of technological, functional, and economic as well as issues of PME. Four parts are contained in the EVS-PME:

- Part 1 European Plant, Machinery & Equipment Valuation Standards and Guidance Notes

  - I.A. European Plant, Machinery & Equipment Valuation Standards, including:

    - EVS-PME 1 considers Market Value and other Bases of Value in the context of Plant, Machinery & Equipment (PME) valuation
    - EVS-PME 2 The Valuation Process, Macro and Micro Identification and Collection of Data
    - EVS-PME 3 The Valuation Approaches and Methods
    - EVS-PME 4 Reporting the Valuation
    - EVS-PME 5 Plant, Machinery & Equipment Valuation and Energy Efficiency

  - I.B. European Plant, Machinery & Equipment Valuation Guidance Notes, including:

    - EVS-PME GN 1 Market Approach
    - EVS-PME GN 2 Cost Approach
    - EVS-PME GN 3 Income Approach
    - EVS-PME GN 4 Useful Life of Plant, Machinery & Equipment
    - EVS-PME GN 5 Functional Obsolescence in Plant, Machinery & Equipment Valuation

- EVS-PME GN 6 Distinguishing between Plant Building and Productive Machinery and Equipment
- EVS-PME GN 7 Inventory Valuation
- EVS-PME GN 8 Issues Regarding Insurable Value, Scrap Value and Salvage Value
- EVS-PME GN 9 Recycling Renewables

■ Part 2 European Plant, Machinery & Equipment Valuation Information Papers. It illustrates four issues:

- ◆ EVS-PME IP 1 PME Maintenance – How it Affects Value and How the Valuer can Verify it
- ◆ EVS-PME IP 2 Equipping Valuers for EU Carbon Reduction Regulation
- ◆ EVS-PME IP 3 PME Servicing Energy Efficiency in Buildings
- ◆ EVS-PME IP 4 Real Estate Valuation and PME Valuation – Valuing the Energy Efficient Transformation of the European Building Stock

■ Part 3 European Plant, Machinery and Equipment Valuers' Code of Conduct

■ Part 4 European Union Legislation and Plant, Machinery & Equipment Valuation, including:

- ◆ General Introduction
- ◆ PME Valuations Imposed by EU Legislation
- ◆ PME Valuation for Company Accounts
- ◆ PME Valuation for Credit Institutions
- ◆ PME Valuation for Insurance and Reinsurance Institutions

Core Words and Expressions 核心术语

European Group of Valuers' Associations (TEGOVA)	欧洲评估师联合会

European Valuation Standards Board (EVSB)	欧洲企业价值评估准则委员会
European Business Valuation Standards (EVS-BV)	欧洲企业价值评估准则
European Plant, Machinery & Equipment Valuation Standards (EVS-PME)	欧洲机器设备评估准则
fast-mutating industrial landscape	快速变化的工业格局
energy efficiency	能源高效
portfolio valuation	资产组合评估
valuation for insurance purposes	以保险为目的的评估
apportionment of value	价值分配
sustainability	可持续性
recurrent property taxation	经常性财产税
multiple interests	多重权益
advanced statistical models	高级统计模型
code of conduct	行为守则
European Union legislation	欧盟立法

Questions and Discussion 问题与讨论

1. Please give a brief introduction of origin and development of the EVS?

2. What is the aim of EVS? What is the applicable scope of EVS?

3. Please list and explain the main parts of the EVS, giving some standards as examples.

Topic 4: Uniform Standards of Professional Appraisal Practice (USPAP) 美国评估准则

Abstract 中文摘要

美国《专业评估执业统一准则》（Uniform Standards of Professional Appraisal Practice, USPAP）由美国评估促进会（The Appraisal Foundation, TAF）制定和发布。该准则致力于维护美国评估师和评估服务使用者利益，并与社会公众、评估师监管机构、评估服务提供方和使用者保持步调上的一致，以满足各方对评估执业统一准则的需求。其不仅是美国专业评估实践公认的准则，适用于全美范围的多数评估行业协会及其会员，而且在美国评估界和国际评估界都具有重要的影响力。例如，在1987年以后，加拿大等一些国家的评估准则也开始接受《专业评估执业统一准则》的主要准则条款或者与之趋同。美国评估促进会拥有众多会员组织，但不设个人会员；目前有超过90个专业组织、企业和政府机构附属于美国评估促进会，超过9万名评估人员应用《专业评估执业统一准则》。

美国评估促进会是由美国国会授权为制定评估准则和认证评估师资格的非营利组织，总部设在美国华盛顿。1986年，在不动产市场和抵押贷款业极端不稳定的情况下，为规范抵押贷款业务中的不当评估行为，防止诱发金融危机，美国八个评估专业组织和加拿大评估师协会联合启动《专业评估执业统一准则》的制定事宜。之后，由美国国会立法认可成立的美国评估促进会（1987年成立，1989年认可）获得授权，负责制定美国评估行业所有专业领域的评估准则。现阶段，美国的资产评估业务涵盖范围广泛，主要可以满足于财产保险、税务、会计处理、资产交易、企业合并、资产抵押贷款、家庭财产分割等多方面的需要。美国评估促进会由理事会（Board of Truste, BOT）管理，其下设评估师认证委员会（Appraiser Qualifications Board, AQB）和评估准则委员会（The Appraisal Standards Board, ASB）。评估师认证委员会负责为评估师建立获得许可或证书必要的教育、工作经验和考试标准；评估准则委员会负责制定美国评估行业一般性的公认准则并负责推广其使用、理解和强制执行，包括对《专业评估执业统一准则》进行制定、出版、解释和修订。

《专业评估执业统一准则》采用的是整版更新的方式。第一版《专业评估执业统一准则》发布于1987年，至今已累计有二十四个版本。其中，该准则在

1992年至2006年期间保持每年更新一版，如《专业评估执业统一准则1992》《专业评估执业统一准则2006》；在2006年至2020保持每两年更新一版，如《专业评估执业统一准则2008-2009》《专业评估执业统一准则2018-2019》。《专业评估执业统一准则2020-2021》是目前的最新版本，经美国评估促进会下设的评估准则委员会于2021年和2022年两次宣布延期，将有效期限由2021年12月31日分别延期至2022年12月31日和延期至2023年12月31日。《专业评估执业统一准则》具有较强的法律效力，美国所有涉及联邦的金融业务都应当遵守其现行版本或适用版本中的规定；美国国税局、证券交易委员会、商业银行和放款机构及各州评估师管理委员会等要求评估师在多数评估业务中遵守该准则的相关规定；加拿大等一些国家的评估准则也接受其主要准则条款或与其趋同。

经过多次修订，随着各方意见逐步达成一致，《专业评估执业统一准则》现已发展为结构相对稳定的综合性评估执业准则。其中，《专业评估执业统一准则2020-2021》由定义、引言、职业规则（Rules）、准则及准则条文（Standards and Standards Rule）、评估准则说明（Statements on Appraisal Standards, SMT）等部分组成。第一部分包括主要术语的含义、注释和说明；第二部分包括准则的宗旨、目的、意义、作用、要求以及准则与准则说明之间的关系；第三部分包括职业道德、档案保管、专业胜任能力、工作范围和管辖除外规则；第四部分包括十项具体准则，是《专业评估执业统一准则》的核心构成部分；第五部分专门用于对准则内容的澄清、阐释和说明。此外，与《专业评估执业统一准则》配套发布的还有咨询意见（Advisory Opinions, AO）和常见问题汇编（Frequently Asked Questions, FAQ），但此二者属于指导性文件，只用于说明该准则在特定情况下的具体应用，并为业务争议和疑问提出解决建议，不属于《专业评估执业统一准则》的构成部分。

对于《专业评估执业统一准则》与《国际评估准则》的关系，国际评估准则委员会（TIAVSC）于2006年同美国评估促进会签署了麦迪逊协议，这一举措促使《专业评估执业统一准则》与《国际评估准则》开始实现协调一致，两者在避免冲突的同时互为补充。但《专业评估执业统一准则》在与《国际评估准则》尽可能协调一致的基础上，仍然保持了框架结构和规则内容方面的独立性与稳定性。为此，美国评估促进会与国际评估准则理事会于2016年6月联合发布了《专业评估执业统一准则》与《国际评估准则》的协调指引（Standards Harmonisation Guide）——"A Bridge from USPAP to IVS: A Guide to Producing IVS-Compliant

Appraisals",作为双方准则制定的执业衔接。对于那些已经习惯和熟悉使用《专业评估执业统一准则》的评估师,该指引规定了其在提供同时符合《国际评估准则》规定的评估服务时所需要采取的附加步骤,以此引导评估师在遵循《专业评估执业统一准则》的同时能够满足《国际评估准则》的执业要求。此后,美国评估促进会与国际评估准则理事会又先后于 2017 年 1 月和 2018 年 1 月两次修订更新了这一协调指引。因此,《专业评估执业统一准则》采用《国际评估准则》的具体方式,实际是在保持其框架结构和规则内容的独立性与稳定性的前提下,通过美国评估促进会与国际评估准则理事会联合发布并适时修订协调指引来为评估师同时遵循两项准则提供执业衔接。

Text 正文

1. Background

Uniform Standards of Professional Appraisal Practice (USPAP) was developed and established by The Appraisal Foundation (TAF). The USPAP is the generally recognized ethical and performance standards for the appraisal profession in the United States. The purpose of the Uniform Standards of Professional Appraisal Practice (USPAP) is to promote and maintain a high level of public trust in appraisal practice by establishing requirements for appraisers.

Found in 1987, headquartered in Washington, DC, TAF is the nation's foremost authority on the valuation profession in U.S.. In 1989, the U.S. Congress enacted the Financial Institutions Reform, Recovery, and Enforcement Act (FiRREA), which authorized the Foundation as the source of appraisal standards and qualifications. Today, with Sponsoring Organizations and Advisory Councils, close to one hundred organizations, corporations and government agencies are affiliated with the Foundation. The foundation also ensures that the profession adapts to changing circumstances and continues to move forward through the work of its two independent boards: the Appraiser Qualifications Board (AQB) and the Appraisal Standards Board (ASB). The ASB of TAF develops, interprets, and amends the USPAP on behalf of appraisers and users of appraisal services.

The first USPAP was developed in 1987 by nine leading professional appraisal organizations in the United States and Canada formed an Ad Hoc Committee and copyrighted in 1987 by TAF, in response to the crisis in the savings and loan industry. The effective date of the original Uniform Standards is April 27, 1987. Prior to the establishment of the ASB in 1989, USPAP had been adopted by major appraisal organizations in North America. At its organizational meeting on January 30, 1989, the ASB unanimously approved and adopted the original USPAP as the initial appraisal standards promulgated by the ASB.

2. Applicable Scope

The USPAP is the extensively recognized ethical and performance standards for the appraisal profession, with significant influence in both the United States and international appraisal fields. In 1989, USPAP had been partly adopted by major appraisal organizations in North America, such as the US and Canada. TAF has many organizations members, but no individual members. At present, there are more than 90 professional organizations, businesses, and government agencies are the members organization of the TAF, and more than 90,000 valuers adopt the USPAP. The USPAP also contains standards for all types of appraisal services, including real estate, personal property, business, and mass appraisal.

In terms of the effectiveness of the standards, although the ASB writes, amends, and interprets USPAP, the Board does not enforce USPAP. However, through the FiRREA, the Federal government has mandated that the states enforce real property appraiser compliance to USPAP; professional appraisal associations also have the legal authority to enforce USPAP compliance by their members. In addition, many users of appraisal services (such as lenders and mortgage companies) have adopted USPAP and require employee or contract appraiser compliance to USPAP.

3. Update Mode

Over the years, USPAP has evolved in response to changes in appraisal practice, in order to help appraisers to have the information they need to deliver unbiased and thoughtful opinions of value. The ASB has developed a process for developing both Standards and guidance based, in part, on written comments submitted in response to exposure drafts and oral testimony presented at public meetings. Today, USPAP contains standards for all types of appraisal services, including real estate, personal property, business, and mass appraisal. Since the first edition in 1987, USPAP has been updated 24 times. In 1992 to 2006, USPAP had been updated every year. During this time, there are USPAP 1992 and USPAP 2006. After 2007, USPAP has been updated every two years, such as USPAP 2008-2009 and USPAP 2018-2019. On 12 August, 2022, the ASB announced that the latest edition, USPAP 2020-2021, would be extended to 31 December, 2023. After that, ASB voted on May 5, 2023 to adopt 2024 USPAP effective January 1, 2024.

Besides, TAF recognizes the importance of interacting with its colleagues from around the globe. TAF is a proud sponsor of the International Valuation and an active participant in the IVSC Advisory Forum and Advisory Forum Working Group. In June, 2006, the IVSC and TAF jointly issued the "Madison Agreement", in which they pledged to work together toward the goal of reconciling the differences between the two sets of standards. Thus, in 2016, a Standards Harmonisation Guide, named "A Bridge from USPAP to IVS - A guide to producing IVS-compliant appraisals" was produced by TAF and IVSC. While the Bridge describes additional steps necessary to ensure compliance with both standards, a full review of both sets of standards is always encouraged. This joint effort unveiled more commonalities than differences in the two sets of standards. After that, this guidance was revised in January 2017 and January 2018. In 2020, the Bridge was updated to be consistent with current IVS and the 2020-2021 USPAP. In conclusion, the way for USPAP adopting the IVS is actually aim at providing a practical connecting for appraisers to adopt both standards, by joint publication and timely revision of the Standards Harmonisation Guide, maintaining theirs independence and stability of framework and standards at the same time.

4. Fundamental Contents

This section takes USPAP 2020-2021 as example, to present the structure of USPAP. The USPAP 2020-2021 consists of three parts, and two guidance documents:

■ Part 1 Uniform Standards of Professional Appraisal Practice:

♦ Forward

♦ Table of Contents

- Preamble
- Definitions
- Ethics Rule
- Record Keeping Rule
- Competency Rule
- Scope of Work Rule
- Jurisdictional Exception Rule

■ Part 2 Standards and Standards Rule, which consists of 10 Standards:

- Standard 1 Real Property Appraisal, Development
- Standard 2 Real Property Appraisal, Reporting
- Standard 3 Appraisal Review, Development
- Standard 4 Appraisal Review, Reporting
- Standard 5 Mass Appraisal, Development
- Standard 6 Mass Appraisal, Reporting
- Standard 7 Personal Property Appraisal, Development
- Standard 8 Personal Property Appraisal, Reporting
- Standard 9 Business Appraisal, Development
- Standard 10 Business Appraisal, Reporting

■ Part 3 Statements on Appraisal Standards (SMT)

These standards are authorized by the by-laws of TAF and are for the purposes of clarification, Interpretation, explanation, or elaboration of the Standards of Professional Appraisal Practice (USPAP). Statements have the full weight of a Standards Rule and can be adopted by the ASB only after exposure and comment. There are currently no active Statements.

■ Advisory Opinions

The USPAP Advisory Opinions (AO) are a reference for appraisers, enforcement officials, users of appraisal services, and the public. Advisory Opinions do not establish new standards or interpret existing standards, so their use is not limited solely to the appraisal discipline(s) specified and is not part of USPAP.

Advisory Opinions are based on presumed conditions without investigation or verification of actual circumstances. Guidance provided in the Advisory Opinions does not represent the only possible solution to the issues discussed and the advice provided may not be applied equally to seemingly similar situations. Each Advisory Opinion applies to one or more appraisal disciplines as identified both in the Advisory Opinion and Table of Contents. However, there may be cases where the guidance in a particular Advisory Opinion could be helpful to an appraiser working in an appraisal discipline that is not specified.

■ Frequently Asked Questions (FAQ)

USPAP Frequently Asked Questions (USPAP FAQ) is a form of guidance issued by the ASB to respond to questions raised by appraisers, enforcement officials, users of appraisal services and the public to illustrate the applicability of USPAP in specific situations and to offer advice from the ASB for the resolution of appraisal issues and problems. The advice presented may not represent the only possible solution to the issues discussed and the advice provided may not be applied equally to seemingly similar situations. USPAP FAQ does not establish new standards or interpret existing standards. USPAP FAQ is not part of USPAP and is approved by the ASB.

Core Words and Expressions 核心术语

The Appraisal Foundation (TAF)	美国评估促进会
Appraisal Standards Board (ASB)	评估准则委员会
preamble	导言
ethics rule	道德条款
record keeping rule	档案保存条款
competency rule	能力条款

jurisdictional exception rule	管辖例外条款
standards rules	准则条文
appraisal review	评估复核
statements on appraisal standards (SMT)	评估标准说明
advisory opinions	咨询意见
frequently asked questions (FAQ)	常见问题汇编

Questions and Discussion 问题与讨论

1. Please list and explain the main parts of the USPAP, giving some standards as examples.

2. Please give a brief introduction of origin and development of the USPAP?

Topic 5: RICS Red Book 英国评估准则

Abstract 中文摘要

英国评估准则由英国皇家特许测量师学会（Royal Institution of Chartered Surveyors, RICS）制定和发布，通常也被称为"红皮书"（The Red Book）。该准则旨在促进和支持全球范围内的评估执业标准，为评估专业人员和其他利益相关者提供有用的参考资源。第一版RICS红皮书发布于1976年。虽然红皮书不是由法律授权制定和发布，但除了评估应用实践指南（Valuation Practice Guidance – Applications, VPGAs）部分外，该准则对于在英国皇家特许测量师学会注册的个人评估师和专业评估机构而言具有强制性。无论其成员在任何地方执业，都应当遵守红皮书的规定，否则将面临谴责、罚款、吊销执业证书甚至取消会员资格等处罚。英国法庭在评估案件判案中通常也会引用和参考红皮书。

英国皇家特许测量师学会成立于1868年，总部设立在英国伦敦，是一家以英国为总部、规管多个国家和地区特许测量师的独立专业团体，其历史可追溯至

1792 年成立的测量师俱乐部。英国皇家特许测量师学会作为英国最大、最具有权威性的评估行业组织，不仅在整个英联邦地区的评估业占据重要地位，而且还是具有全球影响力的专业性学会。该学会得到全球许多地方性协会和联合团体的支持，目前已经拥有遍布全球 146 个国家或地区的 13.4 万多名会员，向会员提供覆盖土地、物业、建造及环境等 17 个专业领域和相关行业的最新发展趋势。其主要职能包括制定行业操作规范和行为准则，对评估人员进行管理、教育和培训，保持与政府部门的联系，提供土地、房地产和建造业的专业资格认证并为会员提供服务。英国皇家特许测量师学会的管理机构是管理委员会，负责批准学会的战略和目标。管理委员会下设"董事会"和"准则与监管理事会"这两个附属组织；管理委员会进一步下设"薪酬委员会""全球区域性委员会和市场顾问小组""审计、风险和财务委员会"，同时保留制定学会战略和目标以及批准修改学会章程文件的职能。"准则与监管理事会"负责制定 RICS 红皮书等准则并监督其执行情况，以及行使学会的监管职能。

RICS 红皮书常常以一"版"多"次"的方式修订，即对一个版本可能进行多次修订。至今，英国皇家特许测量师学会已先后发布十二版红皮书，合计进行二十多次更新。在此期间，RICS 红皮书呈现四个方面的发展特征：（1）1976 年发布的第一版红皮书是以不动产评估业务领域为主，而在 20 世纪 90 年代中期以后，随着评估准则内容的不断丰富，红皮书的适用范围扩展到几乎所有评估业务领域。（2）红皮书包括两类应用范围：一是英国皇家特许测量师学会会员在全球范围从事的不动产和动产评估业务，二是英国皇家特许测量师学会会员在英国范围内从事的不动产和动产评估业务。自 2011 年 4 月第七版起，红皮书开始从准则结构上对全球标准和英国标准加以区分；随后的 2014 年 1 月第九版自 2015 年 6 月修订后，开始对全球版和英国版进行分开出版。（3）为提高国际通用性，英国皇家特许测量师学会还逐渐将国际评估准则（IVS）融入至红皮书：从 2007 年 4 月第五版起，红皮书已经部分采用和执行《国际评估准则》；从 2014 年 1 月的第九版开始，红皮书已经完全采纳 IVS，在此之后的红皮书中也都会将同期最新版的《国际评估准则》全部内容作为组成部分纳入其中。（4）从 2010 年第六版起，红皮书都是由英国皇家特许测量师学会同英国收益评级与估价协会（The Institute of Revenues Rating and Valuation, IRRV）合作出版；后者是英国税务、收益和评估领域最大的专业机构，旨在满足其会员在其职业生涯的每个阶段的需求。

目前，RICS 红皮书全球版的最新版为《RICS 评估——全球标准 2022》（RICS Valuation – Global Standards, 2022），于 2021 年 11 月发布，自 2022 年 1 月 31 日起生效；RICS 红皮书英国版的最新版为《RICS 评估——英国标准 2019》（RICS Valuation – Professional Standards UK, 2019），于 2018 年 11 月发布，自 2019 年 1 月 14 日起生效。总体上，《RICS 评估——全球标准 2022》由引言、术语、专业标准（Professional standards, PS）、评估技术与绩效标准（Valuation technical and performance standards, VPS）、评估应用实践指南（Valuation Practice Guidance – Applications, VPGAs）以及《国际评估准则 2022》六个部分组成。其中，引言主要介绍了红皮书的主要目的、适用范围、编排、制定背景、生效日期和修订方式以及与《国际评估准则》的关系等内容；术语表主要对红皮书所涉及的专业概念进行解释和规范；专业标准主要对评估师需要遵守的准则和操作声明作出规定，对其道德、胜任能力等提出要求；评估技术与绩效标准主要对评估业务的基本程序作出规定；评估应用实践指南主要根据不同的资产类型和评估目的，对评估业务提供指引；《国际评估准则 2022》则是《国际评估准则》的最新版内容。对于《RICS 评估——全球标准 2022》与《国际评估准则 2022》的关系，《RICS 评估——全球标准 2022》实际是以《国际评估准则 2022》作为内容基础和框架范式，在各个部分都引用了《国际评估准则 2022》的最新规定，并且在第六部分对《国际评估准则 2022》进行了全文转载。此外，《RICS 评估——全球标准 2022》还以额外的强制性要求和咨询性质的评估应用实践指南作为补充，从而在《国际评估准则 2022》基础上明确提出对英国皇家特许测量师学会会员的额外执业要求。

Text 正文

1. Background

The Red Book is issued by Royal Institution of Chartered Surveyors (RICS) as part of their commitment to promote and support high standards in valuation delivery worldwide, offering a useful reference resource for valuation users and other stakeholders. RICS is one of the most authoritative and globally recognised professional body in UK. Through their global standards, professional progression and their data and insight, they promoted and enforced the professional standards in the development and management of land, real estate, construction, and infrastructure.

Chapter 11 Valuation Standards 资产评估准则

RICS is a Royal Charter body, founded in 1868, headquartered in London, UK. RICS is also an independent professional body that regulates chartered surveyors in many countries and regions. The history of RICS can be traced back to the Surveyors Club, which was formed as far back as 1792. Royal Charter requires RICS to act in the public interest. Under the Royal Charter, RICS' governing body is the Governing Council, which is responsible for approving RICS strategy and vision, overseeing the effective delivery of the strategy as well as standards and regulation. Governing Council is also responsible for approving changes to RICS' constitution. Governing Council delegates responsibilities to the RICS Board, which retains the function of setting RICS's strategy and vision and approving changes to RICS's constitutional documents. Under the RICS Board, there are the Audit, Risk Assurance and Finance Committee, Nominations and Remuneration Committee, and the World Regional Boards and Market Advisory Panels.

As a globally recognized professional organisation, RICS sets globally recognized standards for professional members and RICS regulated firms to follow when conducting their work. The first edition of RICS Red Book was published in 1976 by RICS, in order to adapt to the promotion of International Accounting Standards (IAS) and to address the inconsistencies in the valuation of real estate in public financial accounts across countries. RICS Red Book reflects the growing importance of successfully combining professional, technical and performance standards in order to deliver high quality valuation advice that meets the expectations and requirements of clients, of governments, regulatory bodies, and other standard-setters, and of the public.

2. Applicable Scope

Although The RICS Red Book is not authorized by law, the publication details mandatory practices for RICS members where they are when undertaking valuation services. Otherwise, the members may face penalties such as reprimands, fines, revocation of practising certificates and even disqualification of membership. The RICS Red Book is also cited and referenced by the courts in valuation cases.

All members providing a written valuation are required to comply with the standards set out in RICS Red Book – in other words, unless stated otherwise, they are mandatory. For members, these global standards set out procedural rules and guidance which impose on individual valuers or firms registered for regulation by RICS certain mandatory obligations regarding competence, objectivity, transparency, and performance. For example, global professional and ethical standards as they expressly apply to valuers are denoted by the use of a PS reference number and are mandatory (unless otherwise stated) for all members providing written valuations; global valuation technical and performance standards are denoted by the use of a VPS reference number and contain specific, mandatory (unless otherwise stated) requirements and related <u>implementation guidance</u>, directed to the provision of a valuation that is IVS-compliant. However, RICS valuation practice guidance – applications, which denoted by the use of a VPGA reference number and provide further implementation guidance in the specific instances listed, are <u>advisory</u>.

With over 134,000 highly qualified trainees, professionals, and offices in every significant financial market from 146 countries or regions, the organisation is ideally placed to influence policy and embed their standards within local marketplaces in order to protect consumers and businesses.

3. Update Mode

RICS Red Book updated in the pattern of <u>amending</u> old editions or developing new editions. Since its first publication in 1976, RICS Valuation has been published for twelve times, and amended for more than 20 times. During this period, the development of RICS Red Book present the following features:

(a) The expansion of the scope: The first edition of the RICS Red Book issued in 1976 focused on the real estate. After the 1920s, the applicable scope of the RICS Red Book was extended to almost all type of assets.

(b) Interact with professionals around the world: There are two types applicable scope for RICS members: those who engaged in real estate and movable property valuation assignment in the UK and those who engaged in real estate and movable property valuation assignment around the world. From April 2011, when the RICS Red Book 7th edition was published, the RICS Red Book began to differentiate the application of the UK and the globe; after RICS Red Book 9th edition in January 2014 was revised in June 2015, RICS issued the UK edition and global edition of the RICS Red Book separately.

(c) Improvement of international generality: The RICS gradually embedded the International Valuation Standards (IVS) in the Red Book. In April 2007, the RICS Red Book 5th edition began to partly adopt the content of IVS, and since January 2014, the of RICS Red Book 9th edition have updated the Global Valuation Standards (Red Book) to incorporate the changes to the IVS's.

(d) Publish with the Institute of Revenues Rating and Valuation (IRRV): Since the RICS Red Book 6th edition published in 2010, the RICS Red Book was joint published by RISC with IRRV. The IRRV is the largest professional body in the field of taxation, earnings and valuation in the UK. It is designed to meet the needs of members at every stage of their careers. A thriving network of Associations is one of the IRRV's main strengths. Their Associations organise programmes of professional and social activities that take place regionally and provide the opportunity for all members to become more involved in the work of the Institute.

The latest edition, RICS Valuation-Global Valuation Standards 2022, was published on November, 2022, and became effective from 31 January, 2022, the same date as the latest edition of IVS became effective. The latest edition RICS Valuation - UK national supplement, was issued on November, 2018, and has been effective from 1 June, 2019.

4. Fundamental Contents

In this section, the fundamental contents of Red Book Global Standards and Red Book UK National Supplement will be introduced.

4.1 RICS Valuation - Global Standards

RICS Valuation - Global Standards reflects the growing importance of successfully combining professional, technical and performance standards in order to deliver high quality valuation advice that meets the expectations and requirements of clients; of governments, regulatory bodies, and other standard-setters, and of the public.

This section takes RICS Valuation - Global Standards 2022 as an example to present the structure of RICS Red Book. It mainly comprises six parts:

- Part 1: Introduction
- Part 2: Glossary

This glossary defines terms used in these global standards that have a special or restricted meaning. Words or phrases not appearing in the glossary follow their common dictionary meaning.

- Part 3: <u>Professional Standards (PS)</u>, which comprises two standards:
  - PS 1 Compliance with standards where a written valuation is provided
  - PS 2 Ethics, competency, objectivity and disclosures.
- Part 4: <u>Valuation technical and Performance Standards (VPS)</u>

With the goal of providing the valuation complying with IVS, global valuation technical and performance standards are listed with VPS numbers, containing specific and mandatory (unless otherwise stated) requirements, as well as related implementation guidance. While VPS 1, 4 and 5 focus more on technical standards, VPS 2 and 3 focus more on performance and delivery standards.

- VPS 1 <u>Terms of engagement</u> (scope of work), investigations and records
- VPS 2 Inspections
- VPS 3 Valuation reports
- VPS 4 Bases of value, assumptions and special assumptions
- VPS 5 Valuation approaches and methods
- Part 5: Valuation Applications

Part 5 covers matters relating to particular valuation applications. This part denoted <u>Valuation Practice Guidance - Applications (VPGAs)</u> reference number and provide further implementation guidance in the specific instances listed. Thus, among the topics covered, they include valuations for specific purposes (of which financial reporting and secured lending are among the most widely encountered), and valuations of certain specific asset types, where particular issues and/or practical considerations expressly need to be taken into account. These VPGAs embody "best practice" that is procedures that in the opinion of RICS meet a high standard of professional competence. While not themselves mandatory, the VPGAs do include links and cross references to the material in the IVS and to material in these global standards that is mandatory. This is intended to assist members in identifying material relevant to the particular valuation assignment they are undertaking.

- ♦ VPGA 1 Valuation for inclusion in financial statements
- ♦ VPGA 2 Valuation of <u>interests for secured lending</u>
- ♦ VPGA 3 Valuation of businesses and business interests
- ♦ VPGA 4 Valuation of individual trade related properties
- ♦ VPGA 5 Valuation of plant and equipment
- ♦ VPGA 6 Valuation of intangible assets
- ♦ VPGA 7 Valuation of personal property, including arts and antiques
- ♦ VPGA 8 Valuation of real property interests
- ♦ VPGA 9 Identification of <u>portfolios, collections and groups of properties</u>
- ♦ VPGA 10 Matters that may give rise to <u>material valuation uncertainty</u>

■ Part 6: International Valuation Standards (IVS)

In this part, RICS cites the core content of IVS including principles of valuation standard setting and core principles of valuation. It also establishes the IVS frame work, IVS general standards and IVS asset standards. Besides, this part summaries the main changes of IVS and its effective date.

4.2 RICS Valuation – Professional Standards, UK

This section takes RICS Valuation – Professional Standards UK, 2019 (published in 2018) as an example to establish the content of Red Book UK National Supplement. This book comprises four parts:

■ Part 1: Introduction

■ Part 2: UK Professional and Valuation Standards – mandatory

- ♦ UK Professional Standards (UK PS)

- UK PS 1 Compliance with valuation standards within the UK jurisdiction
- ♦ UK Valuation Technical and Performance Standards (UK VPSs)
  - UK VPS 1 Terms of engagement (scope of work) and reporting: Red Book compliance
  - UK VPS 2 Terms of engagement (scope of work): supplementary provisions in Scotland
- ■ Part 3: UK Valuation Practice Guidance Applications (UK VPGAs) – advisory
  - ♦ UK VPGA 1 Valuation for financial reporting: general matters
  - ♦ UK VPGA 2 Valuations for other regulated purposes
  - ♦ UK VPGA 3 Valuations for assessing adequacy of financial resources
  - ♦ UK VPGA 4 Valuation of local authority assets for accounting purposes
  - ♦ UK VPGA 5 Valuation of central government assets for accounting purposes
  - ♦ UK VPGA 6 Local authority and central government accounting: existing use value (EUV) basis of value
  - ♦ UK VPGA 7 Valuation of registered social housing providers' assets for financial statements
  - ♦ UK VPGA 8 Valuation of charity assets
  - ♦ UK VPGA 9 Relationship with auditors
  - ♦ UK VPGA 10 Valuation for commercial secured lending purposes
  - ♦ UK VPGA 11 Valuation for residential mortgage purposes
  - ♦ UK VPGA 12 Valuation of residential property for miscellaneous purposes
  - ♦ UK VPGA 13 Residential secured lending guidance for other related purposes including RICS HomeBuyer Service
  - ♦ UK VPGA 14 Valuation of registered social housing for loan security purposes
  - ♦ UK VPGA 15 Valuations for Capital Gains Tax, Inheritance Tax, Stamp Duty Land Tax and the Annual Tax on Enveloped Dwellings

- ◆ UK VPGA 16 Valuations for compulsory purchase and statutory compensation
- ◆ UK VPGA 17 Local authority disposal of land for less than best consideration in England and Wales
- ◆ UK VPGA 18 Affordable rent and market rent under the Housing Acts in a regulatory context
- ■ Part 4: Summary of changes from Red Book UK 2014 (revised January 2015)

Core Words and Expressions 核心术语

Audit, Risk Assurance and Finance Committee	审计、风险保证和财务委员会
Nominations and Remuneration Committee	提名及薪酬委员会
World Regional Boards and Market Advisory Panels	世界区域委员会及市场咨询小组
regulatory body	监管机构
standard-setters	准则制定者
Institute of Revenues Rating and Valuation (IRRV)	英国收益评级与估价协会
Professional Standards (PS)	专业标准
Valuation technical and Performance Standards (VPS)	评估技术与绩效标准
Valuation Practice Guidance – Applications (VPGAs)	评估应用实践指南
mandatory	强制性的
implementation guidance	实践指南

advisory	咨询性的
amending	修订
terms of engagement	聘用条款
interests for secured lending	担保贷款利息
portfolios, collections and groups of properties	房地产投资组合、财产集合和资产组
material valuation uncertainty	重大估值不确定性

Questions and Discussion 问题与讨论

1. Please list and explain the main parts of the RICS, giving some standards as examples.

2. Please give a brief introduction of origin and development of the RICS.

Information Extension

思政微课堂

党的二十大报告强调，要"坚持高水平对外开放，加快构建以国内大循环为主体、国内国际双循环相互促进的新发展格局""推动共建'一带一路'高质量发展""稳步扩大规则、规制、管理、标准等制度型开放""着力形成人才国际竞争的比较优势"。在"十四五"新阶段和"双循环"新格局下，资产评估行业着力于拓宽视野、提升能力，构建行业高端人才、国际化人才、跨专业复合型人才、青年人才等类型多样、结构合理的人才体系，加深对国际评估业务和国际评估准则的了解，加强对新兴业务领域的探索及评估标准的制定，更好地服务企业"走出去"，开辟行业创新之路。

以新发展理念为统领，以高质量发展为主题，中国资产评估协会于2021年发布的《"十四五"时期资产评估行业发展规划》（中评协〔2021〕21号）明确指出，资产评估行业的主要任务之一是"深化国际交流与合作，积极推进资产评估机构国际化发展"。具体而言，一是要深化国际交流与合作，继续积极参与国际评估事务和重大事项决策，主动参与国际规则制定，提升中国资产评估行业的国际话语权和影响力。探索推进国际和地区间会员资格互认、评估准则互认、评估报告互认。推荐资产评估机构和资产评估师加入各类国际评估专业组织，促进国际评估专业经验交流和成果共享；二是要加强国际评估市场和国际评估理论动态跟踪研究，跟踪分析国际评估业务特点，研究总结评估行业发展新态势、新特点、新问题。积极开展国际评估市场与理论研究，为资产评估行业国际化发展提供有力支持，研究国际评估准则"全球采用"政策对我国资产评估准则和资产评估机构国际化的影响；三是要积极提升境外执业能力，研究"一带一路"倡议，紧跟国家重大发展战略，引导资产评估机构服务企业"走出去"，实现行业国际化发展。

与此同时，我国资产评估专业人员遵守资产评估准则的相关要求已上升至法律层面。《中国人民共和国资产评估法》中有九处提到"评估准则"，对我国评估准则体系的完善提出更高要求，为中国参与国际评估标准制定和提升国际话语权奠定了坚实基础。例如，该法律规定，"评估机构及其评估专业人员开展业务应当遵守法律、行政法规和评估准则，遵循独立、客观、公正的原则""评估机构应当建立健全内部管理制度，对本机构的评估专业人员遵守法律、行政法规和评估准则的情况进行监督，并对其从业行为负责""国务院有关评估行政管理部门组织制定评估基本准则和评估行业监督管理办法""评估行业协会""依据评估基本准则制定评估执业准则和职业道德准则"，并"将会员遵守法律、行政法规和评估准则的情况记入信用档案"。为规范资产评估行为，保证执业质量，明确执业责任，保护资产评估当事人合法权益和公共利益，财政部根据《中华人民共和国资产评估法》等于2017年制定了《资产评估基本准则》（财资〔2017〕43号），要求"资产评估机构及其资产评估专业人员应当诚实守信，勤勉尽责，谨慎从业，遵守职业道德规范，自觉维护职业形象，不得从事损害职业形象的活动"。这也是资产评估机构和资产评估专业人员的立身之本。

在此基础上，为规范资产评估机构及其资产评估专业人员的职业道德行为，提高职业素质，维护职业形象，继财政部于2004年发布《资产评估职业道德准则——基本准则》（财企〔2004〕20号）之后，中国资产评估协会在财政部的指导下于2017年制定的《资产评估职业道德准则》（中评协〔2017〕30号）成为中国资产评估准则体系的重要组成部分。该准则从专业能力、独立性、与委托人和其他相关当事人的关系、与其他资产评估机构及资产评估专业人员的关系等方面对资产评估机构及其资产评估专业人员应当具备的道德品质和体现的道德行为进行了规范。例如，"资产评估机构及其资产评估专业人员应当诚实守信，勤勉尽责，谨慎从业，坚持独立、客观、公正的原则，不得出具或者签署虚假资产评估报告或者有重大遗漏的资产评估报告""应当采取恰当措施保持独立性""应当保持公正的态度，以客观事实为依据，实事求是地进行分析和判断，拒绝委托人或者其他相关当事人的非法干预，不得直接以预先设定的价值作为评估结论""应当与委托人进行必要沟通，提醒资产评估报告使用人正确理解评估结论""应当遵守保密原则，对评估活动中知悉的国家秘密、商业秘密和个人隐私予以保密"。"资产评估专业人员应当具备相应的评估专业知识和实践经验，能够胜任所执行的资产评估业务""应当完成规定的继续教育，保持和提高专业能力"。"资产评估机构及其资产评估专业人员不得以恶性压价、支付回扣、虚假宣传，或者采用欺骗、利诱、胁迫等不正当手段招揽业务""不得利用开展业务之便，为自己或者他人牟取不正当利益，不得向委托人或者其他相关当事人索要、收受或者变相索要、收受资产评估委托合同约定以外的酬金、财物等"。基于上述要求，资产评估机构及其资产评估专业人员在从业时严格遵守资产评估职业道德，也有利于提高资产评估作为中介服务行业的公信力。

Appendix I
Glossary 术语表

a class of investors	某一类投资者（chap.6）
a letter of transmittal	提交函（chap.10）
a newly constructed property	全新建造的资产（chap.2）
a signed certification	经评估师签署的评估声明（chap.10）
a value other than market value	非市场价值（chap.2）
a willing buyer	自愿买方（chap.1）
a willing seller	自愿卖方（chap.1）
absolute interest	绝对权益（chap.4）
accompanying work file	作为附件的工作文件（chap.10）
accounting convention	会计惯例，会计原则（chap.2）
Accounting Standard Codification (ASC)	会计准则汇编（chap.7）
accounts receivable	应收账款（chap.6）
accrued depreciation	应计折旧（chap.2）
acquiring firm	收购方（chap.6）
acquisition market	并购市场（chap.2）
acquisition premium	收购溢价（chap.6）

ad valorem tax	从价税（chap.8）
advanced statistical models	高级统计模型（chap.11）
advisory opinions	咨询意见（chap.11）
aging	老化，陈化（chap.6）
algorithms	算法式（chap.9）
allocation of the purchase price	对价分摊，购买价格分配（chap.7）
allowable variance	许可偏差（chap.8）
alternate supplier	备用供应商（chap.6）
alternative taxes	替代税（chap.8）
amending	修订（chap.11）
amortizable	可摊销的，可分批偿还的（chap.5）
amortization	分期偿还，摊销（chap.7）
an arm's length transaction	公平交易（chap.1）
analytical framework	分析框架（chap.5）
analytical methodology	分析方法（chap.2）
analytical procedure	分析程序（chap.2）
analytical process	分析程序（chap.10）
analytical technique	分析技术（chap.6）
analytical tool	分析工具（chap.2）
annual growth rate	年度增长率（chap.6）
annual operating expenses	年运营费用（chap.2）
annuity	年金（chap.2）
anticipation of benefits	收益预期（chap.2）
apportionment of value	价值分配（chap.11）

appraisal institution	评估机构（chap.11）
appraisal professional	评估专业人员（chap.11）
appraisal report	（一般）评估报告（chap.10）
appraisal review	评估复核（chap.11）
appraisal	评估的（chap.1）
Appraisal Standards Board (ASB)	评估准则委员会（chap.11）
appraise	评估（chap.1）
appraiser	评估专业人员，评估师（chap.1）
appurtenance	附属物（chap.4）
arbitrage	套利（chap.1）
are proportional to	与……成比例的（chap.9）
art and collectibles	艺术品，收藏品（chap.9）
articles of incorporation	公司章程（chap.6）
assembled workforce	集合劳动力（chap.5）
assessed, rateable, or taxable value	课税价值（chap.1）
asset standards	资产准则（chap.11）
asset-based approach	资产基础法（chap.6）
asset-specific requirements	资产特定性要求（chap.11）
Assets Standard	实体性准则（chap.11）
assumption	假设（chap.1）
at the end of a lease	租赁到期时（chap.2）
at the end of the forecast period	在预测期末（chap.2）
audit	审计（chap.2）

Audit, Risk Assurance and Finance Committee	审计、风险保证和财务委员会（chap.11）
Automated Valuation Models (AVMs)	自动评估模型（chap.8）
averaging method	平均方法（chap.2）
bad debt	坏账（chap.6）
balance sheet	资产负债表（chap.3）
bargaining power	议价能力（chap.6）
basis of value	价值类型（chap.1）
be weighed and reconciled	经过权衡和综合协调（chap.2）
benchmark	基准，以……为基准（chap.5）
bespoke swap	定制掉期交易（chap.9）
best fitting model	最佳拟合模型（chap.4）
bid	出价（chap.1）
binomial models	二项式模型（chap.7）
block	股票（chap.6）
Bloomberg	彭博社，彭博资讯（chap.6）
bonus	红利，收益（chap.9）
brand	品牌（chap.5）
budgetary decisions	预算决策（chap.9）
business chamber	商会（chap.6）
business model	企业模型（chap.1）
business ownership interests	企业所有者权益（chap.2）
business valuation	企业价值评估（chap.2）
business	企业（chap.2）

businesses and business interests	企业和企业权益（chap.11）
buyout	买断（chap.6）
bylaw	规章制度，制度（chap.6）
capital appreciation	资本增值（chap.4）
Capital Asset Pricing Method (CAPM)	资本资产定价模型（chap.6）
Capital Cities	大都会通讯公司（chap.6）
capital expenditures	资本性支出（chap.2）
capitalization/discount rate	资本化率/折现率（chap.2）
capitalize on	利用（chap.5）
carrying amount	账面值，维持费用（chap.5）
cash flow	现金流（chap.1）
charge made against income	从收入中进行的扣除（额）（chap.2）
chartist	图表分析专家（chap.1）
China Appraisal Society (CAS)	中国资产评估协会（chap.1）
Chinese Valuation Standards (CVS)	中国资产评估准则（chap.11）
closely held corporation	内部持股公司（chap.2）
code of conduct	行为守则（chap.11）
collateral asset quality	抵押资产质量（chap.9）
collateralization	以…作抵押（chap.9）
collinearity	共线性（chap.8）
commercial value	商业价值（chap.1）
commissioning party	委托方（chap.10）
commodity future	期货（chap.9）
company-related characteristics	公司特征（chap.6）

comparability	可比性（chap.10）
comparable data	参照数据（chap.4）
comparable property	可比资产，参照物（chap.2）
comparable sales method	可比交易法（chap.2）
comparable sales	可比交易（案例）（chap.2）
comparables	可比案例（chap.8）
comparative analysis	可比分析（chap.2）
competency rule	能力条款（chap.11）
competing properties	竞争资产（chap.2）
competitive advantage	竞争优势（chap.6）
complementary asset	辅助性资产，互补性资产（chap.3）
comply with	遵从（chap.4）
computer-aided mass appraisal system	计算机辅助批量评估系统（chap.8）
conduct tax	行为税（chap.8）
consolidation	合并（chap.6）
construction methods	施工方法（chap.4）
consumable	消耗品（chap.3）
consumer price index (CPI)	消费者物价指数（chap.6）
contemporary appraisal practice	现代评估实践（chap.2）
contingent liabilities	或有债务（chap.6）
contract rent	合同租金（chap.4）
contractual life	合约期（chap.5）
contractual	合同性的，契约性的（chap.5）
contributory asset	贡献资产（chap.5）

control transaction	控制权交易（chap.7）
controlling interest	控股权益（chap.6）
conversion options	可转换期权（chap.9）
copy	备份（chap.10）
copyright asset	著作权资产（chap.11）
copyright	版权，著作权（chap.5）
corroborate	证实（chap.7）
cost advantage	成本优势（chap.6）
cost approach	成本途径（chap.2）
cost of equity	股权资本成本（chap.6）
cost structure	成本结构（chap.6）
counterparty risk	交易对手风险（chap.9）
credibility	可信性（chap.10）
credit standing	信用地位，商业信誉（chap.7）
criterion	准则（chap.5）
cross-section	横截面（chap.1）
customer relationship	客户关系（chap.5）
data representativeness	数据代表性（chap.8）
data asset	数据资产（chap.11）
dealer brokers	证券交易商之间的经纪人（chap.9）
debt-free net cash flow	无负债现金流（chap.2）
decommission	拆卸，退役（chap.3）
deduct from	扣除（chap.7）
deduction	扣除，减除（chap.3）

default protection	违约保护（chap.9）
default rate	违约率（chap.7）
default risk	违约风险（chap.6）
depreciable amount	折旧额（chap.2）
depreciation and other noncash expense	折旧和其他非现金费用（chap.2）
depreciation charge	折旧费（chap.7）
depreciation/deterioration/obsolescence	折旧，损耗，贬值（chap.2）
derivative assets valuation	衍生品资产评估（chap.11）
derivative instrument	衍生金融工具（chap.9）
detailed documentation	详细的文件（chap.10）
determinate life	确定寿命（chap.5）
development property	开发性房地产（chap.11）
direct capitalization	直接资本化（chap.2）
direct market comparison method	直接市场比较法（chap.2）
direct sales evidence	直接的相关销售证据（chap.2）
disclosure/disclose	披露（chap.2）
discount for lack of marketability	缺乏市场流动性折价（chap.6）
discounted cash flow (DCF)	现金流折现（chap.2）
disposal	清理，处置（chap.3）
distribution channels	分销渠道（chap.6）
distribution contract	分销合同（chap.5）
diversification	多样化，分散投资（chap.6）
dividend discount model	股利折现模型（chap.1）
dividends distribution	股息分配（chap.6）

divorce dispute	离婚争议（chap.6）
downward revaluations	向下重估（chap.3）
draft or final report	报告草稿或终稿（chap.10）
earning power	盈利能力（chap.2）
earnings before interest and tax (EBIT)	息税前利润（chap.2）
earnings capability	获利能力（chap.2）
earnings growth rate	收入增长率（chap.6）
economic depreciation/obsolescence	经济性贬值（chap.2）
economic principle	经济原则，经济原理（chap.2）
economic value	经济价值（chap.1）
economic variables	经济变量（chap.2）
effect of synergy	协同效应（chap.1）
elements of comparison	比较因素（chap.2）
empirical data	经验数据（chap.2）
employment agreements	雇佣协议（chap.5）
encumbrance	财产留置权，产权负担（chap.4）
energy efficiency	能源高效（chap.11）
engagement letter	委托合同（chap.11）
enterprises' state-owned assets	国有资产（chap.11）
equilibrium	均衡（chap.2）
equitable value	公平价值（chap.1）
equity capital market	权益资本市场,股票资本市场（chap.6）
ethical and professional standards	职业道德和行业准则（chap.10）
ethics rule	道德条款（chap.11）

European Business Valuation Standards (EVS-BV)	欧洲企业价值评估准则（chap.11）
European Group of Valuers' Associations (TEGOVA)	欧洲评估师联合会（chap.11）
European Plant, Machinery & Equipment Valuation Standards (EVS-PME)	欧洲机器设备评估准则（chap.11）
European Union legislation	欧盟立法（chap.11）
European Valuation Standards Board (EVSB)	欧洲企业价值评估准则委员会（chap.11）
European Valuation Standards (EVS)	欧洲评估准则（chap.11）
examined	经检验的（chap.10）
excess earnings method	超额收益法（chap.5）
exchange fund note	外汇基金债券（chap.6）
exclusive possession	独占，独有使用权（chap.4）
existing unsold properties	现存未出售的资产（chap.2）
expected benefit	预期收益（chap.7）
expense ratios	费用率（chap.8）
expert testimony	专家作证，专家证词（chap.5）
expiry	终止；满期，届期（chap.5）
exploratory research	探索性研究（chap.5）
explicit duration	有限期（chap.2）
extent of investigation	调查程度（chap.10）
external documentation	外部文件（chap.10）
external source	外部来源（chap.6）
factual or observable inputs	事实的或可观察输入（chap.10）

fair market value	公允市场价值（chap.1）
fair value	公允价值（chap.1）
fall outside	超出，超越（chap.3）
fast-mutating industrial landscape	快速变化的工业格局（chap.11）
file documentation	工作底稿（chap.10）
finance cost	融资费用（chap.4）
finance lease	融资租赁（chap.7）
Financial Accounting Standards Board (FASB)	财务会计准则委员会（chap.5）
financial derivatives	金融衍生品（chap.11）
financial grants	财政拨款（chap.4）
financial interests	金融权益（chap.2）
financial reporting	财务报告（会计）（chap.2）
financial statement	财务报表（chap.2）
financing terms	融资条件，金融条款（chap.2）
fiscal year	会计年度（chap.7）
fixed assets	固定资产（chap.6）
fluctuating	波动的，不稳定的（chap.5）
footnote	财务报表附注（chap.3）
forgery and fraud	伪造和欺诈（chap.9）
form or narrative report	表格型的报告或叙述型的报告（chap.10）
formulae	配方（chap.5）
forward stock option	远期股票期权（chap.9）
framework	框架，结构（chap.1）

franchise buyer	特许买家（chap.1）
fraud case	欺诈案件（chap.6）
free cash flow	自由现金流（chap.6）
frequently asked questions (FAQ)	常见问题汇编（chap.11）
functional depreciation/obsolescence	功能性贬值（chap.2）
fundamental analyst	基本面分析者（chap.1）
future benefits	未来收益（chap.2）
general standards	通用准则（chap.11）
General Valuation Standard	资产评估基本准则（chap.11）
Generally Accepted Accounting Principles (GAAP)	美国一般公认会计准则（chap.3）
goodwill	商誉（chap.5）
government tax base assessment	政府税基评估（chap.8）
gross income	总收入（chap.2）
group or portfolio of assets	资产组或投资组合（chap.10）
guidance note	指导意见（chap.11）
head lease	开头租赁，原始租赁（chap.4）
hedonic price method	特征价格法（chap.8）
hierarchical	分层的，分等级的（chap.7）
historic property	历史建筑（chap.4）
homogenous	同质的（chap.3）
hostile takeover	恶意收购（chap.1）
human capital	人力资本（chap.5）
hypothesis	假说，假设，前提（chap.1）

Appendix I Glossary 术语表

hypothetical exchange	假定的交易（chap.2）
hypothetical licensee	假设的被许可方（chap.5）
identifiable intangible asset	可辨认无形资产（chap.5）
identified investment objectives	特定的投资目标（chap.6）
if the data are averaged	如果所取的数据是平均数（chap.2）
illiquidity	非流动性（chap.6）
immateriality	非物质性（chap.5）
impaired assets	减值资产（chap.3）
impairment loss	减值损失（chap.3）
impairment testing	减值测试（chap.7）
implementation guidance	实践指南（chap.11）
in normal operation	在正常经营情况下（chap.2）
in the context of asset valuation	在资产评估领域（chap.2）
in the terminal year of the forecast	在预测期最后一年（chap.2）
incidental costs	附加成本（chap.4）
income approach	收益法（chap.2）
income capitalization approach	收益资本化途径（chap.2）
income capitalization method	收益资本化法（chap.2）
income multiplier	收益乘数（chap.2）
income per capita	人均收入（chap.6）
income statement	损益表，利润表（chap.2）
income stream	收益流（chap.2）
income tax	所得税（chap.8）
income taxes at the statutory rate	依法定税率征收的所得税（chap.2）

income-producing property	具有获利能力的资产（chap.2）
incorporate	合并，包含（chap.6）
incremental effect	递增效应（chap.5）
incremental income method	增量收益法（chap.5）
indemnification	赔偿，保护，赦免，补偿金（chap.7）
independence and reliability of valuation	评估的独立性和可靠性（chap.2）
indicate a range	形成区间（chap.2）
indirect comparison method	间接比较法（chap.2）
industry-specific risk	行业特有风险（chap.6）
infringement damages	侵权损害赔偿（chap.5）
infusions of cash	现金的投入（chap.2）
inheritance tax	遗产税（chap.8）
initial public offerings (IPO)	首次公开募股（chap.6）
inseparability	不可分离性（chap.5）
insolvency proceeding	破产程序（chap.5）
Institute of Revenues Rating and Valuation (IRRV)	英国收益评级与估价协会（chap.11）
insurable value	保险价值，可保价值（chap.1）
insurance contract	保险合同（chap.6）
intangible asset	无形资产（chap.5）
integrating forward	前向一体化（chap.6）
intellectual assets	知识资产（chap.5）
intellectual capital	智力资本（chap.5）
intellectual property	知识产权（chap.3）

intended use	期望用途（chap.2）
intended user	期望使用者（chap.10）
interests for secured lending	担保贷款利息（chap.11）
intermediary tax base assessment	中介税基评估（chap.8）
internal rate of return	内部收益率（chap.9）
Internal Revenue Service	国内税务局（chap.5）
internal risk	内部风险（chap.9）
internal source	内部来源（chap.6）
International Accounting Standards Board (IASB)	国际会计准则理事会（chap.1）
International Accounting Standards (IAS)	国际会计准则（chap.1）
International Financial Reporting Standards (IFRS)	国际财务报告准则（chap.1）
International Valuation Standards Council (IVSC)	国际评估准则理事会（chap.4）
International Valuation Standards (IVS)	国际评估准则（chap.1）
internet domain name	互联网域名（chap.5）
interval	时间间隔（chap.7）
intrinsic	本质的，固有的（chap.9）
inventory	存货（chap.3）
investment property	投资性房地产（chap.3）
investment securities	投资证券，有价证券（chap.6）
investment value	投资价值（chap.1）
joint venture	合资企业（chap.6）

jurisdiction	行政辖区，管辖权（chap.4）
jurisdictional exception rule	管辖例外条款（chap.11）
key person discount	关键人物折价（chap.6）
know-how	专有技术（chap.5）
lack of market activity	市场活动的缺乏（chap.2）
land value	土地价值（chap.8）
learning curve effect	学习曲线效应（chap.6）
lease classification	租赁分类（chap.7）
lease contract	租赁合约（chap.6）
lease interest	租赁权（chap.4）
lease term	租赁期（chap.7）
legal expense	法律费用（chap.5）
legal interest	法定利率（chap.4）
legal requirements	法律要求（chap.10）
legal rights	法定权利（chap.5）
legitimate rights	合法权益（chap.11）
lessee	承租人（chap.3）
lessor	出租人（chap.3）
level of earnings	盈利水平（chap.2）
leverage	杠杆（chap.2）
levered/unlevered beta	使用/未使用财务杠杆的 β（chap.6）
licensed	得到许可的（chap.5）
licensing arrangement	许可协议（chap.5）
licensing	许可证（chap.5）

life-based method	使用年限法（chap.2）
liquidation or forced sale value	清算价值，强迫出售价值（chap.1）
litigation	官司，诉讼（chap.5）
loan agreement	贷款协议（chap.6）
local standards	当地准则（chap.2）
long-lived asset	长期资产（chap.5）
M&A valuation	并购估值（chap.11）
magnitude	规模（chap.9）
maintenance of existing machinery	对现有设备进行的维护（chap.2）
major premise	重要前提（chap.2）
mandatory	强制性的（chap.11）
market analysis	市场分析（chap.8）
market approach	市场途径（chap.2）
market capitalization	市值，市场资本总额（chap.6）
market comparison approach	市场比较途径（chap.2）
market evidence	市场证据（chap.2）
market index	市价指数，市场指数（chap.6）
market participants	市场参与者（chap.1）
market portfolio	市场投资组合（chap.6）
market rent	市场租金（chap.4）
market risk premium	市场风险溢价（chap.6）
market share	市场份额（chap.2）
market timer	择时交易者（chap.1）
market timing	选时交易（chap.1）

market transaction	市场交易（chap.2）
market value	市场价值（chap.1）
market value	市场价值（chap.8）
marketing effectiveness	市场营销效果（chap.6）
mass appraisal	批量评估（chap.8）
mass asset	大规模资产（chap.5）
material valuation uncertainty	重大估值不确定性（chap.11）
mathematical modelling	数学建模（chap.8）
mathematical procedure	数学程序（chap.2）
mathematical simplification	数学上的简化（chap.6）
maturity	到期（期限）（chap.6）
measure of income or net assets	收益或净资产指标（chap.2）
Mei & Moses All Art Index	梅摩艺术指数（chap.9）
merger & acquisitions (M&A)	兼并与收购（chap.6）
mineral right	矿业权（chap.9）
minerals and land	矿产和土地（chap.9）
minimize taxes	减少税收（chap.2）
Ministry of Finance of the People's Republic of China (MOF of the PRC)	中华人民共和国财政部（chap.11）
minority interest	少数股权（chap.6）
model calibration	模型校准（chap.8）
model specification	模型选择（chap.8）
mortgage lending value	抵押贷款价值（chap.1）
multi-period	多周期（chap.7）

multiple interests	多重权益（chap.11）
multiple regression analysis	多元回归分析（chap.8）
multiple regression	多元回归（chap.4）
near-term growth	近期增长（chap.6）
net cash flow	净现金流（chap.2）
net income	净收益（chap.4）
net receipt	净收入（chap.4）
net selling price	净售价（chap.3）
net working capital	净营运资本（chap.2）
netting agreement	组网协议（chap.9）
newness rate method	成新率法（chap.2）
Nominations and Remuneration Committee	提名及薪酬委员会（chap.11）
non-compete agreement	非竞争协议（chap.5）
non-exclusive right	非独占权益（chap.4）
non-financial liabilities	非金融负债（chap.11）
non-monetary	非货币的（chap.5）
non-performing financial asset	金融不良资产（chap.11）
non-recurrent revenue	非经常收入（chap.6）
non-recurring activities	非经常项目（chap.6）
non-tangible asset	非有形资产（chap.5）
normalized annual economic income	标准化年经济收益（chap.5）
not-for-profit organisation	非营利组织（chap.11）
notional royalty rate	名义提成率（chap.5）

object of tax base assessment	税基评估客体（chap.8）
objective criteria	客观标准（chap.2）
obsolete	废弃的，淘汰的（chap.6）
observation method	观察法（chap.2）
offset	抵消（chap.6）
offshore mineral	近海矿产（chap.9）
offshore	离岸的（chap.9）
oil and gas mineral right	石油和天然气矿产开采权（chap.9）
on the bottom line	在（账表）底栏（chap.2）
ongoing business	持续经营的企业（chap.2）
onshore	陆上的，岸上的（chap.9）
on-site visit	实地勘查（chap.6）
open and competitive market	公开竞争市场（chap.8）
open market hypothesis	公开市场假设（chap.2）
operating leases	经营租赁，营业租赁（chap.6）
operational plant	运作有效的工厂（chap.6）
optimal utility	最佳的功能（chap.2）
option-pricing model	期权定价模型（chap.7）
order book	订货清单（chap.5）
Organisation for Economic Co-operation and Development (OECD)	经济合作与发展组织（chap.1）
organisational capital	组织资本（chap.5）
organisational structure	组织结构（chap.5）
outbid	出价高于（chap.2）

over the counter (OTC) market	场外交易（chap.9）
overall value	整体价值（chap.4）
owners' compensation	所有者的报酬（chap.2）
ownership interests	所有者权益（chap.5）
parameter	参量，参数（chap.5）
paramount	最重要的（chap.4）
particular entity	特定的（会计）主体（chap.2）
patent	专利，专利权（chap.5）
patented technology	专利技术（chap.5）
pending competition/lawsuits	胜负未定的竞争/诉讼（chap.6）
pending litigation	未决诉讼（chap.6）
pending regulatory changes	尚未确定的法规变化（chap.6）
per capita basis	人均基础（chap.9）
periodically	定期地，周期性地（chap.5）
periods of economic development and economic depression	经济发展和经济衰退的周期（chap.2）
personal property	动产，私人财产（chap.2）
physical depreciation/deterioration	实体性贬值（chap.2）
physical life	使用寿命（chap.3）
plant and equipment	厂房和设备，机器设备（chap.3）
Porter's Five Forces Model	波特五力模型（chap.6）
portfolio management	投资组合管理（chap.1）
portfolio valuation	资产组合评估（chap.11）
portfolio	证券投资组合（chap.9）

portfolios, collections and groups of properties	房地产投资组合、财产集合和资产组（chap.11）
postulate	假设（chap.5）
potential pool of buyers	潜在的买方群体（chap.6）
potential users	潜在使用者（chap.2）
Practice Note	指南（chap.11）
preamble	导言（chap.11）
prediction	预报，预测（chap.4）
preliminary data	初始数据（chap.5）
premium for control	控制权溢价（chap.6）
premium profits method	增量收益法（chap.5）
present value/current value	现值（chap.2）
pre-tax	税前（chap.3）
price discount method	价格折扣法（chap.2）
price multiple	价格乘数（chap.6）
price war	价格战（chap.6）
price-book value ratio	市净率（chap.1）
price-earnings ratio	市盈率（chap.1）
price index method	价格指数法（chap.2）
pricing volatility	价格波动（chap.9）
primary assets valuation	原生品资产评估（chap.11）
principle of anticipation	预期原则，预期收益原则（chap.2）
principle of balance	平衡原则（chap.2）
principle of externalities	外部性原则（chap.2）

principle of substitution	替代原则（chap.2）
principle of supply and demand	供求原则（chap.2）
prior transactions	以前的交易（chap.2）
Procedure Standard	程序性准则（chap.11）
process documentation	进程性文件（chap.5）
product cycles	产品周期（chap.2）
product line	生产线（chap.6）
professional affiliation	职业从属关系（chap.10）
Professional Standards (PS)	专业标准（chap.11）
professional valuers	职业评估师（chap.10）
profitability	盈利能力（chap.6）
promulgate	颁布（chap.11）
property market	房地产市场（chap.4）
property ownership	资产所有权（chap.2）
property right	资产权益（chap.2）
property tax	财产税（chap.8）
property types	资产类型（chap.5）
proposed construction	规划中的建筑（chap.2）
prospective owner	准业主（chap.4）
protocol	协议（chap.8）
proviso	附带条件,附文,限制性条款（chap.7）
proxy	代理人，委托书（chap.7）
public interest	公共利益（chap.11）
public relation	公共关系（chap.5）

public stock market	股票市场（chap.2）
Public Valuer (PV)	资产评估师（chap.1）
publicly held corporation	公共持股公司（chap.2）
publicly traded businesses	公开交易的企业（上市公司）（chap.2）
purchasing power	购买力（chap.2）
put rights	卖权，看跌权（chap.6）
qualitative and quantitative business characteristics	企业的数量和质量特征（chap.2）
quality control	质量控制（chap.5）
quality of assets valuation	资产评估质量（chap.11）
quantifiable value	可量化的价值（chap.5）
quantitative	定量的（chap.4）
quasi-government tax base assessment	准政府税基评估（chap.8）
quoted market price	市场报价（chap.7）
quoted price	报价（chap.7）
raider	入侵者（chap.6）
rates of returns	回报率（chap.2）
rates tax	差饷税（中国香港）（chap.8）
raw material	原材料（chap.3）
real estate tax	不动产税（chap.8）
real option	实物期权（chap.11）
real property interest	不动产权益（chap.4）
real property/estate	不动产（chap.2）
reasonable return	合理回报（chap.2）

recipe	食谱，处方（chap.5）
record keeping rule	档案保存条款（chap.11）
recoverable amount	可回收金额（chap.7）
recurrent property taxation	经常性财产税（chap.11）
referring to	参照（chap.6）
refinement	细化，精化（chap.5）
regression model	回归模型（chap.4）
regulatory body	监管机构（chap.11）
related market data	相关市场数据（chap.2）
relevance	相关性（chap.9）
relief-from-royalty method	许可费使用节省法（chap.5）
render …more comparable	使……具有更多的可比性（chap.2）
renewal possibility	续约的可能性（chap.5）
replacement cost	更新重置成本（chap.2）
replacement cost calculation method	重置核算法（chap.2）
replicate	复制（chap.4）
reporting options	报告选择权，报告类型（chap.10）
reporting unit	报告单位（chap.5）
reproduction cost	复原重置成本（chap.2）
requisite element	必要的因素（chap.5）
resale price	转售价格（chap.4）
resale value upon reversion/ reversionary value	终值（chap.2）
residual amount	余额（chap.5）

residual value	剩余价值，残值（chap.7）
resistance line	压力线（chap.1）
resource tax	资源税（chap.8）
restricted use appraisal report	限制用途评估报告（chap.10）
restrictive transfer provisions	限制转让的规定（chap.6）
restructuring	重组（chap.1）
Reuters	路透社（chap.6）
revaluation surplus	重估盈余（chap.3）
revaluation	资产重估（chap.3）
reversion of the property	财产的复归（chap.2）
RICS Red Book	英国评估准则，英国红皮书（chap.11）
risk-free rate	无风险报酬率（chap.6）
Royal Institution of Chartered surveyors (RICS)	英国皇家特许测量师学会（chap.11）
royalty agreement	特许经营协议（chap.5）
sales and purchase agreement	买卖协议（chap.6）
sales comparison approach	销售比较途径（chap.2）
salvage value	残余价值（chap.1）
scale economic benefit index method	规模经济效益指数法（chap.2）
scope of work	工作范围（chap.2）
scoring method	打分法（chap.2）
Securities and Exchange Commission (SEC)	美国证券交易委员会（chap.3）
securities	证券（chap.2）
self-contained appraisal report	完整评估报告（chap.9）

share placement	股份处置（chap.6）
share transaction	股份交易（chap.4）
shareholding in a non-quoted business	非上市公司股权（chap.1）
short sale	卖空（chap.1）
similar businesses	相似企业（chap.2）
similar or substitute properties	相似或可替代资产（chap.2）
single case appraisal	单宗评估（chap.8）
size of block	股份规模（chap.6）
skyrocket	飞涨，猛涨（chap.9）
social resources valuation	社会资源评估（chap.11）
solvency	偿付能力（chap.9）
special assumption	特殊假设（chap.1）
special value	特殊价值（chap.1）
specific risk	特定风险（chap.6）
Specific Standard	具体准则（chap.11）
stand-alone	独立的（chap.5）
standards rules	准则条文（chap.11）
standard-setters	准则制定者（chap.11）
statistical analysis method	统计分析法（chap.2）
statistical principles	统计学原理（chap.2）
start-up business	新开张的企业（chap.2）
Statement of Financial Accounting Standard (SFAS)	财务会计准则的声明（chap.3）
statements on appraisal standards (SMT)	评估标准说明（chap.11）

stepwise regression	逐步回归（chap.4）
stock real estate	存量房地产（chap.8）
stockholder wealth maximization	股东财富最大化（chap.6）
stockholders' equity	股东权益（chap.3）
strategic alliance	战略联盟（chap.6）
stratification	分层（chap.8）
structural capital	结构资本（chap.5）
subject of tax base assessment	税基评估主体（chap.8）
subject property	标的资产（chap.4）
sub-lease interest	转租权，分租权（chap.4）
subordinate interest	次级权益（chap.4）
subset	子集（chap.5）
substantial depreciation	大量贬值，实质性贬值（chap.2）
substantial perks	大量的津贴（chap.2）
summary appraisal report	概述型评估报告（chap.10）
superior interest	最高权益（chap.4）
supplier relationship	供应商关系（chap.5）
supply contract	供应合同（chap.5）
support line	支撑线（chap.1）
sustainability	可持续性（chap.11）
swing vote	关键选票，决定性选票（chap.6）
switching cost	转换成本（chap.6）
synergistic value	协同价值（chap.1）
synergy	协同效应（chap.6）

Appendix I Glossary 术语表

systematic allocation	系统提取（chap.2）
systematic risk	系统性风险（chap.6）
takeover	收购（chap.1）
tariff	关税（chap.8）
tax amortization benefit	税收摊销收益（chap.7）
tax base assessment	税基评估（chap.8）
tax benefit	税收优惠（chap.5）
tax collector	征税人（chap.8）
tax exemptions	免税（chap.4）
tax payer	纳税人（chap.8）
tax savings	税收节约（chap.5）
taxable income	应纳税所得额（chap.5）
technical specification	技术规范（chap.3）
tender offer	要约收购（chap.6）
terms of engagement	聘用条款（chap.11）
The Appraisal Foundation (TAF)	美国评估促进会
the extent of the inspection	勘察的情况（范围／程度）（chap.10）
The International Assets Valuation Standards Committee (TIAVSC)	国际评估准则委员会（chap.11）
the level of detail	详细程度（chap.10）
the nature of the rights	权利的性质（chap.4）
the recoverable amount of an asset	资产可收回金额（chap.3）
the valuer's file	评估专业人员（评估师）的底稿文件（chap.10）

the valuer's signature	评估专业人员（评估师）的签名（chap.10）
thought process	思维过程（chap.4）
threshold	门槛，开端（chap.9）
time cost	时间成本（chap.4）
time frame	时段，期限（chap.6）
time period	时间期间（chap.2）
trade association	行业协会（chap.5）
trade name	商号（chap.5）
trademark	商标（chap.5）
trade-off	权衡（chap.1）
trading price	交易价格（chap.4）
trading volume	交易量（chap.1）
transaction cost	交易成本（chap.1）
turnover tax	流转税（chap.8）
unauthorized use	未经授权使用（chap.5）
unchanged income	等额收益（chap.2）
underlying asset	标的资产（chap.9）
underlying assumption	基本假设（chap.2）
underlying assumptions and limiting conditions	基本假设和限制条件（chap.10）
underlying fundamentals	基本原理（chap.4）
undervalue	低估（chap.6）
undiscovered reserves	未发现的储备（chap.9）
unencumbered	没有阻碍的，不受妨碍的（chap.3）

Uniform Standards of Professional Appraisal Practice (USPAP)	专业评估执业统一准则（chap.1）
unique trade design	专有设计（chap.5）
unleased land	未出租的土地（chap.9）
unlimited duration	无限期（chap.2）
unpatented technology	非专利技术（chap.5）
upward revaluations	向上重估（chap.3）
urban overall assessment method	城市整体评估法（chap.8）
useful life	使用寿命，有效期（chap.7）
vacancy rate	闲置率，空置率（chap.2）
validation	确认（chap.5）
valuation approach	评估途径（chap.2）
valuation certificate	评估声明（chap.10）
valuation date	评估基准日（chap.1）
valuation discipline	评估学科（chap.2）
Valuation Ethical Standard	资产评估职业道德准则（chap.11）
valuation figures	评估数据（chap.10）
valuation for insurance purposes	以保险为目的的评估（chap.11）
Valuation Guidance Note	资产评估指导意见
valuation method	评估方法（chap.2）
Valuation Practice Note	资产评估指南
Valuation Practicing Standard	资产评估执业准则（chap.11）
Valuation Practice Guidance – Applications (VPGAs)	评估应用实践指南（chap.11）
valuation process	评估程序（chap.2）

Valuation technical and Performance Standards (VPS)	评估技术与绩效标准（chap.11）
valuation	评估，估值（chap.1）
value estimate	价值估计（chap.2）
value in use	在用价值（chap.1）
value indication	价值结论（chap.2）
value of control	控制权价值（chap.6）
value	价值，评估（chap.1）
value ratio method	价值比率法（chap.2）
valuer	评估专业人员，评估师（chap.1）
variation	变量（chap.2）
volatile	不稳定的（chap.9）
volatile incomes	不等额收益（chap.2）
voting interest	表决权（chap.6）
waste away	日渐消耗（chap.5）
Weighted Average Cost of Capital (WACC)	加权平均资本成本（chap.6）
withdrawal	退股（chap.6）
working papers	工作文件（chap.10）
World Regional Boards and Market Advisory Panels	世界区域委员会及市场咨询小组（chap.11）
written report	书面报告（chap.10）
yield capitalization	报酬资本化（chap.2）
yield curve	收益曲线（chap.7）
yield rate	收益率（chap.2）

Appendix II
Appraisal Industry Associations and Useful Websites (selected)
资产评估行业组织及实用网站

(1) The International Valuation Standards Council（IVSC）
    国际评估准则理事会
    http://www.ivsc.org/

(2) The World Association of Valuation Organisations（WAVO）
    世界评估组织联合会
    http://www.wavoglobal.org/

(3) The European Group of Valuers Associations（TEOGVA）
    欧洲评估师协会联合会
    http://www.tegova.org/

(4) The International Association of Consultants, Valuators and Analysts（IACVA）
    国际企业价值评估分析师协会
    http://www.iacva.com/

(5) The International Institute of Business Valuers（IIBV）
    国际企业价值评估学会
    http://www.iibv.org/

（6）The International Association of Assessing Officers（IAAO）

　　国际估税官协会

　　http://www.iaao.org/

（7）The International Property Tax Institute（IPTI）

　　国际财产税学会

　　http://www.ipti.org/

（8）China Appraisal Society（CAS）

　　中国资产评估协会

　　http://www.cas.org.cn/

（9）China Real Estate Valuers and Agents Association（CREVA）

　　中国土地估价师与土地登记代理人协会

　　http://www.creva.org.cn/

（10）China Institute of Real Estate Appraisers and Agents（CIREA）

　　中国房地产估价师与房地产经纪人学会

　　http://www.cirea.org.cn/

（11）China Association of Mineral Resources Appraisers（CAMRA）

　　中国矿业权评估师协会

　　http://www.camra2006.org.cn/

（12）Hong Kong Institute of Surveyors（HKIS）

　　香港测量师学会

　　http://www.hkis.org.hk/

（13）The Appraisal Foundation（TAF）

　　美国评估促进会

　　https://www.appraisalfoundation.org/

（14）The American Society of Appraisers（ASA）

美国评估师协会

http://www.appraisers.org/ASAHome.aspx

（15）The National Association of Certified Valuators and Analysts（NACVA）

美国企业价值评估分析师协会

http://www.nacva.com/

（16）The Appraisal Institute（AI）

美国评估学会

http://www.appraisalinstitute.org/

（17）The Royal Institution of Chartered Surveyors（RICS）

英国皇家特许测量师学会

http://www.rics.org/

（18）Institute of Revenues Rating and Valuation（IRRV）

英国收益评级与估价协会

http://www.irrv.net/

（19）The Appraisal Institute of Canada（AIC）

加拿大评估学会

http://www.aicanada.ca/

（20）The Canadian Institute of Chartered Business Valuators（CICBV）

加拿大特许企业价值评估师协会

https://www.cicbv.ca/

（21）Municipal Property Assessment Corporation（MPAC）

加拿大安大略省财产评估公司

https://www.mpac.ca/

（22）The Australian Property Institute（AES）

澳大利亚评估协会

https://www.aes.asn.au/

(23) Property Institute of New Zealand（NZPI）

新西兰资产学会

http://www.property.org.nz/

(24) New Zealand Institute of Valuers（NZIV）

新西兰资产评估师协会

https://propertyinstitute.nz/

(25) The Russian Society of Appraisers（RSA）

俄罗斯评估师协会

http://sroroo.ru/

(26) Korea Association of Property Appraisers（KAPA）

韩国鉴定评估协会

http://www.kapanet.co.kr/

(27) Singapore Institute of Surveyors and Valuers（SISV）

新加坡测量师与评估师协会

http://www.sisv.org.sg/

(28) The Valuation and Property Services Department（JPPH）

马来西亚资产评估与财产服务署

http://www.jpph.gov.my/

(29) The Czech Chamber of Appraisers（CCA）

捷克评估师协会

http://www.ckom.cz/

(30) The National Association of Romanian Valuers（ANEVAR）

罗马尼亚评估师协会

https://www.reval.anevar.ro/

（31）German Association of Publicly Appointed Surveyors（BDVI）

德国公共测量师协会

https://www.bdvi.de/

References 参考文献

(1) Boskin M J and Kumar P, "New Estimates of the Value of Federal Mineral Rights and Land", in Ucla Economics Working Papers, 1986.

(2) Chen Lei, "A Comparative Study of Chinese and Foreign Valuation Standards Based on Investment Value Types", *Appraisal Journal of China*, Vol.246, N.09, 2020.

(3) Chen Lei, "Research on Tax-Related Valuation of Enterprise Restructuring", *Finance and Accounting Monthly*, Vol.64, N.31, 2011.

(4) Chen Lei, Sun Kaimeng, & Li Mengze, "International Comparative Research of Practice Valuation Guidelines During the Covid-19 Pandemic", *State Assets Management*, Vol.383, N.02, 2023.

(5) Chen Lei, *Theoretical Revision and Practical Adjustment of Cyclical Company Valuation: Based on the of Mixed-Ownership Reform Background*, Capital Economic and Trade University Press, 2022.

(6) Chen Lei, *Valuation Principles*, China Financial &Economic Publishing House, 2017.

(7) Chen Lei, Zhou Yanqiu, & He Qing, "Public Service Quality and Real Estate Tax Base Assessment under the Situation of Real Estate Tax Reform Pilot - Simulation Calculation from Empirical Data of 35 Large and Medium Sized Cities in China", *Journal of Macro-quality Research*, Vol.09, N.06, 2021.

(8) Chen Lei, Zhou Yanqiu, & Qin Qizhi, "Benchmark Correction Path for Mass Appraisal of Real Estate Tax Base: Innovation and Practice", *Appraisal Journal of China*, Vol.256, N.07, 2021.

(9) China Appraisal Society (CAS), Chinese Valuation Standards, 2013.

(10) China Appraisal Society (CAS), Chinese Valuation Standards, 2019.

(11) China Appraisal Society (CAS), Fundamentals of Assets Valuation, China

Financial & Economic Publishing House, 2023.

(12) China Appraisal Society (CAS), Practice of Assets Valuation Volume 1, China Financial & Economic Publishing House, 2023.

(13) China Appraisal Society (CAS), Practice of Assets Valuation Volume 2, China Financial & Economic Publishing House, 2023.

(14) Damodaran A., *Acquisitions and Takeover, Handbook of Finance.* John Wiley & Sons, Inc., 2008.

(15) Damodaran A., *Investment Valuation: Tools and Techniques for Determining the Value of Any Asset,* 2nd Edition, John Wiley & Sons, Inc., 2001.

(16) Damodaran A., *Investment valuation: Tools and Techniques for Determining the Value of Any Asset*, 3rd Edition, John Wiley & Sons, Inc., 2012.

(17) Herrmann D., Thomas W. B., & Saudagaran S. M., "The quality of fair value measures for property, plant, and equipment", *Accounting Forum*, Vol.30, N.09, 2006.

(18) International Accounting Standards Board (IASB), The International Accounting Standards, 2003 Edition, 2003.

(19) International Accounting Standards Board (IASB), The International Accounting Standards, 2011 Edition, 2011.

(20) Koller T., Goedhart M., & Wessels D., *Valuation: Measuring and Managing the Value of Companies*, 6th Edition, John Wiley & Sons, Inc., 2015.

(21) Mard M. J., Hitchner J. R., & Hyden S. D., *Valuation for Financial Reporting: Fair Value, Business Combinations, Intangible Assets, Goodwill, and Impairment Analysis*, 3rd edition, John Wiltey & Sons, Inc., 2011.

(22) Mard M. J., Hyden S. D., & Rigby J.S., *Intellectual Property Valuation,* Financial Valuation group of Florida, Inc., 2000.

(23) Pagourtzi E., French N., Hatzichristos T., et al., "Real Estate Appraisal: A Review of Valuation Methods", *Journal of Property Investment & Finance*, Vol.21, N.04, 2003.

(24) Reilly R. F. and Schweihs P. R., Valuing Intangible Assets, Library of Congress Cataloguing-in-Publication Data, 1998.

(25) The Appraisal Foundation (TAF), 2010-2011 Uniform Standards of Professional Appraisal Practice, 2009.

(26) The Appraisal Foundation (TAF), 2012-2013 Uniform Standards of Professional Appraisal Practice, 2011.

(27) The Appraisal Foundation (TAF), 2014-2015 Uniform Standards of Professional Appraisal Practice, 2013.

(28) The Appraisal Foundation (TAF), 2016-2017 Uniform Standards of Professional Appraisal Practice, 2015.

(29) The Appraisal Foundation (TAF), 2018-2019 Uniform Standards of Professional Appraisal Practice, 2017.

(30) The Appraisal Foundation (TAF), 2020-2021 Uniform Standards of Professional Appraisal Practice, 2019.

(31) The European Group of Valuers' Associations (TEGOVA), European Valuation Standards, 8th Edition, 2016.

(32) The European Group of Valuers' Associations (TEGOVA), European Valuation Standards, 9th Edition, 2020.

(33) The International Valuation Standards Council (IVSC), International Valuation Standards, 2007 Edition, 2006.

(34) The International Valuation Standards Council (IVSC), International Valuation Standards, 2011 Edition, 2010.

(35) The International Valuation Standards Council (IVSC), International Valuation Standards, 2013 Edition, 2012.

(36) The International Valuation Standards Council (IVSC), International Valuation Standards, 2017 Edition, 2016.

(37) The International Valuation Standards Council (IVSC), International Valuation Standards, 2020 Edition, 2019.

(38) The International Valuation Standards Council (IVSC), International Valuation Standards, 2022 Edition, 2021.

(39) The International Valuation Standards Council (IVSC), IVSC Investment Property Project: Proposed Amendments to IVS 230 and IVS 300 Exposure Draft, 2014.

(40) The Royal Institution of Chartered Surveyors (RICS), RICS Professional Standards (Red Book), 2014 Edition, 2014.

(41) The Royal Institution of Chartered Surveyors (RICS), RICS Valuation-Global Standards, 2020 Edition, 2019.

(42) The Royal Institution of Chartered Surveyors (RICS), RICS Valuation-Global Standards, 2022 Edition, 2021.

(43) Wang Chengjun, Professional English, *Appraisal Journal of China*, 2005.

(44) Wang Chengjun, Professional English, *Appraisal Journal of China*, 2006.

(45) Wang Chengjun, Professional English, *Appraisal Journal of China*, 2007.

(46) Wang Haisu and Zhang Shiru, *Assets Valuation*, 4th Edition, High Education Press, 2021.

(47) Writing Group of Research Office of the State Council, The Government Work Report of *the First Session of the 14th National People's Congress - Q&A for Study*, China Yan Shi Press, 2023.

(48) Writing Group, *Tutorial Reader of Report to the 20th National Congress of the Communist Party of China*, People's Publishing House, 2022.

(49) Zabihollah Rezaee, *Financial Services Firms: Governance, Regulations, Valuations, Mergers, and Acquisitions*, 3rd Edition, Wiley Online Library, 2012.

(50) Zhonghe Appraisal Company Ltd, *BMI Appraisals Limited Company, Business Valuation and Case Studies*, China Financial &Economic Publishing House, 2010.